VIPASSANA

A Method of Mind Training

Dr. Ch. Venkata Sivasai

PRASHANT PUBLISHING HOUSE
DELHI-110094

Published by :
Prashant Publishing House
C-34, 28 Foota Road, Gali-3,
West Karwal Nagar, Delhi-110094
Phone : 011-22963970, Mob. : 9810396373
e-mail.: prashantpublishinghouse@gmail.com

Vipassana: A Method of Mind Training

First Published 2015

ISBN 978-93-80565-62-0

PRINTED IN INDIA
Published by Mr. R.K. Jha M/s Prashant Publishing House and Published at H.S. Offset House Press, Delhi.

Preface

Vipassana is the oldest science of India. Its rediscovery by Gautama Buddha allowed him to realize the ultimate truth, and he taught this technique for the benefit of humanity. Later on, Emperor Ashoka encouraged the spread of this teaching for the benefit of his subjects, as indicated in the rock edicts. Vipassana goes beyond the barriers of caste, sect, communalism, and narrow nationalism, it brings improves morality so that along with material benefits there can be real happiness. Further, it can be an effective instrument in strengthening national integration and international understanding factors which are of great relevance in today's times.

Vipassana is a great science, the science of understanding mind and matter phenomena. It is a process of mind purification and is free from any sectarian, caste or belief-based approach. Further, it works at the experiential level and leads to a happy life through continuous purification of the mind. It is said that the major part of the mind is the subconscious or unconscious mind. Generally it is difficult to reach this part of the mind, which keeps on reacting according to its past conditioning. Vipassana helps in breaking the barrier between the conscious and unconscious mind. Through the process of observing without reacting, the mind is cleansed of its negativities. With the technique of Vipassana, one reaches deep down to the unconscious level of the mind and experiences sensations within the framework of the body without reacting to them. The law of nature is such that whatever actions we perform are stored in the form of its effect in the unconscious part of the mind.

Need for Meditation: Where exactly does meditation come into the picture? To get an answer, we have to look to more industrialized countries such as the United States and Germany. The nature of the societies produced by advanced industrialization has been characterized by heavy alcohol, drug and cigarette consumption; pandemic divorces and broken families; economic recession and job insecurities; and strong feelings of competition and frustration leading to heart attacks, suicide and so on.

Fragmented Society: People who become business managers come from this fragmented society. Business schools teach them to work for more profits and higher salaries, and the stress involved leads to greater consumption of drugs and alcohol, and various health problems such as hyper-tension. The level of equanimity in such societies deteriorates. The business owners, executives and managers develop feelings of pride, prejudice, jealousy and arrogance and experience their concomitants: depression, anxiety, stress and other harmful effects.

Positive Transformation: The *Vipassana* meditation technique improves the lives of executives and business managers by transforming their attitudes. Prejudice is replaced by compassion; jealousy changes into joy at the success of others; greed and arrogance are replaced by generosity and humility, and so on.

This transformation of attitude results in stress reduction, and mental equanimity and balance. It is a creative force capable of inducing a dynamic work approach in subordinate staff. The positive change is brought about by a change in the attitude and actions of the executive-to polite and compassionate behaviour, gentle speech, and a mind full of love and friendliness. This positive change in consciousness is the aim of genuine meditation practice, and it forms a new and advanced basis for business and industrial management.

Most meditation techniques are unable to reach the subconscious mind, they are not colourless and can therefore "taint" the mind which further complicates the situation. Vipassana bases every step on "reality-as it is." Vipassana allows a meditator to experience moments of "no nutriment to the mind. This starts the process of "detoxifying" the mind of its impurities.

Vipassana meditation is a surgical operation of the mind. When practiced properly the pace of purification can be dramatically increased. The technique frees one's mind from greed. A healthy mind is alert and capable of meeting the demands of a situation. It naturally comes out of addictions and indulgences. The practice of Vipassana results in the diminishment 'of craving. A business conducted with the base of such a mind would have resulted in the growth of the textile industry rather than creating sick production units.

An analysis of the increasing industrial sickness and the failure of business manage merit reveals a pattern. In many cases, over anxiety for export or expansion causes the working capital to be diverted into the generation of fixed assets. The result is an acute shortage of working capital and excessive borrowing-clearly dangerous avenues for business practice. With a mind made mature by meditation, these kinds of desire-driven actions are checked by the calm and cool temper of equanimity, which reduces the possibility of making such mistakes.

Pure Mind: The Basis of Management: The Vipassana technique does not create by itself a new technology of management. It contributes to the improvement of management by correcting the root of the problem-impurity of mind-so that a business is continually nourished by the pure food of right thoughts and action. It is excessive craving and greed which poison the minds of managers; this impurity is corrected by meditation.

I think this book help to everybody, both scholars and the layman, who are interested to know the Vipassana Meditation and its uses for every human beings and their personal and professional life.

— *Dr. Ch. Venkata Sivasai*

Contents

Introduction

As you know, Buddhism is not a unified type of system, or even religion. One could even debate whether or not it actually is a religion. But it spread from India to many, many countries throughout Asia; and in each country, each civilization that it encountered, it was understood and adopted to that culture. And so, we find very different brands of Buddhism around Asia.

There are three general waves of Buddhism. One went to Southeast Asia, the so called Theravada Buddhism. We find that in Sri Lanka, Burma, Thailand, Laos and Cambodia, a little bit in Vietnam (not that much). And then we find one wave went through Central Asia to China and from China to Japan and Korea, and down to Vietnam. And then another wave that went later from India to Tibet and from Tibet to Mongolia, and throughout Central Asia and to the various Mongol groups who came to Russia, so the Buryats, the Kalmyks and also a Turkic group – the Tunisians. So we have a wide diversity, and that is a bit simplifying, because within that there were various waves.

So, I think that in the twenty-first century, Buddhism has a great deal to offer on a global level, which is not restricted to one culture or another, because Buddhism was never restricted to one culture or another. But in these areas of Buddhist science and Buddhist philosophy that it can offer, as I said, methods for developing concentration, methods for developing more discipline. How do you develop discipline? You develop discipline by seeing that there are many disadvantages not to have discipline, and seeing how actually it hinders you not to have discipline. And you deal with motivation and so on. Why would you want to set limits on how often you look at your text messages – this sort of things? Certain limits have to be placed there, that type of discipline and the ethical discipline to take others seriously, not just as people that you can turn on and off with your machine. The critical goal of Buddhist education is to attain wisdom. Buddhism believes that the ultimate wisdom is inherent in each person's nature, stating that everyone has the potential to achieve that wisdom. However, the majorities are distracted by misunderstanding and misconceptions, therefore, are incapable of being aware of this kind of potential. In this sense, Buddhism aims to teach us recognize the intrinsic part of human nature. Buddhist wisdom varies from individual to individual which is related to the degree of one's delusion and there is no inherent difference among all human beings. Buddhism helps us remove delusion and regain the wisdom to remove confusions of individual potential and achieve happiness. Buddhism considers deep meditation and concentration as the crucial factors in order to attain wisdom. Buddhism teaches the way of meditation and the mindfulness of concentration to attain the state of blissful wisdom.

Buddhism values first-hand experience higher than theory. Buddhist education is mainly concerned with handing over of the factual knowledge. The Buddha taught a path of personal inquiry to put an end to suffering, and that path depends on direct experience. Therefore, the traditional methods of Buddhist mind-training i.e. contemplation and meditation, could be taught at schools. The Buddhist view on the integral nature of human experience, where the intellectual and emotional sides of mind are equally appreciated, is highly relevant in the modern world, which is overly fragmented. Since the full meaning of the Buddhist texts and teachings is not fully understood before one has direct experience in meditation, meditation is an indispensable part of Buddhist education. In fact, Buddhist educational institutions, if they have not been tainted by the values of the West, could well define themselves as schools of mental training. The usefulness of mindfulness methods in developing the "seven factors of enlightenment" (such as peace, joy, concentration etc.) has been demonstrated even outside the context of Buddhist education. It has been found indispensable for realizing true education in general.

The development of the mind is central theme in terms of Buddhist Education which helps one to discriminate, for example, between wholesome and unwholesome thoughts and actions. In terms of practicing and internalizing the Dhamma, the affective domain of learning and training is without question an essential ingredient and is linked to harnessing the pool of information and facts in the Dhamma that is to be relied upon for one to arrive at sound conclusions, decisions and actions in our daily life.

Role of Vipassana in Education: We can now understand how *Vipassana* can fill that vital gap in modern education-viz., the training of mind, leading to a balanced, harmonious and purposeful life. *Vipassana* meditation imparts a way to observe all the phenomena of this sensory world. The important benefit of the systematic practice-especially of mindfulness of breath, which is of crucial significance in education-is improvement in one's ability to concentrate on a task. As explained earlier, the essence of the practice is to train the mind to keep the attention continuously on an object (viz., the breath), and to minimize the drifting of the mind into futile daydreams, which are the chief obstacle to concentration. The training of observing the mental states also comes in handy. Once such daydreams have arisen (whether during meditation or during normal activity), if one briefly makes these daydreams themselves an object of close observation, their power of distraction is drastically curtailed and they get quickly dispersed. This results in a quick retrieval of concentration. To achieve this objective, the principal requirement is to develop an insight into the basic characteristics of life. Impermanence (*anicca*) is the fundamental characteristic with which a*Vipassana* student is continually confronted. As this experience becomes ingrained, realization of the other characteristics-viz., of suffering *(dukkha) and* egolessness (*anattaa*)-automatically develops, leading one to a clear understanding of the purpose of life and the way to achieve it-the very acme of spiritual education.

Vipassana helps in breaking the barrier between the conscious and unconscious mind. Through the process of observing without reacting, the mind is cleansed of its negativities. With the technique of Vipassana, one reaches deep down to the unconscious level of the mind and experiences sensations within the framework of the body without reacting to them. The law of nature is such that whatever actions we perform are stored in the form of its effect in the unconscious part of the mind.

Positive Transformation: The *Vipassana* meditation technique improves the lives of executives and business managers by transforming their attitudes. Prejudice is replaced by compassion; jealousy changes into joy at the success of others; greed and arrogance are replaced by generosity and humility, and so on.

This transformation of attitude results in stress reduction, and mental equanimity and balance. It is a creative force capable of inducing a dynamic work approach in subordinate staff. The positive change is brought about by a change in the attitude and actions of the executive-to polite and compassionate behaviour, gentle speech, and a mind full of love and friendliness. This positive change in consciousness is the aim of genuine meditation practice, and it forms a new and advanced basis for business and industrial management.

Right Livelihood: The practice of Right Livelihood is an important aspect of Vipassana meditation. It can become the foundation for business management practice, upon which can be based traditional management techniques of using statistical data such as of cash-flow projections, return on capital, GNP, the turnover of profits, and so on. These parameters are useful if they are based on the concept of Right Livelihood.

Subconscious Mind: Without going into the details of Vipassana meditation, I will touch upon an important aspect of the transformation of consciousness: the subconscious mind. Very little is known about this mind which is filled with negativities which are counter-productive to wealth in its totality. While it is possible to recognize and experience these negativities, it is not possible to empty the mind of these defilements without a proper technique.

Most meditation techniques are unable to reach the subconscious mind, they are not colorless and can therefore "taint" the mind which further complicates the situation. Vipassana bases every step on "reality-as it is." Vipassana allows a meditator to experience moments of "no nutriment to the mind. This starts the process of "detoxifying" the mind of its impurities.

A mind which does not meditate and develops impurity causes grave consequences. When the minds of industry leaders are impure, the ramifications are pervasive and serious. This phenomenon is exemplified by the classic example of the management failure at the Bombay Textile Mills. Twenty years ago, it was a viable, profit-making unit; however ' the greed for quick money caused a financial tragedy. The incoming cash, which could have been used for modernizing the plant and machinery, or for financing working capital was siphoned out for the personal gain of the directors. Their livelihood was not "right livelihood". The defilement of greed killed the best interests of the directors and caused widespread misery to a large section of Bombay's workforce and economic system.

Vipassana meditation is a surgical operation of the mind. When practiced properly the pace of purification can be dramatically increased. The technique frees one's mind from greed. A healthy mind is alert and capable of meeting the demands of a situation. It naturally comes out of addictions and indulgences. The practice of Vipassana results in the diminishment 'of craving.

1

History of Vipassana

Vipassana is the oldest science of India. Its rediscovery by Gautama Buddha allowed him to realize the ultimate truth, and he taught this technique for the benefit of humanity. Later on, Emperor Ashoka encouraged the spread of this teaching for the benefit of his subjects, as indicated in the rock edicts. We are extremely grateful to Goenkaji for bringing this lost wisdom to our country.

Because Vipassana goes beyond the barriers of caste, sect, communalism, and narrow nationalism, it brings improves morality so that along with material benefits there can be real happiness. Further, it can be an effective instrument in strengthening national integration and international understanding factors which are of great relevance in today's times.

Vipassana is a great science, the science of understanding mind and matter phenomena. It is a process of mind purification and is free from any sectarian, caste or belief-based approach. Further, it works at the experiential level and leads to a happy life through continuous purification of the mind. It is said that the major part of the mind is the subconscious or unconscious mind.

Generally it is difficult to reach this part of the mind, which keeps on reacting according to its past conditioning. This reactive mind is the storehouse of our impressions *(sa"mkhaaraa)* of cravings and aversions, and makes our reactions to external events biased and thus lacking in objectivity.

BUDDHIST MEDITATION

The Pali word for meditation practice is *bhavana*, which literally means 'development,' 'cultivation,' or 'culture.' Since this practice has to do directly with the mind, the word *bhavana*therefore refers specifically to a process of mental culture or mental development. In this respect the English word 'meditation' is a rather poor and inadequate equivalent of the word *bhavana*. In employing the term 'meditation' in the Buddhist context, we should be aware of the character and objective of Buddhist practice.

Buddhist meditation is a means to mental development. It deals particularly with the training of the mind, which is the most important composite of the entire human entity. Because mind is the forerunner and prime source of all actions, physical, verbal, or mental, it needs to be properly cultivated and developed. Buddhist meditation is mental development in the real sense of the term*bhavana*, for it aims not only at temporary calm and tranquillity of mind, but at purifying the mind of defilements and negative influences, such as sensual desire, lust, hatred, jealousy, envy, worry, ignorance, restlessness, and indolence.

It cultivates and brings to perfection such wholesome and positive qualities of mind as confidence, compassion, wisdom, energy, mindfulness, concentration, and penetrative insight. Meditation is also a practice through which the Dhamma can be realized and the transcendent bliss of *Nibbana* experienced. It is a useful discipline on all levels of experience, from the ordinary worldly concerns of day-to-day activities up to the highest realization and transcendent spiritual attainment.

Meditation is essentially an experiential activity, not a scholastic subject to be understood through books or secondhand information. It is not an escape from life or evasion from responsibility. Even if the formal meditation practice may appear to the uninformed to be disconnected from real life, its inherent purpose deeply concerns our day-to-day existence and experience.

Meditation means mindfulness and wisdom in what we do, speak, and think; it means greater awareness and higher ability in self-control. It is not, therefore, an irrelevant other-worldly practice meant only for monks and ascetics, but is one of the most valuable practical skills there are for enhancing fulfillment in everyday life.

TYPES OF MEDITATION

Buddhism teaches various methods of meditation practice, but all may be grouped under the two main categories of *samatha* and *vipassana*. The former refers to concentration (*samadhi*) and is a mode of training designed for the specific purpose of cultivating one-pointedness of mind (*cittekaggata*); the latter refers to insight, the penetrative mental faculty which perceives and understands realities the way they really are.

Concentration meditation is designed to produce peace and tranquillity of mind (*cittaviveka*) and stronger powers of will, which can be utilized for practical purposes in daily life. Through constant effort and perseverance the meditator may also be able to attain the higher mystic states called *absorption* (*jhana*). There are eight stages of meditative absorption; the first four are the absorptions of form (*rupajhana*), and the remaining ones are formless absorptions (*arupajhana*), the highest of which is known as the Sphere of Neither-Perception-Nor-Non-Perception (*nevasañña-nasañña-yatana*). However, all these mystic states are created and conditioned by the mind. They are impermanent and still within the sphere of mundane realities.

Concentration meditation was known prior to the establishment of Buddhism, but it was refined and standardized in the Buddhist system of practice. Nevertheless, in itself it does not lead to the extinction of *dukkha* and the realization of *Nibbana*, although it may be useful to a certain extent in mental development. Before enlightenment, the Buddha himself practiced concentration under some highly accomplished teachers of the day, attaining to the very final stage of absorption, the Sphere of Neither-Perception-Nor-Non-Perception, but he soon discovered that it was unsatisfactory and inadequate as a means for achieving the highest spiritual realization. Concentration can be instrumental for a happy life in this existence (*ditthadhamma-sukhavihara*), but it is insight meditation that really enables one to purify the mind and realize*Nibbana*. Insight meditation is essentially a Buddhist contribution to the spiritual wealth of the world. This is a method of analysis in which the emphasis is placed on the development of mindfulness and knowledge of reality. By applying constant awareness to the present reality of existence, the meditator becomes perfectly identified with his own being and experience. He comes to perceive the realities of impermanence, change, unsatisfactoriness, and non-substantiality in all existential phenomena, and intuitively realizes the true nature of his own inner experiences. All things are characterized by emptiness; in the ultimate analysis there is nothing that should be attached to as 'me' or 'mine.' The meditator sees for himself the wholesome and unwholesome thoughts rising and falling in his mind, the defilements, the virtuous qualities, the good, the evil, the noble, and the ignoble — all are 'seen' and recognized in their true nature. Once the realities are directly intuited and experienced, they can be subjected to further analysis and investigation. Self-knowledge and deeper understanding of realities are obtained through consistent effort and perseverance in the practice of this kind of meditation.

POPULARITY OF BUDDHIST MEDITATION IN THE WEST

Prof. Donald K. Swearer, a long-time student of Buddhism, observes: "Buddhist meditation is attractive for many reasons, to be sure. For some it offers a retreat from the chaos and complexity of today's world.

For others it may serve as a means of introspective self-understanding; and for still others it is the means for attempting seriously to grasp the truth of Buddhism." This statement clearly epitomizes how Buddhist meditation can serve a utilitarian objective for people living in the West and how it may hold immense potential for fulfilling their socio-psychological needs. Westerners are, as a rule, practical and goal-oriented people; they are not satisfied with mere theory, but are more interested in experiencing the results of a given principle. Meditation is a discipline that satisfactorily answers to this type of mentality.

The stressful life-style in Western society may be the strongest reason why people are initially attracted to Buddhist meditation. Excessive materialism, the 'rat race,' and the seeking for all the so-called good things in life have combined to produce a society which is full of stress and tension. The need to compete in order to get to the top is relentlessly driving people forward with no time to pause or slow down. The wastefulness of consumerism represents a serious threat to the world's natural resources and environmental stability; unethical commercialism has produced distrust among manufacturers and consumers. Society seems to be more chaotic than we are officially prepared to admit. In such a context, some people are more inclined to find solace and peace in the dynamic quietude of Buddhist meditation. Through the practice they discover that the most practical way to solve man's problems — personal, social, or global — is to begin with their own minds and attitudes. Buddhist meditation offers a variety of techniques for developing mental clarity and an undistorted view of life, and these are fundamental to the real solution of the problems.

In many cases, Western interest in Buddhist meditation is not solely motivated by problems such as stress or tension, but stems from a genuine conviction in the Dhamma and a curiosity about its practices. This group of practitioners consist mainly of intellectuals and students of Buddhism, who find in the religion something that answers their questions and needs. But no matter what the motivation, earnest meditators always stand to benefit from the practice, and that is one of the most attractive features of Buddhist meditation.

PRACTICAL PURPOSE OF BUDDHIST MEDITATION

Doubts about this topic betray a typical misunderstanding concerning Buddhist meditation, prevalent not only among non-Buddhists but also among certain sectors of Buddhists as well. Some people believe that meditation serves no practical purpose and is an escape from the reality of everyday life. Those who embrace this wrong view fail to distinguish between an active training attuned to a state of perfect mental health, tranquillity, and equilibrium, which is Buddhist meditation, and a passive engagement in nothing but mystic musings or recitation of mantras, which has nothing to do with Buddhist meditation. They also fail to understand that sitting with closed eyes or repeating unintelligible phrases does not in itself constitute Buddhist meditation. Buddhist meditation by no means implies an escape from life. Its practice is largely based on life activities and its effects are meant to improve the quality of life. To develop a high level of concentration a certain degree of seclusion or a carefully-structured environment may be more favorable, but Buddhist meditation means much more than just concentration practice. In fact, the Buddha pointed out that concentration for its own sake is an obstacle to the higher realization of the Dhamma. Nevertheless, the image of a meditating monk sitting cross-legged, still as a rock, and deeply absorbed in meditation, may have created a general wrong impression that it is the only way to practice meditation.

Because meditation, as the original Pali term *bhavana,* is the development of the mind, and because mind is the most important determinant by which our physical, verbal, and mental actions are conditioned and controlled, the practice of meditation can bring infinite gains and benefits. The ultimate spiritual benefit attainable through meditation is perfect enlightenment and the realization of *Nibbana*. However, *Nibbana* may appear to be too remote a goal for many meditators who simply aspire to more mundane benefits. Listed below are some of the advantages that can be immediately experienced in meditation practice.

1. Meditation increases awareness of inner potentialities and helps us to be more positive in life.
2. Meditation helps to fortify will power and increase self-confidence.
3. Meditation provides mental calm and tranquillity and frees the mind from restlessness, agitation, fear, and worry.
4. Because meditation promotes mental health, it can positively.influence physical health. People who are free from worry and mental turmoil, whose minds are calm and serene, usually enjoy comparatively good health.

5. By helping the mind to concentrate and become better organized, meditation can help increase efficiency in day-to-day work and in the performance of duties and responsibilities.
6. Meditation promotes virtuous qualities like compassion, good will, confidence (*saddha*), wisdom, energy, perseverance, determination, etc.
7. Meditation helps to purify the mind of defilements (*kilesa*) such as greed, selfishness, hatred, and jealousy, and frees it from the preconceptions and delusions that normally prevent proper insight into reality. A meditator is therefore capable of seeing things the way they really are and can better deal with the life experience.

There are no limits to the benefits that can be derived from the practice of meditation. These benefits can be applied to personal and interpersonal use depending on circumstances and the ability of the meditators themselves. However, it should be added here that the amount of benefit derived from meditation and the measure of success in the practice may be related to such incidental factors as proper understanding of the subject, consistency in the practice, self-confidence, and the degree of perseverance. An experienced teacher can be a great support, especially in the initial stages of training.

COMPARISON OF SAMATHA AND VIPASSANA

Samatha means calm or concentration, and *vipassana bhavana* is a mental training process in which mindfulness is the most important element. Although concentration and mindfulness are two distinct mental faculties, having functions of their own, they do depend on one another and should therefore be cultivated together in a balanced manner. In fact, they may be compared to the two ends of the same stick. If you pick up one, the other will come up. In this way the two are inseparable, although functionally they may constitute two separate roles.

The relationship between concentration and mindfulness is somewhat delicate and sensitive. By definition, concentration refers to the faculty of mind to focus on a single object in a sustained and uninterrupted manner. In order to achieve the state of one-pointedness, it is necessary for the attention to remain unremittingly focused on the meditation object for a long period of time. This presupposes the use of force; the meditator constantly applies his will power to retain mental focus on the object of meditation.

Mindfulness, on the other hand, requires no use of force or will to maintain a mental focus other than the application of bare awareness to the object of experience. Constant practice of mindfulness leads to refined sensibilities and the ability to recognize realities according to their true nature. When developed together with concentration, mindfulness performs the function of selecting an object for concentration and subtly helping to maintain the focus on that particular object. It is a state of bare awareness of the object of experience, involving no desire or aversion, no force of will or attachment.

If mindfulness is strong, it is likely that concentration will become more strengthened, and vice versa. There is the classical analogy of sunlight through a magnifying glass: When sunlight is focused through a magnifying glass, it becomes so concentrated that fire may result. Left to itself, the sun may not be powerful enough to produce that burning effect, although it certainly contains the potential to do so. The lens is therefore instrumental in actualizing the sun's inherent potential. In the same way, the human mind possesses powerful forces and vast potential, which can be harnessed and actualized through the practice of concentration. When the mind is well concentrated, mindfulness is more able to refine the inner sensibilities and to sharpen mental faculties. This finally leads to the development of penetrative insight that enables meditators to perceive all phenomena in their true and undistorted state and to purify their minds of all defilements.

In terms of method and application, mindfulness is broader and more comprehensive than concentration. Mindfulness is inclusive, while concentration is exclusive. Because it is capable of taking all kinds of experiences and phenomena as objects of investigation, mindfulness represents an all-encompassing function. The possibilities of its objects and application are unlimited. Mindfulness is capable of taking in and dealing with everything that comes within the field of sensory and mental experience, leaving nothing aside, while concentration focuses on one single object that has been chosen for the purpose and rejects all others. Basically, it is concentration that generates the mental power and the necessary stillness of mind that mindfulness requires for a deeper penetration into the more profound levels of human consciousness. If concentration is energy, mindfulness provides direction and guidance to that energy. Concentration and mindfulness balanced in proportion will result in greater understanding and insight, which are most vital in spiritual practice.

Right concentration is a wholesome type of one-pointedness which supports wisdom and strengthens other wholesome virtues. Thanks to the power of concentration, mental contaminants such as sensual desire, ill-will, laziness, sloth and torpor, and vacillation, are suppressed, giving an opportunity for wholesome spiritual qualities to arise and grow. If concentration is weakening or the mind drifts from the meditation object, mindfulness immediately takes note of that and assists concentration to regain its footing.

It is the function of concentration to stabilize the mind and hold the mental focus steady onto the object of meditation. Mindfulness plays a supportive role and in addition continues on from where concentration ends. In this way, concentration and mindfulness mutually coordinate and depend on each other throughout the whole process of mental culture which is meditation.

Is meditation selfish?

There are a number of points to be considered here. In the first place, meditation cannot be said to be a selfish activity, or meditators self-centered individuals, any more than one may accuse college students who attend college and concentrate on their studies of being selfish in the face of social problems. Meditation is basically a course of training, and one of the most natural outcomes of the practice is the destruction, partly or wholly, of selfishness. Just as going to college equips one with greater ability to be productive and to contribute to society, training in meditation helps one to do good for others with greater sacrifice and dedication. However, while being more educated does not necessarily imply a lesser degree of selfishness, greater spiritual advancement attainable through meditation does. Higher education may even prove to be more socially counterproductive, if excessive greed and selfishness predominate a person's decisions and actions. Meditation, on the other hand, is free from such drawbacks, since what is actually achieved in the course of training is the elimination of negative mental qualities, especially selfishness, and cultivation of the positive ones like compassion, kindness, and wisdom. Far from being selfish, meditation is an entirely virtuous and positive activity.

Secondly, it must be reiterated here that meditation does not necessarily mean sitting cross-legged with closed eyes, reciting a mantra. Those who think that meditation is only a passive engagement with the mind having nothing to do with worldly existence are greatly mistaken. Buddhist meditation deals with life; it is an intensely vital activity. Meditation can be practiced while eating, drinking, thinking, gardening, farming, and engaging in other kinds of activities, personal or social. It is therefore improper to say that meditation is a selfish activity. As a matter of fact, nothing is farther from the truth.

Thirdly, meditation is something we live with, not simply a practice for its own sake. The Buddha and his noble disciples are said to have dwelled constantly in meditation, but they were most active in working for happiness and welfare of other people, with no thought or expectation of reward. Their activities produced such great benefit for society and humanity at large because their minds were free of greed, selfishness, ill-will, and other kinds of defilements. People who unduly hasten to engage in social activities without sufficiently preparing their own spiritual groundwork are likely to create more harm than help, and whatever service they manage to render may become little more than an extension of their ego. Examples such as the Crusades, the Salem witchcraft trials, and the Inquisition are not lacking in the history of religions, and they stand as clear testimonies of how dangerous human beings can become if their mental defilements are not properly dealt with. By practicing meditation, one becomes aware of one's own mind and thoughts, strengths and weaknesses, and the various subtle manners, including seemingly beneficial social actions, in which egotism may manifest itself.

Is Meditation a kind of running away?

This question demonstrates yet another serious misunderstanding concerning Buddhist meditation. Mental purification is one of the many benefits of meditative practice; it is not the only objective of the discipline. To purify the mind is not to reject existential realities or to run away from them. On the contrary, the process of training requires that meditators learn to recognize realities as they occur from one moment of experience to another. Meditation is, in fact, the most daring kind of practice, one in which one learns to squarely encounter realities; there is no better way to deal with them than through meditation.

The existential realities that we have to contend with are not only external phenomena like earthquakes, flash floods, the AIDS epidemic, child prostitution, or high crime rates. More intimate and closer to ourselves are the inner experiences that we feel and perceive in each and every moment. These experiences are no less real and tangible than other seemingly more concrete events that are happening in other parts of the world. They are the most immediate realities we have to contend with, and if they are not handled properly, chances are that we will add more problems and cause more suffering to ourselves and the world.

Buddhist meditation, especially insight meditation, represents a unique mode of practice by which meditators are trained to recognize realities without bias and fully experience life as it is. We learn to go beyond our inherent preconceptions and illusions, and try to analytically deal with our experiences in an objective manner. This enables us to perceive things as they really are, not as we are conditioned, positively or negatively, to see them. Most importantly, we learn how to see ourselves in a clear, straightforward way, understanding our own character and temperaments, weaknesses and shortcomings. Buddhist meditation is a noble method of accepting reality. It is the most practical way to deal with the realities of life.

Can meditation cause insanity?

To say that meditation causes insanity is as true as the assertion that eating can cause death or brushing teeth may cause mouth injury. Actually, insanity can be produced in many different ways. Normal activities such as studying in college, business dealings, playing the stock market, and even love affairs, all hold the potential to induce insanity. It really depends on one's attitude of mind and on how these activities are carried out. If you stretch yourself to an extreme by studying all day and night without a rest or working nonstop without going to sleep, then there are good chances of developing mental problems or neuroses. There are also reports of those whose sweet love turns sour and, through the agony of a broken heart, suffer emotional imbalance and insanity. Practically anything can be cited as a potential cause for mental derangement.

Those who assert that meditation can cause insanity do not really understand what Buddhist meditation is and how it is practiced. Far from being a cause for mental disorder or the loss of sanity, meditation is rather a subtle art for promoting mental health of the highest order. We have seen that in meditation practice, mindfulness is the most important factor, and it is mindfulness that has to be constantly developed and applied to one's psycho-physical experiences in each and every moment. This leads to the growth of other virtuous qualities such as compassion, generosity, morality, wisdom, energy, perseverance, and selflessness.

It is therefore appropriate to assert that meditation is, in fact, not only conducive to emotional stability and psychological well-being, but also greatly contributes to spiritual advancement and enhances personal and social lives.

It is most probable that people whose mental constitutions are abnormal, who are afflicted with a severe case of mental disorder, such as paranoid schizophrenia, may not be ready for meditation practice. These individuals are prone to display uncontrollable and erratic behavior and are likely to suffer some degree of insanity no matter what spiritual discipline they undertake or what activities they may engage in. If they indulge in meditation practice without first taking sufficient professional care of their problems, one would not expect them to fare very well in the training.

There are also those who profess certain ideas about meditation and start an intensive practice on their own. Without proper background knowledge or guidance, it is possible that such practice may result in a loss of mental equilibrium and hallucinations. But meditation cannot be held accountable for these negative effects. Buddhist meditation is completely safe and wholesome when undertaken with the proper frame of mind and under the guidance of a capable teacher.

MEDITATION TECHNIQUE

Because of lack of space, not all the methods or details of the practice of concentration meditation can be given here. However, we may discuss the most fundamental concepts and techniques of training to give readers a clear understanding of how meditation is undertaken in the initial stages; those who are interested in putting these techniques into practice may do so without harm or adverse effects if moderation is duly observed.

Concentration is developed by single-mindedly focusing the attention on a selected object. There is a wide range of objects that can be used for meditation, and forty have been specifically recommended in Buddhist literature, although it is quite possible that other things may be included in the list as well. Classical examples are one's own breaths, a Buddha image, a candlelight, a painted disc or dyed cloth stretched on a round frame (*kasina*), water, empty space, etc. The reason why a rather large variety of objects is described is to provide a wide choice for practitioners with different preferences and temperaments. A suitable object of meditation facilitates the practice and ensures better progress.

The meditator can, if so desired, initially experiment with different objects of concentration to see which is most suitable. Very often this may not be necessary if one chooses to commence the practice with a more convenient device, like one's own breaths. A good meditation object is one on which the practitioner finds it easier to concentrate. With the help of an experienced teacher, a right decision is made much easier. On one's own, a student of meditation may experiment until satisfied with the choice. However, once the decision has been made, it makes more sense to stick to whatever has been selected rather than keep changing the meditation object, otherwise the practitioner will become confused and the practice will not progress as well as it should.

The concentration technique which involves a prolonged and constant focus on one's own breaths has been praised by the Buddha as being suitable to all types of temperaments. This technique is so popular that it is virtually taught in all Buddhist traditions. It is so convenient to practice that even children, properly instructed, can do it.

There are different ways by which concentration on the breath is developed. In other words, one may say that there are numerous ways and means to use one's breaths as the object of concentration practice. These may be regarded simply as different variations of the same method, and they are so many that it is impossible to list all of them here. Individual meditation centers may have a specific preference for one variation over others, although all are equally valid and beneficial. For the sake of illustration, we may cite the method in which the two-syllable Pali word *bud-dho* is employed as an aid to cultivate concentration. This is how it is done:

Sit cross-legged, placing the right foot on the left. Keep the back straight and upright, but not uncomfortably rigid. If your legs are stiff, being unaccustomed to the cross-legged maneuver, and you find this posture uncomfortable, try using a cushion to support yourself from underneath so that the weight of the body will be less pressing on the legs and your feet enjoy a little more room. If this is still a problem, you may sit on a chair, although this is not a traditional posture. (Most people in Asia can sit cross-legged with ease.) Sitting in the traditional way is said to effect a sense of stability and helps to prepare you for the task of meditation that will follow. In any case you should feel sufficiently comfortable that you do not have to move for a specific period of time during the practice.

Having properly settled down, put your hands on your lap, the right one on the left, palms upward. Close your eyes and begin to relax your body. You may will the different parts of the body to relax, starting from the head downward and working with all the muscles in each part. Do it slowly, in a leisurely manner, and systematically, avoiding nothing in the process. This will take roughly two to three minutes, and by the time you have completed this preparatory stage, your mind should have been appropriately attuned to the meditation practice proper. You should be completely relaxed, otherwise meditation will become more of a burden than the enjoyable spiritual experience that it is. Not only should you feel physically relaxed, you should also train your mind to be free from psychological tension by putting down for the time being any cares and concerns that may cause mental disturbance or restlessness. Careful attention to small details prior to the sitting, like making sure that the door is locked, the gas stove or television set turned off, and the telephone unplugged or moved to another area where it will not be a nuisance, can add much to the pleasure of the practice and further ensure success in the endeavor.

When you have gained a certain amount of relaxation and composure, turn your attention to the in- and out-breaths. Now you become clearly conscious of your own respiration, which has hardly been noticed before. Keep focusing on your in- and out-breaths to the exclusion of anything else until your mind becomes further composed and still. Mentally repeat the syllable*bud* (as in Buddha) as you breathe in and *dho* as you breathe out. Synchronize each syllable of*bud-dho* with the in- and out-breath so that they become completely identified with one another. Keep the body unmoved and the mind still through the time assigned for the practice. In the likely event that your mind gets distracted or starts to roam about, gently bring it back to the object of meditation which is your in- and out-breaths. Continue to do this and your mind will gradually become one with your breaths and attain the state of one-pointedness.

In this technique of concentration practice, inhalation and exhalation are employed as a tool to keep the mind still and focused. The mental recitation of *bud-dho* serves to fortify the practice. Some meditators may find this a more convenient concept on which to retain their attention. For Buddhists, it adds a distinct flavor of faith to the training, because the Pali word *bud-dho* really signifies the Buddha. Some meditators prefer to use the nose-tip as a point of mental focus; others may like to follow the inhalation movement down from the nostrils to the abdomen and the exhalation movement up from the abdomen through the nostrils, especially if they are newcomers to meditation. The breathing technique is the most popular form of Buddhist meditation; its practicality and usefulness have been universally recognized wherever Buddhism is taught. The incorporation of *bud-dho* into the practice is distinctly a Thai contribution and the technique is very widespread in the country.

Different Levels of Concentration

Obviously, the strength of concentration differs in different stages of training. The Buddhist commentaries mention three levels of concentration. The first, momentary concentration (*khanika samadhi*), is a quality of mind that is inherently common in all sentient beings. This is an essential faculty that we all need in our everyday activities, and we can experience it even when we are engaged in the most mundane chores like eating, drinking, reading, writing a letter, or driving. In fact, it seems impossible to perform any function effectively without a certain amount of concentration. In the same way, it may also be said that our capacity and efficiency to work depend largely on the amount of concentration we are able to mobilize in the fulfillment of our duties. Thus a higher degree of concentration almost invariably means a better performance of actions. However, this type of concentration is hard to control and not very stable. It is momentary. Normally, it is sustained by the interest we pay to objects of sense stimuli at the moment of experience; as soon as the interest weakens, we will also begin to lose concentration and will have to refocus our attention.

The second level, called access or approximate concentration (*upacara samadhi*), is a more developed form of concentration attainable through the process of mental development mentioned above. At this stage, the mind of the meditator is elevated beyond the ordinary level of consciousness but is not as yet well established in deep concentration. The state of one-pointedness of mind is still subject to some degree of instability and fluctuation, although it can be better controlled than in the first type of concentration.

Concentration at this particular level provides the necessary basis for the practice of insight meditation, and one need not develop it further should one chose to develop insight. However, if the meditator prefers to continue with concentration training, this stage will prove an important juncture where his consciousness has reached a higher stratum of spiritual accomplishment and is acutely attuned to attain higher, more steady one-pointedness of mind.

The third level is attainment concentration (*appana samadhi*). This is a stage where the meditator's mind becomes well established in one-pointedness and is completely under control. This means that at this level the meditator is in a position to retain concentration for as long as he or she wishes, and the concentration reached is so profound and deep it cannot be disturbed by any external elements. It is total mastery over oneself, a mastery that is potentially capable of defying even the known laws of nature. Here the meditator has become so entirely absorbed in the object of meditation that he or she appears to be wholly identified with it. This kind of concentration is the foundation of *jhana* or absorption. From this level of concentration, the meditator enters into the first absorption, and if one continues to persevere in one's effort, one will progress even further to higher stages of absorption.

Higher Benefits of Concentration

We have seen from the above discussion that concentration meditation involves force, will power, and mastery of mind. The inner powers generated through a high intensity of concentration may be used to influence other people and events. This is still rudimentary compared to what the higher states of mental development can achieve, and such powers are not the real objective of meditation practice and were not encouraged by the Buddha. Due to the limitations of modern life-styles, few people can afford the luxury of full-time practice as ascetics in mountain caves or forests. However, if one consistently perseveres until attainment concentration (*appana samadhi*) is gained, one may continue to achieve any of the eight levels of absorption.

The first four (five, according to the Abhidhamma) absorptions result from meditation on some concrete form such as earth, fire, water, or a *kasina* (colored disc), etc. A state of absorption achieved through the practice in this way is called absorption of form (*rupajhana*).

The other four are called absorptions of the formless sphere (*arupajhana*) because, rather than focusing the mind on any concrete form, the meditator employs abstract concepts as objects of concentration. These conceptual objects are the sphere of infinity of space (*akasanañcayatana*), the sphere of infinity of consciousness (*viññanañcayatana*), the sphere of nothingness (*akiñcaññayatana*), and the sphere of neither perception nor non-perception (*nevasaññanasaññayatana*). To practice the absorptions of the formless sphere one has to be first thoroughly accomplished in the four absorptions of form.

Concentration increases the power of mind. This can be brought to such a high level that psychic wonders, or what one may call 'miracles,' can be performed through it, although we should again emphasize that psychic powers or miracles are neither the purpose nor the goal of Buddhist meditation. In fact, the Buddha even laid down rules for the monks against the display of such feats, for they are likely to distract the uninformed and mislead them from the path of enlightenment and deliverance from *Samsara*, which is the true goal of Buddhism. In the Buddhist system of meditation, right concentration is that which serves as the basis for insight. It is a means to an end, not an end in itself.

PRACTICE OF INSIGHT MEDITATION

This properly requires a long description, but for reasons of space and balance we shall have to limit our discussion only to a brief description of this uniquely Buddhist meditation practice.

For the sake of clarity we may begin by briefly comparing some salient features in the two types of meditation, concentration and insight, which we have been discussing at some length. To practice concentration, a properly structured environment or atmosphere is required. For example, the environment should be relatively secluded and quiet, somewhat segregated from other activities, and completely free from disturbances.

Insight meditation does not need any of these requirements, although in the initial stages of practice they may prove valuable. Concentration training employs only one object as a tool for cultivating one-pointedness of mind, whereas insight meditation uses all available experiences as the primary matrix by which mindfulness and insight may be developed. The fact that insight meditation can take in all experiences, physical, emotional, and psychological, as its objects of training also means that one can practice it in all activities and situations. Concentration does not enjoy this kind of free range. So we may assert that insight meditation is one spiritual discipline that can be practiced at all times, in all places, and under all circumstances. Concentration and insight are also different in terms of the objectives and goals each aims to achieve. The former is connected with one-pointedness of mind, tranquillity, psychic powers, and miracles, whereas the latter aims at increased awareness, knowledge, wisdom, right understanding, virtues, purification of the mind, and the realization of *Nibbana*.

One of the most important discourses by the Buddha dealing with insight meditation is the*Satipatthana Sutta*, or the Discourse on the Foundations of Mindfulness. This discourse contains what is considered by all Buddhist traditions to be the classical explanation of how insight meditation should be practiced. In the opening words of the discourse, the Buddha categorically affirms that the development of mindfulness in accordance with the *Satipatthana Sutta* constitutes the direct way, the only way, to purification, the extinction of suffering, and the realization of *Nibbana*. It is one of the few discourses in which the Buddha has so explicitly and unequivocally given such a strong assurance.

According to the *Satipatthana Sutta*, mindfulness is the key factor in the development of insight. This mindfulness is the quality of awareness which is applied to four groups of experiences, namely, the body, the sensations, the mind, and mental objects (particularly in reference to moral and spiritual experiences or the Dhamma). Thus the discourse is divided into four principal sections, each dealing with an individual class of experiences on which mindfulness should be cultivated.

The first of the Four Foundations of Mindfulness deals with the body (*kaya*). This includes the breaths, the physical postures, the bodily activities, the analysis of various physical components, the material elements, and death. These are the realities of life one has to deal with. A student of insight meditation should practice by constantly applying mindfulness to all these experiences founded on the body. For instance, he should be attentively mindful of his breaths, noting their ever-changing characteristics to see if they are short or long, shallow or deep, refined or gross, regular or irregular, and so forth. The purpose is to train the mind to dwell in the present, by being constantly aware of what goes on at the moment. The same principle may be applied to the bodily posture, such as standing, walking, sitting, or lying down, as well as to other physical activities like eating and drinking, or even the movements of feet and hands. In the words of the Buddha:

"Monks, a monk should further apply full attention to the act of going forward or going back, looking straight or looking away, bending or stretching, putting on his robes or holding the bowl, eating, drinking, chewing or savoring food, attending to the calls of nature, walking, standing, sitting, falling asleep, waking up, speaking, or being silent. In all these activities he should be fully aware and attentive."

The second section deals with feelings (*vedana*), which are of three types, pleasant, unpleasant, and neutral. These feelings keep arising one after the other and the meditator should apply mindfulness to them at the moment they arise, understanding them objectively as conditioned phenomena that arise and fall according to the law of causality, not subjectively as 'my feeling.'

Sensations or feelings have a peculiar way of misleading us into a false sense of individuality. Because of feelings, man tends to conceptualize an essential agent within that feels or does the act of feeling, the recipient of various experiences, including the results of *kamma*. This is called a soul or self. According to the Buddha, the false belief in the existence of self is largely due to our feelings. It is therefore important that the meditator trains himself to perceive reality as it is by simply observing his own feelings for what they really are, natural phenomena that constantly arise and disappear in accordance with their conditionality.

Another way to consider feelings is the careful analysis of their nature and their origination and dissolution. The meditator is fully mindful whether he experiences pleasant, unpleasant, or neutral feeling. He is aware of the feelings but does not become attached to them. Says the Buddha:

"Here, a meditating monk dwells observing feelings internally, externally, or internally and externally. He dwells observing the nature of origination, dissolution, or origination and dissolution of feelings. His mindfulness is established merely to an extent necessary for knowledge and awareness that feelings exist. He lives unattached and clings to nothing in the world. In this way a monk dwells observing feelings."

The next section in the discourse deals with the mind. If part of the spiritual practice involves the ability to understand and control one's own thoughts, this is, perhaps, one of the most effective methods to realize that objective. Here, the meditator dwells observing his own mind and thoughts, ever mindful of their origination and dissolution. He also observes how they change and are conditioned. The meditator should constantly apply full awareness to the present moment of experiences only, not the past or the future, and simply acknowledge the existence and nature of those mental phenomena. There is no conscious intervention involved to suppress one thought or encourage another. It is a simple, uncomplicated process of recognizing the realities as they are, a pure psychological act of detached understanding and acceptance.

The *Satipatthana Sutta* gives an elaborate explanation of the techniques for observing the mind and recognizing its conditions in the present moment. We quote below some examples from the text:

"Here a meditating monk recognizes the lustful mind as lustful; the non-lustful mind as non-lustful; the hateful mind as hateful; the non-hateful mind as non-hateful; the deluded mind as deluded; the non-deluded mind as non-deluded; the depressed state of mind as depressed; the distracted state of mind as distracted; the cultivated state of mind as cultivated; the uncultivated state of mind as uncultivated ..."

It is clear from this short passage how a practitioner may train in insight meditation by steadfastly being mindful of his own mental states. By continually practicing according to this method, one not only comes to understand oneself better but will eventually be able to penetrate deeply into the most remote reaches of one's own consciousness. Thus one learns to come to terms with oneself, and a genuine effort to improve oneself and do away with weaknesses may now begin. This kind of practice is not only valuable as far as insight is concerned, but substantially contributes to peace and harmony, both within the individual and within society. If one, for instance, keeps taking mindful note of one's own greed, lust, anger, or aggression as they arise in the mind, it is most probable that the thoughts or actions associated with such negative qualities will be recognized as quickly as they originate and will subsequently be kept under control or eliminated. It is like having your hitherto clandestine enemies duly exposed so you can take appropriate action against them. There is no better way to deal with them than this.

The last section of the *Satipatthana Sutta* discusses the Dhamma as the system of ethical and spiritual experiences. In practical terms, this may also include mindfulness in contemplation, deliberation, and investigation of the Buddha's teachings in the context of one's own perception at the present moment. Because these Dhamma experiences are subjected to the contemplation and investigation of mind, they are referred to as mental objects. A few categories of Dhamma are listed in the *Satipatthana Sutta*: the Five Hindrances, the Five Aggregates, the Six Sense Bases, the Seven Factors of Enlightenment, and the Four Noble Truths. Detailed explanations illustrative of the practice are also given, for example:

"How, monks, does a monk dwell observing the Five Hindrances as mental objects? Here, when sense desire is present, a monk comprehends, "Sense desire is present in me;" when sense desire is not present, he comprehends, "Sense desire is not present in me." He comprehends how non-arisen sense desire arises; he comprehends how arisen sense desire disappears. He comprehends how abandoned sense desire will not arise in the future ..."

Broadly speaking, most of the deliberate intellectual exercises pertaining to ethics and truth come within the scope of this mode of insight meditation. To be more precise, however, each of the aforementioned categories of the Dhamma should not be viewed merely as a subject for academic scrutiny or an article for purely abstract contemplation. Rather, they are specific mental objects to which a meditator should apply mindfulness as and when they are actually experienced and comprehended, right at the moment of their arising and disappearing. In this way the meditator will be able to understand the Dhamma not as some abstract concept, but as the actual reality of personal experience which it truly is.

The Four Foundations of Mindfulness as described by the Buddha can be practiced simultaneously, depending on which of the four is more prominent or conspicuous at the moment of experience. The present moment is what counts, not the past or the future.

Beginners may find it more practicable to begin training with mindfulness on the body, particularly the breathing exercises. Once the basic technique has been mastered, it becomes increasingly more natural to 'ever dwell in meditation,' constantly and effortlessly observing the body, the feelings, the mind, and the mental objects while carrying on their duties and responsibilities.

Concentration in Insight Meditation

Concentration in *samatha bhavana* is characterized by its mundane nature and objective, whereas the same in *vipassana* is directed toward the transcendent goal of *Nibbana*. Concentration in insight meditation, moreover, assists the meditator to penetrate into the three existential realities in all experiences to which he applies his mindfulness. These are the characteristics common to all existence, namely, impermanence, unsatisfactoriness, and non-substantiality. Based on these three signs of reality, *vipassana* concentration is therefore divided into three types as follows:

The first kind of concentration is called *suññata samadhi*, meaning concentration on the void. This is the concentration which is specifically based on *anattalakkhana* or the characteristic of soullessness. It supports and identifies with the insight that contemplates on the relative, non-substantial nature of realities.

This insight aims primarily at liberation through penetration into the soulless nature of all things.

The second category of *vipassana* concentration is known as *animittasamadhi. Animitta*means "signless," an expression referring to the transitoriness of existence. This concentration supports insight which contemplates the impermanent nature of all things (*aniccalakkhana*), particularly the experiences to which the meditator's awareness is applied in the training of insight meditation. Here, liberation is achieved through seeing things in their true nature as impermanent and ever-changing.

The third kind of *vipassana* concentration, called in Pali *appanihitasamadhi*, is one which is directed toward the characteristic of unsatisfactoriness of all things (*dukkhalakkhana*). The word *appanihita* means "desireless." Where this type of concentration is involved in insight meditation, the meditator directs mindfulness to the unsatisfactory aspect of experiences pertaining to the Four Foundations of Mindfulness in order to perceive things in their true nature. Such contemplation enables one to relinquish desire and attachment and leads to the realization of*Nibbana*.

Strictly speaking, the three characteristics of existence are but different aspects of one and the same reality. As the Buddha often stressed, "Whatever is impermanent is unsatisfactory; whatever is unsatisfactory is nonself." The practitioner of insight meditation may therefore select that characteristic which is most suitable to his temperament and concentrate on that in order to make greater progress in his endeavor. For instance, a person with inherent propensity for sensual desire may practice profitably by constantly applying mindfulness to the unsatisfactory nature of things. This would serve as a direct antidote to that weakness and enable one to advance more satisfactorily on the spiritual path.

EXPERIENCES IN MEDITATION

It was eight years ago, amid the material comforts of city living and the demanding pressures of academic pursuits, that I first encountered the gentle and profound teachings of the Buddha. At that time a natural curiosity about the nature of the mind, and encounters with the concepts of biology and theoretical physics, had awakened in me a healthy appetite for intellectual nourishment. It is therefore not surprising that I was immediately attracted to the philosophical and psychological genius of the Buddha. What I at that time accepted intellectually of Buddhism led me, in due course, to the practice of meditation, which is the central axis of Buddhist spiritual life.

I began my meditation practice with mindfulness of breathing (*anapana-sati*) and cultivation of loving-kindness (*metta-bhavana*), two techniques widely practised by Theravada Buddhists in Sri Lanka, Thailand, and Burma. As I had no teacher at the time, and consequently had to rely on a small paperback manual on Buddhist meditation, my practice did not really take off. It remained intermittent and rather unenthusiastic until some five years ago, when I met my Buddhist teacher, the Venerable Shravasti Dhammika. He became instrumental in launching me into serious and committed meditation practice, practice that has continued to the present day.

The above preamble sets the background for this account of my subjective experiences during some two years of practising mindfulness of breathing and loving-kindness meditation. In the first half-year, this comprised a daily average of fifteen minutes of mindfulness of breathing followed by ten minutes of loving-kindness meditation. By the second year, the daily average for the two types of meditation had increased to about forty minutes and twenty minutes respectively. That second year also included two semi-intensive retreats. The first retreat lasted four days, during which the daily practice time totalled four and a half hours; the second was of three days duration, with the daily practice time increased to six hours. This, however, was not the whole of my meditative regime during the period in question. I was also practising general mindfulness (*satipatthana*) as far as possible when not engaged in formal mindfulness of breathing and loving-kindness meditation. However, that mindfulness practice is not described here.

The Meditative Techniques

Mindfulness of breathing, or anapana-sati, is a traditional Buddhist meditation technique aimed at purifying and unifying the mind through sustained concentration on the breath during inhalation and exhalation. Attention is fixed at the nostrils, at the point against which the moving air strikes, because it is there that the entry and exit of breath can be observed. No attempt is made to hold or stop the breath, or to deliberately deepen or force it into a definite time rhythm. As Nyanaponika Thera states, "The only task here is to follow the natural flow of the breath mindfully and continuously, without a break or without unnoticed break." Any thoughts that arise in the course of the meditation are merely noted, and attention is gently returned to the point of observation. A major goal of the practice is the attainment of states of deep unification called*jhanas*, characterised by total immersion of the mind in its object and a progressive elimination of thoughts and emotions.

Meditation on loving-kindness, or metta-bhavna, is another traditional Buddhist meditation technique. It has the twofold aim of (a) strengthening the quality of unbounded and universal loving-kindness within the mind, and (b) attaining the first three jhanas. The practice begins with sitting quietly with fully or half closed eyes and back erect, and arousing within oneself the emotion of joy and kindness. One then silently wishes "May I be well and happy," while suffusing oneself with kind and loving emotions. This is followed by evoking the image of someone that one respects or likes, and extending these emotions to him or her, while wishing, "May you be well and happy." The same procedure is then used in turn for a neutral person, a disliked person, and finally for all sentient beings. It thus involves a gradual progression in the extension of loving-kindness, from the individual to all living beings without exception, and in all directions: in front, to the right, behind, to the left, below and above. The commentarial advice given for beginners in this practice is not to extend loving-kindness to someone of the opposite sex, as this might evoke emotions of lust or attachment. A dead person who was dear to one is also an unsuitable object, as this might arouse emotions of grief and sadness. It is stressed that the first person to be suffused with loving-kindness should be oneself, since self-acceptance forms the basis of any genuine acceptance of other beings.

The First Four Months

I began meditating with fifteen minutes of mindfulness of breathing each day. During the first few weeks of practice, I was overwhelmed by the barrage of thoughts, images, emotions, and even sounds or voices, that were constantly "swimming" in the mind. This was not evident to me until I had to make repeated attempts to focus attention on a single object (the breathing). I started to become aware of how unaware I had always been of these ubiquitous mental states and contents. The constant flow of images and inner sounds would so often occupy the entire field of consciousness that it was extremely difficult to pay concentrated attention to the breath. This led to a gradual build-up of frustration and doubt, which on certain days grew almost unbearable. On such days I would abandon my fruitless attempts to attend to the breath and instead engage in chanting traditional praises to the Buddha, Dhamma and Sangha. This would often result in a certain degree of upliftment and purity of mind that imparted a quiet tranquility to my otherwise difficult practice.

Devotional practices, such as chanting and symbolic offerings of light, flowers and incense, while not essential to Buddhist practice, have often been found useful in calming and unifying the mind — a valuable preliminary to formal meditation practice. With persistent effort, and a firm, affirming confidence in Dhamma, I was gradually able to maintain concentration on the breath for increasingly longer periods without unnoticed break. By the end of the fourth month of practice, I was able to maintain concentration for twenty minutes at a time with comparative ease.

Each day, following my mindfulness of breathing, I would proceed to the practice of loving-kindness meditation. This involved extending loving thoughts and feelings to myself and others without undue thinking and emotional involvement. My initial attempts brought the feeling that the whole procedure was rather contrived and artificial. I had felt, at the time, that the practice was not very different from the psychological technique of auto-suggestion and therefore was suspect. Nevertheless, I decided to temporarily suspend my scepticism and critical appraisal of the practice so as to give it a fair trial.

Another difficulty I encountered in the course of this practice was constant emotional involvement in the images I had evoked, whether of a loved one or of a disliked one, often resulting in a whole train of discursive thinking connected with the images. At such times I would forget the aim of the practice and become completely immersed in my personal mental melodramas. It usually took me some time to notice that I had wandered. This recognition had the effect of automatically re-establishing the practice. By the end of the first two months, I was feeling increasingly doubtful about the value of this practice. The sense of its artificiality came to me with greater intensity than before. I persisted nevertheless. By the fourth month of practice, I found myself more able to stay with the practice without being sidetracked. I also began to feel more natural and at ease with the procedure.

The First Year

By this time in my breath-watching practice, the flow of thoughts was no longer the main problem. Instead, the increased ability to sustain attention elicited an intensifying boredom in the observation process. The breath was by nature not at all interesting to watch, and I was very quickly overcome by a dullness and drowsiness of mind. There came a point when brief periods of awareness would be interrupted by longer periods of a semi-consciousness, sleep-like state, during which the mind was totally inattentive to the breath. The meditation sessions often resulted in a heavy, uncomfortable pressure in the head that would subside whenever the mind was aroused by some object or activity of great interest. This made me more aware of the intimate link between the body and the mind, and of how profoundly psychological states influence one's physical condition.

By the beginning of the seventh month of practice, I was sitting in meditation for a total of forty-five minutes per day: half an hour of mindfulness of breathing, followed by fifteen minutes of loving-kindness meditation. Drowsiness continued to be a problem in observing the breath, but never seemed to interfere with the practice of extending kind and loving thoughts. This seemed to be because radiating loving-kindness to mentally-evoked images aroused more interest than watching the breath at the nostrils. It was not until the end of the seventh month of breathing practice that I began to experience a relative freedom from drowsy episodes, except on days when I was physically tried.

There were days when the benefits of meditation practice became apparent to me, as the mind began to grow in calmness and alertness. Such times were often characterized by a pliancy and lightness of mind coupled with a seemingly effortless attention to the breathing process. During these periods, I noted a sense of enthusiastic interest in the practice. Whenever this mental quality was present, boredom and drowsiness would be absent. With this noticing of the mutual exclusivity of incompatible mental states, I felt I had realized a simple but significant and fundamental aspect of the nature of the mind. On certain occasions, this enthusiastic interest in Dhamma practice would manifest as an emotion of uplifting joy which would pervade the whole upper body. Any thoughts that were still present seemed to have lost much of their force and energy, such that they no longer had the power to distract the focused attention.

Upon terminating the meditation session, I would experience a deep sense of peace and relaxation, which would linger on throughout the day, as long as activities were not too rushed or emotionally intense. Also, such occasions would result in a spontaneous and expansive flow of warm and kind feelings, which naturally led to a deep and genuine experience of loving-kindness for all beings. On such days, and for a long time after that, my earlier doubts about, and resistance to, loving-kindness practice dissolved. I was finally able to touch a deep and loving part of my heart to a degree I never thought possible. The gradual extension of loving-kindness from myself to all beings resulted in a state of consciousness which, though brief, was blissful, expansive, and non-limiting.

The Second Year

In the second year of practice, I increased the mindfulness of breathing to forty minutes daily and the loving-kindness meditation to twenty minutes. It was also during this period that I did the two semi-intensive retreats mentioned earlier. My ability to attend to the breath without unnoticed break steadily improved, though it was still not without the regressions into excessive discursive thinking, worries, fantasies, and occasional bouts of drowsiness. I noticed that whenever the mind was immersed in trains of thoughts, there was almost invariably some underlying emotional state that seemed to be generating these thoughts: worry, fear, anticipation, excitement, or (more subtly) a state of apathy or lack of interest (resulting in thoughts as a means of distraction or entertainment). Generally, however, there was improved concentration and a heightened capacity to be relaxed yet alert and relatively tranquil in the course of my daily life.

In loving-kindness practice there was becoming evident an increased ability to feel genuine and sincere acceptance of, even warmth for, a disliked person. As I practised looking deeply at the image of the disliked person in question, with a non-judgemental mind, and without entering into unprofitable conceptual proliferation about her faults and weaknesses, I found myself more able to appreciate her as another being who shares in the universal ailments of greed, aversion, delusion, and hence suffering. With this change in perspective came a corresponding decrease in dislike and an increase in warm, positive feeling for the person. These manifested in an improved and more harmonious relationship between us. It was also becoming increasingly easy for me to extend deep feelings of love and acceptance to myself, to those dear to me, and in fact to all beings. While it was technically impossible to conceptualize each and every living being in the universe, it remained possible for me to visualize as many beings as I could recall (both human and non-human) and to relate similar feelings of warmth and love to them without judging or discriminating.

One profound experience I had in the course of this practice left a deep and lasting impression on me. On the occasion in question, I sat and commenced with mindfulness of breathing as usual, which left my mind with a sense of lightness and happiness. As I proceeded to wish myself well and happy, a sudden gush of rapturous joy welled up within me in the region of the middle chest, then spread and permeated my neck, face, head, shoulders, hands, and even down to my lower abdomen. With this pervasive and uplifting feeling came a momentary one-pointedness and an expansion of the spatial boundaries of consciousness. In retrospect, I realised that in that moment of oneness and expansion the mind was totally still with not a single thought. However, slight trickles of thought soon re-emerged as the experience of mental concentration and expansion gradually faded. These thoughts seemed to move much more slowly than usual and lacked the power to disturb my tranquillity. In such a state, I continued with the expansion of loving-kindness to a dear one, a neutral person, a disliked person, and finally to all beings, with a depth, authenticity, and naturalness that previous sessions had lacked. I was left with an openness of heart and a sensitivity of spirit that carried over into the next two days or so.

There were also three related experiences worth mentioning here. The first was an ability to notice increasingly minute details of the breathing process. I noticed that every inhalation ended with a short pause, during which no movement of the breath occurred; then followed the movement of exhalation, which ended in another short pause.

This cycle repeated itself with the commencement of the next inhalation. I also observed that even the fleeting phenomenon of a single breath (one inhalation or exhalation) had extension in time, a distinct beginning, middle, and end of movement. The attention, however, was not equally keen and clear in all three phases, the middle and end of each breath often being more distinct than the beginning. It seemed to me that the reason for this was that breathing had been so much an unconscious and involuntary process that I was normally unaware of its existence, let alone of the distinct phases of the whole process. It was thus to be expected that any attempt to observe the process keenly would result in an intermittent awareness, which often arose somewhat more slowly than the inhalation itself. The task was, therefore, to cultivate an evenly-applied mindfulness that would sustain itself through all three phases of the inhalation — and indeed through the whole breathing cycle, incorporating the pauses and and the three phases of each inhalation and exhalation. The recognition that an evenly-applied mindfulness was my next task proved to be another important insight into how the mind is to be focused — an insight that has greatly facilitated my concentration practice since then.

I therefore put an increased amount of energy into watching clearly the distinct phases of both inhalation and exhalation together with the pauses, with the aim of sustaining an even, continuous attention throughout. With repeated effort, I finally succeeded in achieving this for an extended period. Following this a new type of sensory experience became apparent. I felt vivid tactile sensations, in the form of subtle rapid vibrations, at the tip of each nostril and around the upper lip. These tactile sensations became more distinct and concrete whenever mindfulness increased in intensity and duration. At this stage, when strong continuous mindfulness was present, the three phases of the breathing were no longer apparent, as they seemed to have dissolved into a rapid succession of minute vibrations. The flow of rapid vibrations occupied the whole field of consciousness, and there was a deep one-pointedness and an immense vacuity of mind. For an instant, my whole physical world would seem to have collapsed into oblivion, with a total loss of bodily perceptions except for the concentrated awareness of rapid vibrations.

From this second experience, and apparently as a direct consequence of it, there immediately followed the third experience. Sustained application of attention to the vibratory sensations would gradually lead to a point where the vibrations would suddenly disappear, leaving a spacious ground of greatly expanded awareness that seemed to have no distinct boundaries. It was as if the threshold of consciousness had been reached.

This altered state of consciousness was, however, very short-lived, lasting only for a finger-snap. Its termination was followed by the preceding experience of tactile vibrations. This profound experience occurred very rarely, and mostly during the periods of retreat when the pressures and distractions of mundane existence were largely absent. It would invariably result in a state of strong mindfulness and mental clarity, heightened perceptual sensitivity and calmness, which would then persist for hours or even days on end.

Critical Appraisal

The above is a phenomenological account of my experience with mindfulness of breathing and loving-kindness meditation. It is of interest to compare this account with the Buddha's descriptions of meditative experience as recorded in the Pali suttas.

The first jhana, the first stage in the process of mental unification, is repeatedly described in the suttas as follows:

> Being thus detached from sense desires, detached from unwholesome states, he enters and remains in the first jhana, which is with thinking, and pondering, born of detachment, filled with delight and joy. [D.i, 73]

As mentioned earlier, there was a time during my breath-watching practice when, in the absence of certain "unwholesome" states (namely frustration, doubt, drowsiness, excessive thinking) and the presence of enthusiasm and joy, the mind was effortlessly attentive to the breathing process, pliant, and light. "Thinking" and "pondering" were present but the thoughts lacked the energy and power to distract the mind from its object of concentration. This experience seems to correspond very closely to the Buddha's description of first jhana.

In the Tevijja Sutta, the Buddha describes how the noble disciple goes forth into the holy life, practises the moralities, attains the first jhana (account similar to the one above), and then proceeds to loving-kindness meditation:

> Then, with his heart filled with loving-kindness, he dwells suffusing one quarter, the second, the third, the fourth. Thus he dwells suffusing the whole world, upwards, downwards, across, everywhere, always with a heart filled with loving-kindness, abundant, unbounded without hate or ill-will.
>
> [D.i, 250-251]

As mentioned before, when my loving-kindness meditation was preceded by a pliancy and lightness of mind with relative freedom from thoughts, spontaneous feelings of joy and warmth would arise from within and lead to an almost effortless pervasion of the whole world with loving-kindness. In that state, the mind was filled with a sense of delight and openness. This experience seems to correspond to the Buddha's description just quoted.

More importantly, it lends credence to the idea of sequential progression in meditative training: prior attainment of the first jhana greatly facilitates successful practice of extending loving-kindness.

The sutta description of the second jhana is as follows:

Again, a monk, with the subsiding of thinking and pondering, by gaining inner tranquillity and oneness of mind, enters and remains in the second jhana, which is without thinking and pondering, born of concentration, filled with delight and joy. [D.i, 74]

In describing one profound experience I had in the course of loving-kindness practice, I mentioned three specific mental factors present, namely an uplifting joy permeating my body, mental one-pointedness, and a momentary but total absence of thoughts. This experience was, therefore, significantly similar to the Buddha's description of the second jhana.

The sutta describe a further set of advanced meditative attainments, namely the *arupa* or formless jhanas, four distinct and progressively more subtle stages. The first arupa jhana is described as follows:

By completely transcending all perception of matter, by the vanishing of the perception of sense reactions, and by non-attention to the perception of variety, realising: "Space is infinite," one enters and abides in the Sphere of Infinite Space. [D.ii, 71]

I described above the experience of rapid subtle vibrations that occupied the whole field of consciousness, with loss of body sense and of perception of distinct breath phases. This bears a loose similarity to the sutta account just quoted. The disappearance of body sense and of distinct breath phases seems to correspond to the "vanishing of the perception of sense reactions" and "non-attention to the perception of variety." The sense of limitless expansion of the mind-space — filled completely by the perception of subtle vibrations — and the apparent disappearance of the breath and the physical world, further suggest that my experience was of the first arupa jhana.

The second arupa jhana is described thus:

By transcending the Sphere of Infinite Space, thinking:

"Consciousness is infinite," one enters and abides in the Sphere of Infinite Consciousness. [D.ii, 70]

This invites comparison with the third set of experiences described earlier. The sudden disappearance of the vibrations, accompanied by dissolution of the boundaries of consciousness and thus attainment of a wider-encompassing awareness, can be seen as corresponding to the characteristics of the second arupa jhana as just quoted.

Some Final Thoughts

Diligent and sustained practice of mindfulness of breathing and loving-kindness meditation is a fruitful and spiritually fulfilling endeavour that results in an enhanced state of awareness and a transformation of unwholesome mental patterns in one's daily life. The above comparison indicates, furthermore, that the altered states of consciousness to which these practices lead correspond closely to certain of the jhanas as described in the Pali texts.

An important point to note is that the jhanas are not permanent states which, once arisen, will remain unfluctuating. Persistent diligent, and insightful practice is essential to the consolidation of such positive mental states in one's meditation and life.

Personally, I find that these practices have brought a deeper understanding of the following words of the well-known meditation master, Sumedho Thera:

[The Buddhist texts] are not meant to be "sacred scriptures" that tell us what to believe. One should read them, listen to them, think about them, contemplate them, and investigate the present reality, the present experience with them. Then, and only then, can one insightfully know the truth beyond words.

BREATH MEDITATION CONDENSED

There are lots of people who are ashamed to talk about their own defilements but who feel no shame at talking about the defilements of others. Those who are willing to report their own diseases — their own defilements — in a straightforward manner are few and far between. As a result, the disease of defilement is hushed up and kept secret, so that we don't realize how serious and widespread it is. We all suffer from it, and yet no one is open about it. No one is really interested in diagnosing his or her own defilements....

We have to find a skillful approach if we hope to wipe out this disease, and we have to be open about it, admitting our defilements from the grossest to the most subtle levels, dissecting them down to their minutest details. Only then will we gain from our practice.

If we look at ourselves in a superficial way, we may feel that we're already fine just as we are, already know all we need to know. But then when the defilements let loose with full force as anger or delusion, we pretend that nothing is wrong — and this way the defilements become a hidden disease, hard to catch hold of, hard to diagnose....

We have to be strong in fighting off defilements, cravings, and illusions of every sort. We have to test our strength against them and bring them under our power. If we can bring them under our power, we can ride on their backs. If we can't, they'll have to ride on *our* backs, making us do their work, pulling us around by the nose, making us want, wearing us out in all sorts of ways.

So are we still beasts of burden? Are we beasts of burden because defilement and craving are riding on our backs? Have they put a ring through our noses? When you get to the point when you've had enough, you have to stop — stop and watch the defilements to see how they come into being, what they want, what they eat, what they find delicious. Make it your sport — watching the defilements and making them starve, like a person giving up an addiction....See if it gets the defilements upset. Do they hunger to the point where they're salivating? Then don't let them eat. No matter what, don't let them eat what they're addicted to. After all, there are plenty of other things to eat. You have to be hard on them — hard on your "self" — like this...."Hungry? Well go ahead and be hungry! You're going to die? Fine! Go ahead and die!" If you can take this attitude, you'll be able to win out over all sorts of addictions, all sorts of defilements — because you're not pandering to desire, you're not nourishing the desire that exists for the sake of finding flavor in physical things. It's time you stopped, time you gave up feeding these things. If they're going to waste away and die, let them die. After all, why should you keep them fat and well fed?

No matter what, you have to keep putting the heat on your cravings and defilements until they wither and waste away. Don't let them raise their heads. Keep them under your thumb. This is the sort of straightforward practice you have to follow. If you're steadfast, if you put up a persistent fight until they're all burned away, then there's no other victory that can come anywhere near, no other victory that's anywhere near a match for victory over the cravings and defilements in your own heart.

This is why the Buddha taught us to put the heat on the defilements in all our activities — sitting, standing, walking, and lying down. If we don't do this, *they'll* burn *us* in all our activities....

If you consider things carefully, you'll see that the Buddha's teachings are all exactly right, both in how they tell us to examine the diseases of defilement and in how they tell us to let go, destroy, and extinguish defilement.

All the steps are there, so we needn't go study anywhere else. Every point in his doctrine and discipline shows us the way, so we needn't wonder how we can go about examining and doing away with these diseases. This becomes mysterious and hard to know only if you study his teachings without making reference to doing away with your own defilements. People don't like to talk about their own defilements, so they end up completely ignorant. They grow old and die without knowing a thing about their own defilements at all.

When we start to practice, when we come to comprehend how the defilements burn our own hearts, that's when we gradually come to know ourselves. To understand suffering and defilement and learn how to extinguish defilement gives us space to breathe....

When we learn how to put out the fires of defilement, how to destroy them, it means we have tools. We can be confident in ourselves — no doubts, no straying off into other paths of practice, because we're sure to see that practicing in this way, contemplating inconstancy, stress, and not-selfness in this way at all times, really gets rid of our defilements.

The same holds true with virtue, concentration, and discernment. They're our tools — and we need a full set. We need the discernment that comes with Right View and the virtue that comes with self-discipline. Virtue is very important. Virtue and discernment are like our right and left hands. If one of our hands is dirty, it can't wash itself. You need to use both hands to keep both hands washed and clean.

Thus wherever there's virtue, you have to have discernment. Wherever there's discernment, you have to have virtue. Discernment is what enables you to know; virtue is what enables you to let go, to relinquish, to destroy your addictions. Virtue isn't just a matter of the five or eight precepts, you know. It has to deal with the finest details. Whatever your discernment sees as a cause of suffering, you have to stop, you have to let go. Virtue is something that gets very subtle and precise. Letting go, giving up, renouncing, abstaining, cutting away, and destroying: All of these things are an affair of virtue. This is why virtue and discernment have to go together, just as our right and left hands have to help each other. They help each other wash away defilement. That's when your mind can become centered, bright, and clear. These things show their benefits right at the mind. If we don't have these tools, it's as if we had no hands or feet: We wouldn't be able to get anywhere at all. We have to use our tools — virtue and discernment — to destroy defilement. That's when our minds will benefit....

This is why the Buddha taught us to keep training in virtue, concentration, and discernment. We have to keep fit in training these things. If we don't keep up the training as we should, our tools for extinguishing suffering and defilement won't be sharp, won't be of much use. They won't be a match for the defilements. The defilements have monstrous powers for burning the mind in the twinkling of an eye. Say that the mind is quiet and neutral: The slightest sensory contact can set things burning in an instant by making us pleased or displeased. Why?

Sensory contact is our measuring stick for seeing how firm or weak our mindfulness is. Most of the time it stirs things up. As soon as there's contact by way of the ear or eye, the defilements are very quick. When this is the case, how can we keep things under control? How are we going to gain control over our eyes? How are be going to gain control over our ears, nose, tongue, body, and mind? How can we get mindfulness and discernment in charge of these things? This is a matter of practice, pure and simple...our own affair, something by which we can test ourselves, to see why defilements flare up so quickly when sensory contact takes place.

Say, for instance, that we hear a person criticizing someone else. We can listen and not get upset. But say that the thought occurs to us, "She's actually criticizing *me.*" As soon as we conjure up this "me," we're immediately angry and displeased. If we concoct very much of this "me," we can get very upset. Just this fact alone should enable us to observe that as soon as our "self" gets involved, we suffer immediately. This is how it happens. If no sense of self comes out to get involved, we can remain calm and indifferent. When they criticize other people, we can stay indifferent; but as soon as we conclude that they're criticizing us, our "self" appears and immediately gets involved — and we immediately burn with defilement. Why?

You have to pay close attention to this. As soon as your "self" arises, suffering arises in the very same instant. The same holds true even if you're just thinking. The "self" you think up spreads out into all sorts of issues. The mind gets scattered all over the place with defilement, craving, and attachments. It has very little mindfulness and discernment watching over it, so it gets dragged every which way by craving and defilement.

And yet we don't realize it. We think we're just fine. Is there anyone among us who realizes that this is what's happening? We're too weighted down, weighted down with our own delusions. No matter how much the mind is smothered in the defilement of delusion, we don't realize it, for it keeps us deaf and blind....

There are no physical tools you can use to detect or cure this disease of defilement, because it arises only at sensory contact. There's no substance to it. It's like a match in a matchbox. As long as the match doesn't come into contact with the friction strip on the side of the box, it won't give rise to fire. But as soon as we strike it against the side of the box, it bursts into flame. If it goes out right then, all that gets burned is the matchhead. If it doesn't stop at the matchhead, it'll burn the matchstick. If it doesn't stop with the matchstick, and meets up with anything flammable, it can grow into an enormous fire.

When defilement arises in the mind, it starts from the slightest contact. If we can be quick to put it out right there, it's like striking a match that flares up — *chae* — for an instant and then dies down right in the matchhead. The defilement disbands right there. But if we don't put it out the instant it arises, and let it start concocting issues, it's like pouring fuel into a fire. We have to observe the diseases of defilement in our own minds to see what their symptoms are, why they're so quick to flare up. They can't stand to be disturbed. The minute you disturb them, they flare up into flame. When this is the case, what can we do to prepare ourselves beforehand? How can we stock up on mindfulness before sensory contact strikes?

The way to stock up is to practice meditation, as when we keep the breath in mind. This is what gets our mindfulness prepared so that we can keep ahead of defilement, so that we can keep it from arising as long as we have our theme of meditation as an inner shelter for the mind.

The mind's outer shelter is the body, which is composed of physical elements, but its inner shelter is the theme of meditation we use to train its mindfulness to be focused and aware. Whatever theme we use, that's the inner shelter for the mind that keeps it from wandering around, concocting thoughts and imaginings. This is why we need a theme of meditation. Don't let the mind chase after its preoccupations the way ordinary people who don't meditate do. Once we have a meditation theme to catch this monkey of a mind so that it becomes less and less willful, day by day, it will gradually calm down, calm down until it can stand firm for long or short periods, depending on how much we train and observe ourselves.

Now, as for how we *do* breath meditation: The texts say to breathe in long and out long — heavy or light — and then to breathe in short and out short, again heavy or light. Those are the first steps of the training. After that we don't have to focus on the length of the in-breath or out-breath. Instead, we simply gather our awareness at any one point of the breath and keep this up until the mind settles down and is still. When the mind is still, you then focus on the stillness of the mind at the same time you're aware of the breath.

At this point you don't focus directly on the breath. You focus on the mind that is still and at normalcy. You focus continuously on the normalcy of the mind at the same time that you're aware of the breath coming in and out, without actually focusing on the breath. You simply stay with the mind, but you watch it with each in-and-out breath. Usually when you are doing physical work and your mind is at normalcy, you can know what you're doing, so why can't you be aware of the breath? After all, it's part of the body.

Some of you are new at this, which is why you don't know how you can focus on the mind at normalcy with each in-and-out breath without focusing directly on the breath itself. What we're doing here is practicing how to be aware of the body and mind, pure and simple, in and of themselves....

Start out by focusing on the breath for about 5, 10, or 20 minutes. Breathe in long and out long, or in short and out short. At the same time, notice the stages in how the mind feels, how it begins to settle down when you have mindfulness watching over the breath. You've got to make a point of observing this, because usually you breathe out of habit, with your attention far away. You don't focus on the breath; you're not really aware of it. This leads you to think that it's hard to stay focused here, but actually it's quite simple. After all, the breath comes in and out on its own, by its very nature. There's nothing at all difficult about breathing. It's not like other themes of meditation. For instance, if you're going to practice recollection of the Buddha, or *buddho,* you have to keep on repeating *buddho, buddho, buddho.*

Actually, if you want, you can repeat *buddho* in the mind with each in-and-out breath, but only in the very beginning stages. You repeat *buddho* to keep the mind from concocting thoughts about other things. Simply by keeping up this repetition you can weaken the mind's tendency to stray, for the mind can take on only one object at a time. This is something you have to observe. The repetition is to prevent the mind from thinking up thoughts and clambering after them.

After you've kept up the repetition — you don't have to count the number of times — the mind will settle down to be aware of the breath with each in-and-out breath. It will begin to be still, neutral, at normalcy.

This is when you focus on the mind instead of the breath. Let go of the breath and focus on the mind — but still be aware of the breath on the side. You don't have to make note of how long or short the breath is. Make note of the mind staying at normalcy with each in-and-out breath. Remember this carefully so that you can put it into practice.

The posture: For focusing on the breath, sitting is a better posture than standing, walking, or lying down, because the sensations that come with the other postures often overcome the sensations of the breath. Walking jolts the body around too much, standing for a long time can make you tired, and if the mind settles down when you're lying down, you tend to fall asleep. With sitting it's possible to stay in one position and keep the mind firmly settled for a long period of time. You can observe the subtleties of the breath and the mind naturally and automatically.

Here I'd like to condense the steps of breath meditation to show how all four of the tetrads mentioned in the texts can be practiced at once. In other words, is it possible to focus on the body, feelings, the mind, and the Dhamma all in one sitting? This is an important question for all of us. You could, if you wanted to, precisely follow all the steps in the texts so as to develop strong powers of mental absorption *(jhana),* but it takes a lot of time. It's not appropriate for those of us who are old and have only a little time left.

What we need is a way of gathering our awareness at the breath long enough to make the mind firm, and then go straight to examining how all formations are inconstant, stressful, and not-self, so that we can see the truth of all formations with each in-and-out breath. If you can keep at this continually, without break, your mindfulness will become firm and snug enough for you to give rise to the discernment that will enable you to gain clear knowledge and vision. So what follows is a guide to the steps in practicing a condensed form of breath meditation....Give them a try until you find they give rise to knowledge of your own within you. You're sure to give rise to knowledge of your very own.

The first thing when you're going to meditate on the breath is to sit straight and keep your mindfulness firm. Breathe in. Breathe out. Make the breath feel open and at ease. Don't tense your hands, your feet, or any of your joints at all. You have to keep your body in a posture that feels appropriate to your breathing. At the beginning, breathe in long and out long, fairly heavily, and gradually the breath will shorten — sometimes heavy and sometimes light. Then breathe in short and out short for about 10 or 15 minutes and then change.

After a while, when you stay focused mindfully on it, the breath will gradually change. Watch it change for as many minutes as you like, then be aware of the whole breath, all of its subtle sensations. This is the third step, the third step of the first tetrad: *sabba-kaya-patisamvedi* —focusing on how the breath affects the whole body by watching all the breath sensations in all the various parts of the body, and in particular the sensations related to the in-and-out breath.

From there you focus on the sensation of the breath at any one point. When you do this correctly for a fairly long while, the body — the breath — will gradually grow still. The mind will grow calm. In other words, the breath grows still together with the awareness of the breath. When the subtleties of the breath grow still at the same time that your undistracted awareness settles down, the breath grows even more still. All the sensations in the body gradually grow more and more still. This is the fourth step, the stilling of bodily formations.

As soon as this happens, you begin to be aware of the feelings that arise with the stilling of the body and mind. Whether they are feelings of pleasure or rapture or whatever, they appear clearly enough for you to contemplate them.

The stages through which you have already passed — watching the breath come in and out, long or short — should be enough to make you realize — even though you may not have focused on the idea — that the breath is inconstant. It's continually changing, from in long and out long to in short and out short, from heavy to light and so forth. This should enable you to read the breath, to understand that there's nothing constant to it at all. It changes on its own from one moment to the next.

Once you have realized the inconstancy of the body — in other words, of the breath — you'll be able to see the subtle sensations of pleasure and pain in the realm of feeling. So now you watch feelings, right there in the same place where you've been focusing on the breath. Even though they are feelings that arise from the stillness of the body or mind, they're nevertheless inconstant even in that stillness. They can change. So these changing sensations in the realm of feeling exhibit inconstancy in and of themselves, just like the breath.

When you see change in the body, change in feelings, and change in the mind, this is called*seeing the Dhamma,* i.e., seeing inconstancy. You have to understand this correctly. Practicing the first tetrad of breath meditation contains all four tetrads of breath meditation. In other words, you see the inconstancy of the body and then contemplate feeling. You see the inconstancy of feeling and then contemplate the mind. The mind, too, is inconstant. This inconstancy of the mind is the Dhamma. To see the Dhamma is to see this inconstancy.

When you see the true nature of all inconstant things, then keep track of that inconstancy at all times, with every in-and-out breath. Keep this up in all your activities to see what happens next.

What happens next is dispassion. Letting go. This is something you have to know for yourself.

This is what condensed breath meditation is like. I call it condensed because it contains all the steps at once. You don't have to do one step at a time. Simply focus at one point, the body, and you'll see the inconstancy of the body. When you see the inconstancy of the body, you'll have to see feeling. Feeling will have to show its inconstancy. The mind's sensitivity to feeling, or its thoughts and imaginings, are also inconstant. All of these things keep on changing. This is how you know inconstancy....

If you can become skilled at looking and knowing in this way, you'll be struck with the inconstancy, stressfulness, and not-selfness of your "self," and you'll meet with the genuine Dhamma. The Dhamma that's constantly changing like a burning fire — burning with inconstancy, stress, and not-selfness — is the Dhamma of the impermanence of all formations. But further in, in the mind or in the property of consciousness, is something special, beyond the reach of any kind of fire. There, there's no suffering or stress of any kind at all. This thing that lies "inside": You could say that it lies within the mind, but it isn't really in the mind. It's simply that the contact is there at the mind. There's no way you can really describe it. Only the extinguishing of all defilement will lead you to know it for yourself.

This "something special" within exists by its very nature, but defilements have it surrounded on all sides. All these counterfeit things — the defilements — keep getting in the way and take possession of everything, so that this special nature remains imprisoned inside at all times. Actually, there's nothing in the dimension of time that can be compared with it. There's nothing by which you can label it, but it's something that you can pierce through to see — i.e., by piercing through defilement, craving, and attachment into the state of mind that is pure, bright, and silent. This is the only thing that's important.

But it doesn't have only one level. There are many levels, from the outer bark to the inner bark and on to the sapwood before you reach the heartwood. The genuine Dhamma is like the heartwood, but there's a lot to the mind that isn't heartwood: The roots, the branches and leaves of the tree are more than many, but there's only a little heartwood. The parts that aren't heartwood will gradually decay and disintegrate, but the heartwood doesn't decay. That's one kind of comparison we can make. It's like a tree that dies standing. The leaves fall away, the branches rot away, the bark and sapwood rot away, leaving nothing but the true heartwood. That's one comparison we can make with this thing we call deathless, this property that has no birth, no death, no changing. We can also call it *nibbana* or the Unconditioned. It's all the same thing.

THE PRACTICAL ASPECTS OF BUDDHIST MEDITATION

The mental exercise known as meditation is found in all religious systems. Prayer is a form of discursive meditation, and in Hinduism the reciting of slokas and mantras is employed to tranquilize the mind to a state of receptivity. In most of these systems the goal is identified with the particular psychic results that ensue, sometimes very quickly; and the visions that come in the semi-trance state, or the sounds that are heard, are considered to be the end-result of the exercise. This is not the case in the forms of meditation practiced in Buddhism.

There is still comparatively little known about the mind, its functions and its powers, and it is difficult for most people to distinguish between self-hypnosis, the development of mediumistic states, and the real process of mental clarification and direct perception which is the object of Buddhist mental concentration. The fact that mystics of every religion have induced on themselves states wherein they see visions and hear voices that are in accordance with their own religious beliefs indicates that their meditation has resulted only in bringing to the surface of the mind and objectifying the concepts already embedded in the deepest strata of their subconscious minds. The Christian sees and converses with the saints of whom he already knows; the Hindu visualizes the gods of the Hindu pantheon, and so on. When Sri Ramakrishna Paramahamsa, the Bengali mystic, began to turn his thoughts towards Christianity, he saw visions of Jesus in his meditations, in place of his former eidetic images of the Hindu Avatars.

The practiced hypnotic subject becomes more and more readily able to surrender himself to the suggestions made to him by the hypnotiser, and anyone who has studied this subject is bound to see a connection between the mental state of compliance he has reached and the facility with which the mystic can induce whatever kind of experiences he wills himself to undergo. There is still another possibility latent in the practice of meditation; the development of mediumistic faculties by which the subject can actually see and hear beings on different planes of existence, the Devalokas and the realm of the unhappy ghosts, for example.

These worlds being nearest to our own are the more readily accessible, and this is the true explanation of the psychic phenomena of Western Spiritualism.

The object of Buddhist meditation, however, is none of these things. They arise as side-products, but not only are they not its goal, but they are hindrances which have to be overcome. The Christian who has seen Jesus, or the Hindu who has conversed with Bhagavan Krishna may be quite satisfied that he has fulfilled the purpose of his religious life, but the Buddhist who sees a vision of the Buddha knows by that very fact that he has only succeeded in objectifying a concept in his own mind, for the Buddha after his Parinibbana is, in his own words, no longer visible to gods or men.

There is an essential difference, then, between Buddhist meditation and concentration and that practiced in other systems. The Buddhist embarking on a course of meditation does well to recognize this difference and to establish in his own conscious mind a clear idea of what it is he is trying to do.

The root-cause of rebirth and suffering is *avijja* conjoined with and reacting upon *tanha.* These two causes form a vicious circle; on the one hand, concepts, the result of ignorance, and on the other hand, desire arising from concepts. The world of phenomena has no meaning beyond the meaning given to it by our own interpretation.

When that interpretation is conditioned by *avijja,* we are subject to the state known as*vipallasa,* or hallucination. *Sañña-vipallasa,* hallucination of perception; *citta-vipallasa,*hallucination of consciousness, and *ditthi-vipallasa,* hallucination of views, cause us to regard that which is impermanent *(anicca)* as permanent, that which is painful *(dukkha)* as a source of pleasure, and that which is unreal *(anatta),* or literally without any self existence, as being a real, self-existing entity. Consequently, we place a false interpretation on all the sensory experiences we gain through the six channels of cognition, that is, the eye, ear, nose, tongue, sense of touch and mind *cakkhu, sota, ghana, jivha, kaya* and *mano (ayatana).* Physics, by showing that the realm of phenomena we know through these channels of cognition does not really correspond to the physical world known to science, has confirmed this Buddhist truth. We are deluded by our own senses. Pursuing what we imagine to be desirable, an object of pleasure, we are in reality only following a shadow, trying to grasp a mirage. It is *anicca, dukkha, anatta* — impermanent, associated with suffering, an insubstantial. Being so, it can only be the cause of impermanence, suffering and insubstantiality, since like begets like; and we ourselves, who chase the illusion, are also impermanent, subject to suffering and without any persistent ego-principle. It is a case of a shadow pursuing a shadow.

The purpose of Buddhist meditation, therefore, is to gain more than an intellectual understanding of this truth, to liberate ourselves from the delusion and thereby put an end to both ignorance and craving. If the meditation does not produce results tending to this consummation — results which are observable in the character and the whole attitude to life — it is clear that there is something wrong either with the system or with the method of employing it. It is not enough to see lights, to have visions or to experience ecstasy. These phenomena are too common to be impressive to the Buddhist who really understands the purpose of Buddhist meditation. There are actual dangers in them which are apparent to one who is also a student of psychopathology.

In the Buddha's great discourse on the practice of mindfulness, the Maha-Satipatthana Sutta, both the object and the means of attaining it are clearly set forth. Attentiveness to the movements of the body, to the ever-changing states of the mind, is to be cultivated in order that their real nature should be known. Instead of identifying these physical and mental phenomena with the false concept of "self," we are to see them as they really are: movements of a physical body, an aggregate of the four elements, *(mahabhutas)* subject to physical laws of causality on the one hand, and on the other, a flux of successive phases of consciousness arising and passing away in response to external stimuli. They are to be viewed objectively, as though they were processes not associated with ourselves but belonging to another order of phenomena.

From what can selfishness and egotism proceed if not from the concept of "self"*(sakkayaditthi)*? If the practice of any form of meditation leaves selfishness or egotism unabated, it has not been successful. A tree is judged by its fruits and a man by his actions; there is no other criterion. Particularly is this true in Buddhist psychology, because the man *is* his actions. In the truest sense they, or the continuity of kamma and *vipaka* which they represent, are the only claim he can make to any persistent identity, not only through the different phases of this life but also from one life to another. Attentiveness with regard to body and mind serves to break down the illusion of self; and not only that, it also cuts off craving and attachment to external objects, so that ultimately there is neither the "self" that craves nor any object of craving. It is a long and arduous discipline, and one that can only be undertaken in retirement from the world and its cares.

Yet even a temporary retirement, a temporary course of this discipline, can bear good results in that it establishes an attitude of mind which can be applied to some degree in the ordinary situations of life. Detachment, objectivity, is an invaluable aid to clear thinking; it enables a man to sum up a given situation without bias, personal or otherwise, and to act in that situation with courage and discretion. Another gift it bestows is that of concentration — the ability to focus the mind and keep it steadily fixed on a single point *(ekaggata,* or one-pointedness), and this is the great secret of success in any undertaking. The mind is hard to tame; it roams here and there restlessly as the wind, or like an untamed horse, but when it is fully under control, it is the most powerful instrument in the whole universe. He who has mastered his own mind is indeed master of the Three Worlds.

In the first place he is without fear. Fear arises because we associate mind and body *(nama-rupa)* with "self"; consequently any harm to either is considered to be harm done to oneself. But he who has broken down this illusion by realizing that the five *khaṇdha* process is merely the manifestation of cause and effect, does not fear death or misfortune. He remains equable alike in success and failure, unaffected by praise or blame. The only thing he fears is demeritorious action, because he knows that no thing or person in the world can harm him except himself, and as his detachment increases, he becomes less and less liable to demeritorious deeds. Unwholesome action comes of an unwholesome mind, and as the mind becomes purified, healed of its disorders, bad kamma ceases to accumulate. He comes to have a horror of wrong action and to take greater and greater delight in those deeds that are rooted in *alobha, adosa,* and*amoha* — generosity, benevolence and wisdom.

Anapana Sati

One of the most universally-applicable methods of cultivating mental concentration is*anapanasati,* attentiveness on the in-going and out-going breath. This, unlike the Yogic systems, does not call for any interference with the normal breathing, the breath being merely used as a point on which to fix the attention, at the tip of the nostrils. The attention must not wander, even to follow the breath, but must be kept rigidly on the selected spot. In the initial stages it is advisable to mark the respiration by counting, but as soon as it is possible to keep the mind fixed without this artificial aid, it should be discontinued and only used when it is necessary to recall the attention.

As the state of mental quiescence *(samatha)* is approached, the breath appears to become fainter and fainter, until it is hardly discernible. It is at this stage that certain psychic phenomena appear, which may at first be disconcerting. A stage is reached when the actual bodily *dukkha,*the sensation of arising and passing away of the physical elements in the body, is felt. This is experienced as a disturbance, but it must be remembered that it is an agitation that is always present in the body but we are unaware of it until the mind becomes stabilized. It is the first direct experience of the *dukkha* (suffering) which is inherent in all phenomena — the realization within oneself of the first of the Four Noble Truths, *Dukkha Ariya Sacca.* When that is passed there follows the sensation of *piti,* rapturous joy associated with the physical body. The teacher of*vipassana,* however, is careful never to describe to his pupil beforehand what he is likely to experience, for if he does so, there is a strong possibility that the power of suggestion will produce a false reaction, particularly in those cases where the pupil is very suggestible and greatly under the influence of the teacher.

Devices in Meditation

In *kammattana,* it is permissible to use certain devices, such as the earth or colour *kasina,* as focal points for the attention. A candle flame, a hole in the wall, or some metal object can also be used, and the method of using them is found in the Pali texts and the *Visuddhi-magga.* In the texts themselves it is to be noted that the Buddha gave objects of meditation to disciples in accordance with their individual characteristics, and his unerring knowledge of the right technique for each came from his insight into their previous births. Similarly with recursive meditation, a subject would be given which was easily comprehensible to the pupil, or which served to counteract some strong, unwholesome tendency in his nature. Thus, to one attracted by sensual indulgence, the Buddha would recommend meditation on the impurity of the body, or the "cemetery meditation." Here the object is to counterbalance attraction by repulsion, but it is only a "skillful means" to reach the final state, in which attraction and repulsion both cease to exist. In the Arahant there is neither liking nor disliking: he regards all things with perfect equanimity, as did Thera Maha Moggallana when he accepted a handful of rice from a leper.

Beads

The use of the rosary in Buddhism is often misunderstood. If it is used for the mechanical repetition of a set formula, the repeating of so many phrases as an act of piety, as in other religions, its value is negligible. When it is used as means of holding the attention and purifying the mind, however, it can be a great help. One of the best ways of employing it, because it calls for undivided attention, is to repeat the Pali formula of the qualities of Buddha, Dhamma and Sangha, beginning *"Iti'pi so Bhagava — "* with the first bead, starting again with the second and continuing to the next quality: *"Iti'pi so Bhagava, Arahan — "* and so on until with the last bead the entire formula is repeated from beginning to end. This cannot be carried out successfully unless the mind is entirely concentrated on what is being done. At the same time the recalling of the noble qualities of Buddha, Dhamma and Sangha lifts the mind to a lofty plane, since the words carry with them a meaning the impresses itself on the pattern of the thought-moments as they arise and pass away. The value of this in terms of Abhidhamma psychology lies in the wholesome nature of the *cittakkhana*, or "consciousness-moment" in its *uppada* (arising), *thiti*(static) and *bhanga* (disappearing) phases. Each of these wholesome *cittakkhana* contributes to the improvement of the *sankhara;* or aggregate of tendencies; in other words, it directs the subsequent thought-moments into a higher realm and tends to establish the character on that level.

Samatha Bhavana

Samatha bhavaṅa, the development of mental tranquillity with concentration, is accompanied by three benefits; it gives happiness in the present life, a favorable rebirth, and the freedom from mental defilements which is a prerequisite for attainment of insight. In *samatha* the mind becomes like a still, clear pool completely free from disturbance and agitation, and ready to mirror on its surface the nature of things as they really are, the aspect of them which is hidden from ordinary knowledge by the restlessness of craving. It is the peace and fulfillment which is depicted on the features of the Buddha, investing his images with a significance that impresses even those who have no knowledge of what it means. Such an image of the Buddha can itself be a very suitable object of meditation, and is, in fact, the one that most Buddhists instinctively use. The very sight of the tranquil image can calm and pacify a mind distraught with worldly hopes and fears. It is the certain and visible assurance of Nibbana.

Vipassana Bhavana

Vipassana bhavana is realization of the three signs of being, *anicca, dukkha,* and *anatta,* by direct insight. These three characteristics, impermanence, suffering and non-self, can be grasped intellectually, as scientific and philosophical truth, but this is not in itself sufficient to rid the mind of egoism and craving. The final objective lies on a higher level of awareness, the direct "intuitional" plane, where it is actually experienced as psychological fact. Until this personal confirmation is obtained, the sphere of sense perception *(ayatana)* and sensory-responses remain stronger than the intellectual conviction; the two function side by side on different levels of consciousness, but it is usually the sphere dominated by *avijja* which continues to determine the course of life by volitional action. The philosopher who fails to live according to his philosophy is the most familiar example of this incompatibility between theory and practice. When the direct perception is obtained, however, what was at its highest intellectual level still merely a theory becomes actual knowledge, in precisely the same way that we "know" when we are hot or cold hungry or thirsty. The mind that has attained it is established in the Dhamma, and *paññа,* wisdom, has taken the place of delusion.

Discursive meditation, such as that practiced in Christian devotion, is entirely on the mental level, and can be undertaken by anyone at any time. It calls for no special preparation or conditions. For the more advanced exercises of *samatha* and *vipassana,* however, the strictest observance of *sila,* the basic moral rules, becomes necessary. These techniques are best followed in seclusion, away from the impurities of worldly life and under the guidance of an accomplished master. Many people have done themselves psychic harm by embarking on them without due care in this respect. It is not advisable for anyone to experiment on his own; those who are unable to place themselves under a trustworthy teacher will do best to confine themselves to discursive meditation. It cannot take them to enlightenment but will benefit them morally and prepare them for the next stage.

The Practice of Metta Bhavana

Metta bhavana is the most universally beneficial form of discursive meditation, and can be practiced in any conditions. Thoughts of universal, undiscriminating benevolence, like radio waves reaching out in all directions, sublimate the creative energy of the mind. With steady perseverance in *metta bhavana* a point can be reached at which it becomes impossible even to harbor a thought of ill-will. True peace can only come to the world through minds that are at peace, If people everywhere in the world could be persuaded to devote half an hour daily to the practice of *metta bhavana,* we should see more real advance towards world peace and security than international agreements will ever bring us. It would be a good thing if, in this new era of the Buddha Sasana, people of all creeds could be invited to take part in a world-wide movement for the practice of *metta bhavana* and pledge themselves to live in accordance with the highest tenets of their own religion, whatever it may be. In so doing they would be paying homage to the Supreme Buddha and to their own particular religious teacher as well, for on this level all the great religions of the world unite. If there is a common denominator to be found among them, it is surely here, in the teaching of universal loving-kindness which transcends doctrinal differences and draws all being together by the power of a timeless and all-embracing truth.

The classic formulation of *metta* as an attitude of mind to be developed by meditation is found in the *Karaniya Metta Sutta* (Sutta Nipata, Khuddaka-patha) [See appendix]. It is recommended that this sutta be recited before beginning meditation, and again at its close, a practice which is invariably followed in the Buddhist countries. The verses of the sutta embody the highest concept to which the thought of loving-kindness can reach, and it serves both as a means of self-protection against unwholesome mental states and as a subject of contemplation*(kammatthana).*

It is taught in Buddhism that the cultivation of benevolence must begin with oneself. There is a profound psychological truth in this, for no one who hates or despises himself consciously or unconsciously can feel true loving-kindness for others. To each of us the self is the nearest object; if one's attitude towards oneself is not a wholesome one, the spring of love is poisoned at its source. This does not mean that we should build up an idealized picture of ourselves as an object of admiration, but that, while being fully aware of our faults and deficiencies, we should not condemn but resolve to improve ourselves and cherish confidence in our ability to do so.

Metta bhavana, therefore, begins with the thought: "May I be free from enmity; may I be free from ill-will; may I be rid of suffering; may I be happy."

This thought having been developed, the next stage is to apply it in exactly the same form and to the same degree, to someone for whom one has naturally a feeling of friendship.

In so doing, two points must be observed: the object should be a living person, and should not be one of the opposite sex. The second prohibition is to guard against the feeling of *metta* turning into its "near enemy," sensuality. Those whose sensual leanings have a different orientation must vary the rule to suit their own needs.

When the thought of *metta* has been developed towards a friend, the next object should be someone towards whom one has no marked feelings of like or dislike. Lastly, the though of*metta* is to be turned towards someone who is hostile. It is here that difficulties arise. They are to be expected, and the meditator must be prepared to meet and wrestle with them. To this end, several techniques are described in the *Visuddhimagga* and elsewhere. The first is to think of the hostile personality in terms of *anatta* — impersonality. The meditator is advised to analyze the hostile personality into its impersonal components — the body, the feelings, the perceptions, the volitional formations and the consciousness. The body, to begin with, consists of purely material items: hair of the head, hair of the body, skin, nails, teeth and so on. There can be no basis for enmity against these. The feelings, perceptions, volitional formations and consciousness are all transitory phenomena, interdependent, conditioned and bound up with suffering. They are *anicca, dukkha* and *anatta,* impermanent, fraught with suffering and void of selfhood. There is no more individual personality in them than there is in the physical body itself. So towards them, likewise, there can be no real ground for enmity.

If this approach should prove to be not altogether effective, there are others in which emotionally counteractive states of mind are brought into play, as for example regarding the hostile person with compassion. The meditator should reflect: "As he (or she) is, so am I. As I am, so is he. We are both bound to the inexorable Wheel of Life by ignorance and craving. Both of us are subject to the law of cause and effect, and whatever evil we do, for that we must suffer. Why then should I blame or call anyone my enemy? Rather should I purify my mind and wish that he may do the same, so that both of us may be freed from suffering."

If this thought is dwelt upon and fully comprehended, feelings of hostility will be cast out. When the thought of loving-kindness is exactly the same, in quality and degree, for all these four objects — oneself, one's friend, the person toward whom one is neutral, and the enemy — the meditation has been successful.

The next stage is to widen and extend it. This process is a threefold one: suffusing *metta* without limitation, suffusing it with limitation, and suffusing it in all of the ten directions, east, west, north, south, the intermediate points, above and below.

In suffusing *metta* without limitation *(anodhiso-pharana),* the meditator thinks of the objects of loving-kindness under five heads: all sentient beings; all things that have life; all beings that have come into existence; all that have personality; all that have assumed individual being. For each of these groups separately he formulates the thought: "May they be free from enmity; may they be free from enmity; may they be free from ill will; may they be rid of suffering; may they be happy. For each object he specifies the particular group which he is suffusing with *metta:* "May all sentient beings be free from enmity, etc... May all things that have life be free from enmity, etc." This meditation embraces all without particular reference to locality, and so is called "suffusing without limitation."

In suffusing *metta* with limitation *(odhiso-pharana),* there are seven groups which form the objects of the meditation. They are: all females; all males; all Noble Ones (those who have attained any one of the states of Sainthood); all imperfect ones; all Devas; all human beings; all beings in states of woe. Each of the groups should be meditated upon as described above: "May all females be free from enmity, etc." This method is called "suffusing *metta* with limitation" because it defines the groups according to their nature and condition.

Suffusing with *metta* all beings in the ten directions is carried out in the same way. Directing his mind towards the east, the meditator concentrates on the thought: "May all beings in the east be free from enmity; may they be free from ill will; may they be rid of suffering; may they be happy!" And so with the beings in the west, the north, the south, the north-east, south-west, north-west, south-east, above and below.

Lastly, each of the twelve groups belonging to the unlimited and limited suffusions of *metta* can be dealt with separately for each of the ten directions, using the appropriate formulas.

It is taught that each of these twenty-two modes of practicing *metta bhavana* is capable of being developed up to the stage of a *appana-samadhi,* that is, the concentration which leads to jhana, or mental absorption. For this reason it is described as the method for attaining release of the mind through *metta (metta cetovimutti).* It is the first of the Four Brahma Viharas, the sublime states of which the Karaniya Metta Sutta: *"Brahmam etam viharam idhamahu"* — "Here is declared the Highest Life."

Metta, karuna, mudita, upekkha: [see Nyanaponika Thera, *The Four Sublime States,* Wheel 6.] loving-kindness, compassion, sympathetic joy and detachment, these four states of mind represent the highest levels of mundane consciousness. One who has attained to them and dwells in them is impervious to the ills of life. Like a god he moves and acts in undisturbed serenity, armored against the blows of fate and the uncertainty of worldly conditions. And the first of them to be cultivated is *metta,* because it is through boundless love that the mind gains its first taste of liberation.

THE NATURE OF THE SELF

While there was much of interest in the details of content and process revealed under the spotlight of awareness, it all seemed of minor importance compared with one over-riding insight which constituted the very essence of the experience. That insight provided the answer to a number of interrelated questions, some of which had preoccupied me since my earliest encounter with meditation: Who — or what — is doing the thinking? What is it that is aware? Who is observing all these processes? What is the nature of this observing?

It seemed natural to describe awareness with the statement, "I am observing the mental processes." But at the same time, that statement was self-evidently misleading. It suggested a situation analogous to that of a spectator watching a street parade, which was not at all the situation that existed in awareness. It was not a case of an observer, "I," engaged in observing a spectacle, "the mental processes." Rather — and this was the central insight of awareness — the observer *was* the mental processes. Instead of saying, "I am observing the mental processes," one ought to say, "I *am* the mental processes." In fact I verbalized this startling revelation in more or less the following words: "Good grief, this is *me*! I'm *all this*!" The supposed observer was identical with the object being observed. And the same was true of the supposed act of observing: the observing of the mental processes was nothing other than those processes. Observer, observed, and observing were all one and the same.

The moment awareness broke down, this vision was lost. Without awareness the split returned; there was again the sense of being "I, the thinker"; and there were again the mental contents or thoughts that I was thinking. While there was no awareness, there existed the feeling of being an "I" or thinker, separate and distinct from the thoughts. But when there *was* awareness, this feeling vanished, and it became self-evident that there was no "I" or thinker separate from the thinking process. The feeling of being an "I" separate from the thoughts coincided with failure to see thoughts as process. The seeming reality of "I, the thinker" coincided with the seeming reality of the contents of images. The two arose and ceased together, as two aspects of the same fundamental illusion.

Awareness was, I was certain, the ultimate meditative technique. As long as awareness was maintained, there was uninterrupted insight into the functioning of the mind. It was not exactly the case that that functioning was not thereby interfered with. Clearly, mental events did not go on just as they would have done in the absence of awareness. Awareness implied recognition of the true nature of images, and hence absence of any affective involvement in their contents; and this would certainly influence the direction taken by thought sequences. Nevertheless, awareness was a maximally non-intrusive technique for observing the thought-stream in operation.

In retrospect I saw that my four years of meditative effort had in one respect led me in a circle. I had begun by attempting to stop the thought-stream (through concentration), then I had tried making it go backwards (retracing), and finally I had let it flow normally again (link-watching, awareness). The mind had thus arrived back at its starting-point. However, in the process it had acquired an important new skill: it had learned to be aware of itself in action.

As for the way ahead, that now seemed clear and beyond doubt: awareness must be perfected. The intermittent, brief periods of awareness must become progressively more frequent and must last progressively longer. Other techniques learned earlier in my meditative career still had their place; basic concentration, together with general mindfulness of the body, feelings, and emotional states, would always be valuable as a foundation. However, awareness of the thought-stream was the real practice. The practice would be perfected when the mind had become fully and uninterruptedly aware of itself. The achievement of that condition would surely be the culmination of the entire meditative endeavour.

Insight by the Nature Method

Now we shall see how concentration can come about, naturally on the one hand, and as a result of systematic practice on the other. The end result is identical in the two cases: the mind is concentrated and fit to be used for carrying out close introspection. One thing must be noticed, however. The intensity of concentration that comes about naturally is usually sufficient and appropriate for introspection and insight, whereas the concentration resulting from systematic training is usually excessive, more than can be made use of. Furthermore, misguided satisfaction with that highly developed concentration may result. While the mind is fully concentrated it is likely to experience such a satisfying kind of bliss and well-being that the mediator may become attached to it or imagine it to be the fruit of the path. Naturally occurring concentration which is sufficient and suitable for use in introspection is harmless, having none of the disadvantages inherent in concentration developed by means of intensive training.

In the Tipitaka there are numerous references to people attaining naturally all stages of path and fruit. This generally came about in the presence of the Buddha himself but also happened later with other teachers. These people did not go into the forest and sit, assiduously practising concentration on certain objects in the way described in later manuals. No systematic effort was involved when arahantship was attained by the first five disciples of the Buddha on hearing the Discourse on Non-selfhood, or by the one thousand hermits on hearing the Fire Sermon. In these cases keen, penetrating insight came about quite naturally. These examples clearly show that natural concentration is liable to develop of its own accord while one is attempting to understand clearly some question; and that the resulting insight, as long as it is firmly established, is sure to be quite intense and stable. It happens naturally, automatically, in just the same way that the mind becomes concentrated the moment we set about doing arithmetic. The same happens when firing a gun. When we take aim the mind automatically becomes concentrated and steady.

Normally we completely overlook this naturally occurring concentration because it does not appear the least bit magical, miraculous, or awe-inspiring. But through the power of just such concentration, most of us could actually attain liberation. We could attain the path, the fruit, nirvana, and arahantship, just by means of natural concentration. It is something most of us either already have or can readily develop. We ought to do everything we can to cultivate it, to make it function perfectly and yield the appropriate results. That is just what most of those people did who succeeded in attaining enlightenment without knowing anything of modern concentration techniques.

Now let us look at the nature of the stages of inner awareness leading to full insight into the world, that is, into the five aggregates (*khandhas*). The first stage is joy (*piti*), mental happiness, or spiritual well-being. Doing good in some way, even giving alms, considered the most basic form of merit-making, can be a source of joy. Higher up, at the level of morality, completely blameless conduct by way of word and deed brings an increase of joy. We also discover that joy of a definite kind is associated with the lower stages of concentration.

This joy or rapture has in itself the power to induce tranquillity. Normally the mind is quite unrestrained, continually falling slave to all sort of thoughts and feelings associated with enticing things outside. It is normally restless, not calm. But as spiritual joy becomes established, calm and steadiness are bound to increase in proportion. When steadiness has been perfected, the result is full concentration. The mind becomes tranquil, steady, flexible, manageable, and at ease. It is then ready to be used for any chosen purpose, in particular for the elimination of the defilements.

It is not a case of the mind's being rendered silent, hard, and rocklike. Nothing like that happens at all. The body feels normal, but the mind is especially calm and suitable for use in reflection and introspection. It is perfectly clear, cool, still, and restrained. This is quite unlike sitting in deep concentration. A deeply concentrated mind is in no position to investigate anything. It cannot practise introspection at all; it is in a state of unawareness and is of no use for insight. *Deep concentration is a major obstacle to insight practice.* To practise introspection one must first return to the shallower levels of concentration; then one can make use of the power the mind has acquired. Insight so developed is natural insight, the same sort as was gained by some individuals while sitting listening to the Buddha expounding the Dharma. It is conducive to reflection and introspection of the right kind, the kind that brings understanding, and it involves neither ceremonial procedures nor miracles.

This does not mean, however, that insight will arise instantaneously. One cannot be an *arahant*straight off. The first stage in insight may come about at any time, depending once again on the intensity of the concentration. It may happen that what arises is not true insight because one has been practising incorrectly or is enveloped in too many false views. If insight develops in only small measure, it may convert a person into an *ariya* at the lowest stage. Or, if it is not sufficient to do that, it will at least make him or her a high-minded individual, an ordinary person of good qualities. If conditions are right and good qualities have been properly and adequately established, it is possible to become an *arahant*, a fully enlightened being.

The expression "insight into the true nature of things" refers to realizing transience (*anicca*), unsatisfactoriness or suffering (*dukkha*), and non-selfhood (*anatta*). It means seeing that nothing is worth getting, that no object whatsoever should be grasped at and clung to as being a self or as belonging to a self, as being good or bad, attractive or repulsive. Liking or disliking anything, even an idea or a memory, is clinging. To say that nothing is worth getting or being is the same as saying that nothing is worth clinging to. "Getting" refers to setting one's heart on properly, position, wealth, or any attractive object. "Being" refers to the awareness of one's status as husband, wife, rich man, poor man, winner, loser, or even the awareness of being oneself. If one can completely give up clinging to the idea of being oneself, then being oneself will no longer be subject to suffering.

If we were to give up trying to get or to be anything, how could we continue to exist? The words "getting" or "being" as used here refer to getting and being based on mental defilements, craving, the idea of "worth getting," "worth being," so that the mind does get and be in real earnest. These factors lead to depression, anxiety, and distress, or at least to a heavy burden on the mind from beginning to end. Knowing this truth, we shall be constantly on the alert, keeping watch over the mind to see that it does not fall slave to getting and being through the influence of grasping and clinging.

The world and all things have the property of impermanence, of worthlessness, and of not belonging to anyone.

A skeptic may ask: "If nothing at all is worth getting or being, does it follow that nobody ought to do any work or build up wealth, position, and property?" Anyone who comprehends this subject can see that a person equipped with right knowledge and understanding is actually in a far better position to carry out any task than one subject to strong desires and lacking in understanding. Very briefly, in becoming involved in things, we must do so mindfully, and our actions must not be motivated by craving.

The Buddha and all the other *arahants* were completely free of desire; yet they succeeded in doing many things far more useful than what any of us are capable of. If we look at accounts of how the Buddha spent his day, we find that he slept for only four hours and spent the rest of the time working. We spend more than four hours a day just amusing ourselves. If the defilements responsible for the desire to be and get things had been completely eliminated, what was the force that motivated the Buddha and all *arahants* to act? They were motivated by discrimination coupled with loving-kindness (*metta*). Even actions based on natural bodily wants, such as receiving and eating alms food, were motivated by discrimination. They were free of defilements, free of all desire to keep on living in order to be this or to get that. They had the ability to discriminate between what was worthwhile and what was not; this was the motivating force in all they did. If they found food, well and good. If not, it made no difference. When they were suffering with fever, they knew how to treat it and did so as well as possible on the basis of this knowledge. If the fever was quite overpowering, they recalled that to die is natural. Whether they lived or died was of no significance to them. The two were of equal value in their eyes.

If one is to be completely free of suffering, this is the best attitude to have. There is no need for a self as master of the body. Discrimination alone enables the body to carry on by its natural power. The example of the Buddha shows that the power of pure discrimination and pure goodwill alone is sufficient to keep an *arahant* living in the world and, what is more, doing far more good to others than people who are still subject to craving. People with defilements are likely to do only what benefits themselves, since they act out of selfishness. By contrast, the deeds of enlightened beings are entirely self-less and so are perfectly pure.

To come to know the true nature of things is the objective of every Buddhist. It is the means by which we can liberate ourselves. Regardless of whether we are hoping for worldly benefits, wealth, position, and fame; or for benefits in the next world such as heaven; or for supramundane benefit, the path, the fruit, and nirvana; whatever we are hoping for, the only way to achieve it is by means of right knowledge and insight. In the texts it is said that we become purified through insight and not by any other means. Our path to freedom lies in gaining the insight, the clear vision, which sees that in all things there neither is nor has ever been anything at all worth grasping at or clinging to, worth getting or being, worth risking life and limb for. We *have* things and we*are* things only in terms of worldly, relative truth.

In worldly language we say we are this or that, just because in any society it is expedient to recognize by names and occupations. But we must not believe that we really are this or that, as is assumed at the level of relative truth. To do so is to behave like crickets, which, when their faces become covered with dirt, become disoriented and muddled and proceed to bite one another until they die. We humans, when our faces become covered in dirt, when we are subject to all sorts of delusions, become so bewildered and disoriented that we do things no human being would ever do under ordinary circumstances — killing, for instance. So let us not go blindly clinging to relative truths; rather, let us be aware that they are just relative truths, essential for society but nothing more. We have to be aware of what this body-and-mind really is, what its true nature is. In particular we have to be aware of its impermanence, unsatisfactoriness, and non-selfhood, and make sure we always remain independent of it.

As for the wealth and position that we cannot do without, let us regard these too as relative truths, so that we can break free from the existing custom of saying, "This belongs to So-and-so" or "That belongs to Such-and-such." The law watches over ownership rights for us; there is no need for us to cling to the idea of "mine." We ought to possess things purely and simply for the sake of convenience and ease, not so they can be master over our minds.

When we have really come to perceive clearly that nothing is worth getting or being, disenchantment (*nibbida*) develops in proportion to the intensity of the insight. This is a sign that the clinging has become less firm and is starting to give way. It is a sign that we have been slaves for so long that the idea of trying to escape has at last occurred to us. This is the onset of disenchantment and disillusionment, when one becomes fed up with one's own stupidity in grasping and clinging to things, believing things to be worth having and being. As soon as disenchantment has set in, there is bound to come about a natural, automatic process of disentanglement (*viraga*), as if a rope with which one had been tightly bound were being untied, or a rinsing out, as when the dye that had been firmly fixed in a piece of cloth is removed by soaking it in the appropriate substances. This process, whereby clinging gives way to a breaking free or a dissolving out from the world or from the objects of that clinging, was called by the Buddha emancipation (*vimutti*). This stage is most important. Though not the final stage, it is an essential step toward complete liberation. When one has broken free to this extent, complete liberation from suffering is assured.

Once broken free from slavery, one need never again be a slave to the world. One becomes pure and uncontaminated where previously one was defiled in every way. To be enslaved to things is to be defiled in body, speech, and mind. To break free from slavery to the delightful tastes of the world is to achieve a condition of purity and never be defiled again. This purity (*visuddhi*), once it has been attained, will give rise to a genuine calm and coolness free from all turbulence, strife, and torment. This state of freedom from oppression and turbulence was called by the Buddha simply Peace (*santi*), that is, stillness, coolness in all situations. It is virtually the same thing as nirvana.

The word "nirvana" (*nibbana*) has been translated as "absence of any instrument of torture." Taken another way, it means "extinction without remainder." So the word "nirvana" has two very important meanings: first, absence of any source of torment and burning, freedom from all forms of bondage and constraint; and second, extinction, with no fuel for the further arising of suffering. The combination of these meanings indicates a condition of complete freedom from suffering. The word "nirvana" also has several other useful meanings. It can be taken to mean the extinction of suffering, or the complete elimination of defilements, or the state of coolness, or the condition that is the cessation of all suffering, all defilements and all karmic activity. The word "nirvana" is used by various sects, but often in quite different senses. For instance, one group takes it to mean simply calm and coolness, because they identify nirvana with deep concentration. Other groups even consider nirvana to be total absorption in sensuality.

The Buddha defined nirvana as simply that condition of freedom from bondage, torment, and suffering which results from seeing the true nature of the worldly condition of all things, and so being able to give up clinging to them. It is essential, then, that we recognize the great value of insight into the true nature of things, and that we endeavour to cultivate this insight by one means or another. Using one method we simply encourage it to come about of its own accord, naturally, by developing, day and night, the joy that results from mental purity, until the qualities we have described gradually evolve. The other method consists in developing mental power by following an organized system of concentration and insight practice. This latter technique is appropriate for people with a certain kind of disposition who may make rapid progress with it if conditions are right. But we can practise the development of insight by the nature method in all circumstances and at all times. We do it just by making our own way of daily living so pure and honest that there arise in succession spiritual joy, calm, insight into the true nature of things, disenchantment, disentanglement, escape, purification from defilements, and finally peace, nirvana.

2

Buddhism: A Method of Mind Training

When you hear something about Buddhism in the daily news you usually think of it having a background of huge idols and yellow-robed monks, with a thick atmosphere of incense fumes. You never feel that there is anything in it for you, except, maybe, an exotic spectacle.

But is that all there is in Buddhism? Do the news photographers take pictures of the real Buddhism? Do the glossy magazines show you the fundamentals, or only the externals?

Let us see, then, what Buddhism really is, Buddhism as it was originally expounded and as it still exists underneath the external trappings and trimmings.

Although generally regarded as a religion, Buddhism is basically a method of cultivating the mind. It is true that, with its monastic tradition and its emphasis on ethical factors, it possesses many of the surface characteristics that Westerners associate with religion. However, it is not theistic, since it affirms that the universe is governed by impersonal laws and not by any creator-god; it has no use for prayer, for the Buddha was a teacher and not a god; and it regards devotion not as a religious obligation but as a means of expressing gratitude to its founder and as a means of self-development. Thus it is not a religion at all from these points of view.

Again, Buddhism knows faith only in the sense of confidence in the way recommended by the Buddha. A Buddhist is not expected to have faith or to believe in anything merely because the Buddha said it, or because it is written in the ancient books, or because it has been handed down by tradition, or because others believe it. He may, of course, agree with himself to take the Buddha-doctrine as a working hypothesis and to have confidence in it; but he is not expected to accept anything unless his reason accepts it. This does not mean that everything can be demonstrated rationally, for many points lie beyond the scope of the intellect and can be cognized only by the development of higher faculties. But the fact remains that there is no need for blind acceptance of anything in the Buddha-doctrine.

Buddhism is a way of life based on the training of the mind. Its one ultimate aim is to show the way to complete liberation from suffering by the attainment of the Unconditioned, a state beyond the range of the normal untrained mind. Its immediate aim is to strike at the roots of suffering in everyday life.

All human activity is directed, either immediately or remotely, towards the attainment of happiness in some form or other; or, to express the same thing in negative terms, all human activity is directed towards liberation from some kind of unsatisfactoriness or dissatisfaction. Dissatisfaction, then, can be regarded as the starting point in human activity, with happiness as its ultimate goal.

Dissatisfaction, the starting point in human activity, is also the starting point in Buddhism; and this point is expressed in the formula of the Four Basic Statements, which set out the fact of dissatisfaction, its cause, its cure, and the method of its cure.

The First Basic Statement can be stated thus:

DISSATISFACTION IS INESCAPABLE IN EN-SELF-ED LIFE

In its original meaning, the word which is here rendered as "dissatisfaction" and which is often translated as "suffering" embraces the meanings not only of pain, sorrow, and displeasure, but also of everything that is unsatisfactory, ranging from acute physical pain and severe mental anguish to slight tiredness, boredom, or mild disappointment.

Sometimes the term is rendered as "dissatisfaction" or "unsatisfactoriness"; in some contexts these are perhaps more accurate, while at other times the word "suffering" is more expressive. For this reason we shall use both "suffering" and "dissatisfaction" or "unsatisfactoriness" according to context.

In some translations of the original texts it is stated that birth is suffering, sickness is suffering, old age is suffering, and pleasure is suffering. In English, this last statement fails to make sense; but if we restate it as "pleasure is unsatisfactory" it becomes more readily understandable, for all pleasure is impermanent and is eventually succeeded by its opposite, and from this point of view at least it is unsatisfactory.

Now the Buddha-doctrine teaches that dissatisfaction or suffering is inescapable in en-self-ed life; and the term "en-self-ed life" needs some explanation. In brief, the doctrine teaches that the self, considered as a fixed, unchanging eternal soul, has no reality.

The central core of every being is not an unchanging soul but a life-current, an ever-changing stream of energy which is never the same for two consecutive seconds. The self, considered as an eternal soul, therefore, is a delusion, and when regarded from the ultimate standpoint it has no reality; and it is only within this delusion of selfhood that ultimate suffering can exist. When the self-delusion is finally transcended and the final enlightenment is attained, the ultimate state which lies beyond the relative universe is reached. In this ultimate state, the Unconditioned, suffering is extinguished; but while any element of selfhood remains, even though it is a delusion, suffering remains potentially within it.

We must understand, then, that the First Basic Statement does not mean that suffering is inescapable; it means that suffering is inescapable in enselfed life, or while the delusion of selfhood remains. We can now move on to the Second Basic Statement, which says:

The Origin of Dissatisfaction is Craving

If you fall on a slippery floor and suffer from bruises, you say that the cause of your suffering is the slippery floor. In an immediate sense you are right, of course, and to say that the cause of your bruises is craving fails to make sense.

But the Second Statement does not refer to individual cases or to immediate causes. It means that the integrating force that holds together the life-current is self-centered craving; for this life-current — this self-delusion — contains in itself the conditions for suffering, while the slippery floor is merely an occasion for suffering.

It is obviously impossible, by the nature of the world we live in, to cure suffering by the removal of all the occasions for suffering; whereas it is possible in Buddhism to strike at its prime or fundamental cause. Therefore the Third Basic Statement states:

Liberation May Be Achieved by Destroying Craving

It is self-centered craving that holds together the forces which comprise the life-current, the stream of existence which we call the self; and it is only with self-delusion that unsatisfactoriness or suffering can exist. By the destruction of that which holds together the delusion of the self, the root cause of suffering is also destroyed.

The ultimate aim of Buddhist practice, then, is to annihilate the self. This is where a great deal of misunderstanding arises, and naturally so; but once it is realized that to annihilate the self is to annihilate a delusion, this misunderstanding disappears. When the delusion is removed, the reality appears; so that to destroy delusion is to reveal the reality. The reality cannot be discovered while the delusion of self continues to obscure it.

Now what is this reality which appears when the delusion is removed? The ultimate reality is the Unconditioned, called also the Unborn, the Unoriginated, the Uncreated, and the Uncompounded. We can, inadequately and not very accurately, describe it as a positive state of being.

It is characterized by supreme bliss and complete freedom from suffering and is so utterly different from ordinary existence that no real description of it can be given. The Unconditioned can be indicated — up to a point — only by stating what it is not; for it is beyond words and beyond thought.

Hence, in the Buddhist texts, the Unconditioned is often explained as the final elimination' from one's own mind, of greed, hatred and delusion. This, of course, also implies the perfection of the opposite positive qualities of selflessness, loving-kindness, and wisdom.

The attainment of the Unconditioned is the ultimate aim of all Buddhist practice, and is the same as complete liberation from dissatisfaction or suffering. This brings us to the last of the Four Basic Statements:

THE WAY OF LIBERATION IS THE NOBLE EIGHTFOLD PATH

The eight factors of the path are these:

1. Right understanding, a knowledge of the true nature of existence.
2. Right thought, thought free from sensuality, ill-will and cruelty.
3. Right speech, speech without falsity, gossip, harshness, and idle babble.
4. Right action, or the avoidance of killing, stealing and adultery.
5. Right livelihood, an occupation that harms no conscious living being.
6. Right effort, or the effort to destroy the defilements of the mind and to cultivate wholesome qualities.
7. Right mindfulness, the perfection of the normal faculty of attention.
8. Right concentration, the cultivation of a collected, focussed mind through meditation.

Now you will see that in this Noble Eightfold Path there is nothing of an essentially religious nature; it is more a sort of moral psychology.

But in the East as well as in the West people as a whole demand external show of some sort, and — on the outside at least — the non-essentials have assumed more importance than the essentials.

While some external features in the practice of Buddhism must of necessity vary according to environment, the essential and constant characteristics of that practice are summed up in the following outline of the Noble Eightfold Path, the Middle Way between harmful extremes, as taught by the Buddha.

Although it is convenient to speak of the various aspects of the eightfold path as eight steps, they are not to be regarded as separate steps, taken one after another. On the contrary, each one must be practiced along with the others, and it might perhaps be better to think of them as if they were eight parallel lanes within the one road rather than eight successive steps.

The first step of this path, right understanding, is primarily a matter of seeing things as they really are — or at least trying to do so without self-deceit or evasion. In another sense, right understanding commences as an intellectual appreciation of the nature of existence, and as such it can be regarded as the beginning of the path; but, when the path has been followed to the end, this merely intellectual appreciation is supplanted by a direct and penetrating discernment of the principles of the teaching first accepted intellectually.

While right understanding can be regarded as the complete understanding of the Buddha doctrine, it is based on the recognition of three dominating characteristics of the relative universe, of the universe of time, form and matter. These three characteristics can briefly be set out in this way:

1. Impermanence: All things in the relative universe are unceasingly changing.
2. Dissatisfaction: Some degree of suffering or dissatisfaction is inherent in en-selfed life, or in life within the limitations of the relative universe and personal experience.
3. Egolessness: No being — no human being or any other sort of being — possesses a fixed, unchanging, eternal soul or self. Instead, every being consists of an ever-changing current of forces, an ever-changing flux of material and mental phenomena, like a river which is always moving and is never still for a single second.

The self, then, is not a static entity but an ever-changing flux. This dynamic concept of existence is typical of deeper Buddhist thought; there is nothing static in life, and since it is ever-flowing you must learn to flow with it.

Another aspect of right understanding is the recognition that the universe runs its course on the basis of a strict sequence of cause and effect, or of action and reaction, a sequence just as invariable and just as exact in the mental or moral realm as in the physical. In accordance with this law of moral action and reaction all morally good or wholesome will actions eventually bring to the doer happiness at some time, while unwholesome or morally bad will-actions bring suffering to the doer.

The effects of wholesome and unwholesome will-actions — that is to say, the happiness and suffering that result from them — do not generally follow immediately; there is often a considerable time-lag, for the resultant happiness and suffering can arise only when appropriate conditions are present. The results may not appear within the present lifetime. Thus at death there is normally a balance of "merit" which has not yet brought about its experience of happiness; and at the same time there is also a balance of "demerit" which has not yet given rise to the suffering which is to be its inevitable result.

After death, the body disintegrates, of course, but the life-current continues, not in the form of an unchanging soul, but in the form of an ever-changing stream of energy. Immediately after death a new being commences life to carry on this life current; but the new being is not necessarily a human being, and the instantaneous rebirth may take place on another plane of existence. But in any case, the new being is a direct sequel to the being that has just died.

Thus the new being becomes an uninterrupted continuation of the old being, and the life-current is unbroken. The new being inherits the balance of merit built up by the old being, and this balance of merit will inevitably bring happiness at some future time. At the same time, the new being inherits the old being's balance of demerit, which will bring suffering at some time in the future.

In effect, in the sense of continuity, the new being is the same as the old being. In just the same way — that is, in the sense of continuity only — an old man is the same as the young man he once was, the young man is the same as the boy he once was, and the boy is the same as the baby he once was. But the identity of the old man with the young man, and with the boy, and with the baby, is due only to continuity; there is no other identity.

Everything in the universe changes from day to day and from moment to moment, so that every being at this moment is a slightly different being from that of the moment before; the only identity is due to continuity. In the same way, the being that is reborn is different from the previous one that died; but the identity due to continuity remains as before.

These teachings are basic to the Buddha-doctrine — the illusory nature of the self, the law of action and reaction in the moral sphere, and the rebirth of the life-forces — but there is no need for anyone to accept anything that does not appeal to his reason. Acceptance of any particular teaching is unimportant; what is important is the continual effort to see things as they really are, without self-deceit or evasion.

So much for a brief outline of the doctrine under the heading of right understanding. The second step, right thought or aim, is a matter of freeing the intellectual faculties from adverse emotional factors, such as sensuality, ill-will, and cruelty, which render wise and unbiased decisions impossible.

Right speech, right action, and right livelihood together make up the moral section of the path, their function being to keep the defilements of the mind under control and to prevent them from reaching adverse expression. These defilements, however, cannot be completely eradicated by morality alone, and the other steps of the path must be applied to cleanse the mind completely of its defilements.

Now in the next step — right effort — we enter the sphere of practical psychology, for right effort in this context means effort of will. In other words, the sixth step of the path is self-discipline, the training of the will in order to prevent and overcome those states of mind that retard development, and to arouse and cultivate those that bring about mental progress. The seventh step of the path is also one of practical psychology; this is the step called right mindfulness, and it consists of the fullest possible development of the ordinary faculty of attention. It is largely by the development of attention — expanded and intensified awareness — that the mind can eventually become capable of discerning things as they really are.

The primary function of the, seventh step, right mindfulness, is to develop an increasing awareness of the unreality of the self. However, it functions also by continually improving the normal faculty of attention, thus equipping the mind better to meet the problems and stresses of the workaday world.

In the Buddha-way, mindfulness consists of developing the faculty of attention so as to produce a constant awareness of all thoughts that arise, all words that are spoken, and all actions that are done, with a view to keeping them free from self-interest, from emotional bias, and from self-delusion.

Right mindfulness has many applications in the sphere of everyday activities. For example, it can be employed to bring about a sharpened awareness, a clear comprehension, of the motives of these activities, and this clear comprehension of motive is extremely important.

In right concentration, the last of the eight steps, the cultivation of higher mind-states — up to the meditative absorptions — is undertaken, and these higher mind-states serve to unify, purity, and strengthen the mind for the achievement of liberating insight.

In this ultimate achievement the delusion of selfhood, with its craving and suffering, is transcended and extinguished.

This penetrating insight is the ultimate goal of all Buddhist practices, and with it comes a direct insight into the true nature of life, culminating in realization of the Unconditioned. While the Unconditioned is the extinction of self, it is nevertheless not mere non-existence or annihilation, for the extinction of self is nothing but the extinction of a delusion. Every description of the Unconditioned must fail, for it lies not only beyond words but beyond even thought; and the only way to know it is to follow the Noble Eightfold Path to its end.

This, then, is the original Buddhism; this is the Buddhism of the Noble Eightfold Path, of the path that leads from the bondage of self to liberating insight into reality.

Meditating on No-Self

In Buddhism we use the words "self" and "no-self," and so it is important to understand just what this "no-self," *anatta,* is all about, even if it is first just an idea, because the essence of the Buddha's teaching hinges on this concept. And in this teaching Buddhism is unique. No one, no other spiritual teacher, has formulated no-self in just this way. And because it has been formulated by him in this way, there is also the possibility of speaking about it. Much has been written about no-self, but in order to know it, one has to experience it. And that is what the teaching aims at, the experience of no-self.

Yet in order to experience no-self, one has first to fully know self. Actually know it. But unless we do know what this self is, this self called "me," it is impossible to know what is meant by "there is no self there." In order to give something away, we have to first fully gave it in hand.

We are constantly trying to reaffirm self. Which already shows that this "self" is a very fragile and rather wispy sort of affair, because if it weren't why would we constantly have to reaffirm it? Why are we constantly afraid of the "self" being threatened of its being insecure, of its not getting what it needs for survival? If it were such a solid entity as we believe it to be, we would not feel threatened so often.

We affirm "self" again and again through identification. We identify with a certain name, an age, a sex, an ability, an occupation. "I am a lawyer, I am a doctor. I am an accountant, I am a student." And we identify with the people we are attached to. "I am a husband, I am a wife, I am a mother, I am a daughter, I am a son." Now, in the manner of speech, we have to use "self" in that way — but it isn't only in speech. We really think that that "self" is who we are. We really believe it. There is no doubt in our mind that that "self" is who we are. When any of these factors is threatened, if being a wife is threatened, if being a mother is threatened, if being a lawyer is threatened, if being a teacher is threatened — or if we lose the people who enable us to retain that "self" — what a tragedy!

The self-identification becomes insecure, and "me" finds it hard to say "look at me," "this is me." Praise and blame are included. Praise reaffirms "me." Blame threatens "me." So we like the praise and we dislike the blame. The ego is threatened. Fame and infamy — same thing. Loss and gain. If we gain, the ego gets bigger; if we lose, it gets a bit smaller. So we are constantly in a quandary, and in constant fear. The ego might lose a little bit of its grandeur. It might be made a bit smaller by someone. And it happens to all of us. Somebody is undoubtedly going to blame us for something eventually. Even the Buddha was blamed.

Now the blame that is levied at us is not the problem. The problem is our reaction. The problem is that we feel smaller. The ego has a hard time reasserting itself. So what we usually do is we blame back, making the other's ego a bit smaller too.

Identification with whatever it is that we do and whatever it is that we have, be it possessions or people, is, so we believe, needed for our survival. "Self" survival. If we don't identify with this or that, we feel as if we are in limbo. This is the reason why it is difficult to stop thinking in meditation. Because without thinking there would be no identification. If I don't think, what do I identify with? It is difficult to come to a stage in meditation in which there is actually nothing to identify with any more.

Happiness, too, may be an identification. "I am happy." "I am unhappy." Because we are so keen on survival, we have got to keep on identifying. When this identification becomes a matter of the life or death of the ego, which it usually is, then the fear of loss becomes so great that we can be in a constant state of fear. Constantly afraid to lose either the possessions that make us what we are, or the people that make us what we are. If we have no children, or if they all die, we are no longer a mother. So fear is paramount. The same goes for all other identifications. Not a very peaceful state of living and what is it due to? Only one thing: ego, the craving to be.

This identification results, of course, in craving for possessing. And this possessing results in attachment. What we have, what we identify with, we are attached to. That attachment, that clinging, makes it extremely difficult to have a free and open viewpoint. This kind of clinging, whatever it may be that we cling to — it may not be clinging to motor cars and houses, it may not even be clinging to people — but we certainly cling to views and opinions. We cling to our world view. We cling to the view of how we are going to be happy. Maybe we cling to a view of who created this universe. Whatever it is we cling to, even how the government should run the country, all of that makes it extremely difficult to see things as they really are. To be open-minded. And it is only an open mind which can take in new ideas and understanding.

Lord Buddha compared listeners to four different kinds of clay vessels. The first clay vessel is one that has holes at the bottom. If you pour water into it, it runs right out. In other words, whatever you teach that person is useless. The second clay vessel he compared to one that had cracks in it. If you pour water into it, the water seeps out. These people cannot remember. Cannot put two and two together. Cracks in the understanding. The third listener he compared to a vessel that was completely full. Water cannot be poured in for it's full to the brim. Such a person, so full of views he can't learn anything new! But hopefully, we are the fourth kind. The empty vessels without any holes or cracks. Completely empty.

I dare say we are not. But may be empty enough to take in enough. To be empty like that, of views and opinions, means a lack of clinging. Even a lack of clinging to what we think is reality. Whatever we think reality is, it surely is not, because if it were, we would never be unhappy for a single moment. We would never feel a lack of anything. We would never feel a lack of companionship, of ownership. We would never feel frustrated, bored. If we ever do, whatever we think is real, is not. What is truly reality is completely fulfilling. If we aren't completely fulfilled, we aren't seeing complete reality. So, any view that we may have is either wrong or it is partial.

Because it is wrong or partial, and bounded by the ego, we must look at it with suspicion. Anything we cling to keeps us bound to it. If I cling to a table-leg, I can't possibly get out the door.

There is no way I can move. I am stuck. Not until I let go will I have the opportunity to get out. Any identification, any possession that is clung to, is what stops us from reaching transcendental reality. Now we can easily see this clinging when we cling to things and people, but we cannot easily see why the five *khandhas* are called the five clung-to aggregates. That is their name, and they are, in fact, what we cling to most. That is an entire clinging. We don't even stop to consider when we look at our body, and when we look at our mind, or when we look at feeling, perception, mental formations, and consciousness — *vedana, sañña, sankhara,* and*viññana.* We look at this mind-and-body, *nama-rupa,* and we don't even doubt the fact that this is *my* feeling, *my* perception, *my* memory, *my* thoughts, and *my* awareness of *my*consciousness. And no one starts doubting until they start seeing. And for that seeing we need a fair bit of empty space apart from views and opinions.

Clinging is the greatest possessiveness and attachment we have. As long as we cling we cannot see reality. We cannot see reality because clinging is in the way. Clinging colors whatever we believe to be true. Now it is not possible to say "all right, I'll stop clinging." We can't do that. The process of taking the "me" apart, of not believing any more that this is one whole, is a gradual one. But if meditation has any benefit and success, it must show that first of all there is mind and there is body. There isn't one single thing acting in accord all the time. There is mind which is thinking and making the body act. Now that is the first step in knowing oneself a little clearer. And then we can note "this is a feeling" and "I am giving this feeling a name" which means memory and perception. "This is the thought that I am having about this feeling. The feeling has come about because the mind-consciousness has connected with the feeling that has arisen."

Take the four parts of the *khandhas* that belong to the mind apart. When we do that while it is happening — not now when we are thinking about at-but while it is happening, then we get a inkling that this isn't really *me,* that these are phenomena that are arising, which stay a moment, and then cease. How long does mind-consciousness stay on one object? And how long do thoughts last? And have we really invited them?

The clinging, the clung-to, are what make the ego arise. Because of clinging the notion of "me" arises and then there is me, and *me* having all the problems. Without *me* would there be problems? If there weren't anyone sitting inside me — as we think there is — who is called I or me or John, Claire, then who is having the problem? The *khandhas* do not have any problems. The *khandhas* are just processes. They are phenomena, and that is all. They are just going on and on and on. But because I am grasping at them, and trying to hold on to them, and saying: "it's*me,* it's *me* feeling, it's *me* wanting,." then problems arise.

If we really want to get rid of suffering, completely and totally, then clinging has to go. The spiritual path is never one of achievement; it is always one of letting go. The more we let go, the more there is empty and open space for us to see reality. Because what we let go of is no longer there, there is the possibility of just moving without clinging to the results of the movement. As long as we cling to the results of what we do, as long as we cling to the results of what we think, we are bound, we are hemmed in.

Now there is a third thing that we do: we are interested in becoming something or somebody. Interested in becoming an excellent meditator. Interested in becoming a graduate. Interested in becoming something which we are not. And becoming something stops us from being. When we are stopped from being, we cannot pay attention to what there really is. All this becoming business is, of course, in the future. Since whatever there is in the future is conjecture, it is a dream world we live in. The only reality we can be sure of is this particular moment right now; and this particular moment as you must be able to be aware of — has already passed and this one has passed and the next one has also passed. See how they are all passing! That is the impermanence of it all. Each moment passes, but we cling, trying to hold on to them. Trying to make them a reality. Trying to make them a security. Trying to make them be something which they are not. See how they are all passing. We cannot even say it as quickly as they are doing it.

There is nothing that is secure. Nothing to hold on to, nothing that is stable. The whole universe is constantly falling apart and coming back together. And that includes the mind and the body which we call "I." You may believe it or not, it makes no difference. In order to know it, you must experience it; when you experience it, it's perfectly clear. What one experiences is totally clear. No one can say it is not. They may try, but their objections make no sense because you have experienced it. It's the same thing as biting into the mango to know its taste.

To experience it, one needs meditation. An ordinary mind can only know ordinary concepts and ideas. If one wants to understand and experience extraordinary experiences and ideas, one has to have an extraordinary mind. An extraordinary mind comes about through concentration. Most meditators have experienced some stage that is different then the one they are use to. So it is not ordinary any more. But we have to fortify that far more than just the beginning stage. To the point where the mind is truly extraordinary. Extraordinary in the sense that it can direct itself to where it wants to go. Extraordinary in the sense that it no longer gets perturbed by everyday events. And when the mind can concentrate, then it experiences states which it has never known before. To realize that your universe constantly falls apart and comes back together again is a meditative experience. It takes practice, perseverance and patience. And when the mind is unperturbed and still, equanimity, evenmindedness, peacefulness arise.

At that time the mind understands the idea of impermanence to such an extent that it sees itself as totally impermanent. And when one sees one's own mind as being totally impermanent, there is a shift in one's viewpoint. That shift I like to compare with a kaleidoscope that children play with. A slight touch and you get a different picture. The whole thing looks quite different with just a slight shift.

Non-self is experienced through the aspect of impermanence, through the aspect of unsatisfactoriness, and through the aspect of emptiness. Empty of what? The word "emptiness" is so often misunderstood because when one only thinks of it as a concept, one says "what do you mean by empty?" Everything is there: there are the people, and there are their insides, guts and their bones and blood and everything is full of stuff — and the mind is not empty either. It's got ideas, thoughts and feelings. And even when it doesn't have those, what do you mean by emptiness? The only thing that is empty is the emptiness of an entity.

There is no specific entity in anything. That is emptiness. That is the nothingness. That nothingness is also experienced in meditation. It is empty, it is devoid of a specific person, devoid of a specific thing, devoid of anything which makes it permanent, devoid of anything which even makes it important. The whole thing is in flux. So the emptiness is that. And the emptiness is to be seen everywhere; to be seen in oneself. And that is what is called *anatta,* non-self. Empty of an entity. There is nobody there. It is all imagination. At first that feels very insecure.

That person that I've been regarding with so much concern, that person trying to do this or that, that person who will be my security, will be my insurance for a happy life — once I find that person — that person does not really exist. What a frightening and insecure idea that is! What a feeling of fear arises! But as a matter of fact, it's just the reverse. If one accepts and bears that fright and goes through it, one comes to complete and utter relief and release.

I'll give you a simile: Imagine you own a very valuable jewel which is so valuable that you place your trust in it so that should you fall upon hard times, it will look after you. It's so valuable that you can have it as your security. You don't trust anybody. So you have a safe inside your house and that is where you put your jewel. Now you have been working hard for a number of years and you think you deserve a holiday. So now, what to do with the jewel? Obviously you cannot take it with you on your seaside holiday. So you buy new locks for the doors to your house and you bar your windows and you alert your neighbors. You tell them about the proposed holiday and ask them to look after you house — and the safe in it. And they say they will, of course. You should be quite at ease and so you go off on your holiday.

You go to the beach, and it's wonderful. Marvelous. The palm trees are swaying in the wind, and the spot you've chosen on the beach is nice and clean. The waves are warm and it's all lovely. The first day you really enjoy yourself. But on the second day you begin to wonder; the neighbors are very nice people, but they do go and visit their children. They are not always at home, and lately there has been a rash of burglaries in the neighborhood. And on the third day you've convinced yourself that something dreadful is going to happen, and you go back home. You walk in and open the safe. Everything is all right. You go over to the neighbors and they ask, "Why did you come back? We were looking after your place. You didn't have to come back. Everything is fine."

The next year, the same thing. Again you tell the neighbors, "Now this time I am really going to stay away for a month. I need this holiday as I've been working hard." So they say, "Absolutely no need to worry, just take off. Go to the beach." So once more you bar the windows, lock the doors, get everything shipshape, and take off for the beach. Again, it's wonderful, beautiful. This time you last for five days. On the fifth day you are convinced that something dreadful must have happened. And you go home. You go home, and by golly, it has. The jewel is gone. You are in a state of complete collapse. Total desperation. Depressed. So you go to the neighbors, but they have no idea what has happened. they've been around all the time. Then you sit and consider the matter and you realize that since the jewel is gone, you might as well go back to the beach and enjoy yourself!

That jewel is *self.* Once it is gone, all the burden of looking after it, all the fears about it, all the barring of doors and windows and heart and mind is no longer necessary. You can just go and enjoy yourself while you're still in this body. After proper investigation, the frightening aspect of losing this thing that seemed so precious turns out to be the only relief and release from worry that there is.

There are three doors to liberation: the signless, the desireless, and emptiness. If we understand impermanence, *anicca,* fully, it is called the signless liberation. If we understand suffering,*dukkha,* fully, it is the desireless liberation. If we understand no-self, *anatta,* fully, then it is the emptiness liberation. Which means we can go through any of these three doors. And to be liberated means never to have to experience an unhappy moment again. It also means something else: it means we are no longer creating kamma. A person who has been completely liberated still acts, still thinks, still speaks and still looks to all intents and purposes like anybody else, but that person has lost the idea that *I am* thinking, *I am* speaking, *I am* acting. Kamma is no longer being made because there is just the thought, just the speech, just the action. There is the experience but no experiencer. And because no kamma is being made any longer, there is no rebirth. That is full enlightenment.

In this tradition, three stages of enlightenment have been classified before one comes to the fourth stage, full enlightenment. The first stage, the one we can concern ourselves with — at least theoretically — is called *sotapanna.* Stream-enterer. It means a person who has seen Nibbana once and has thereby entered the stream. That person cannot be deterred from the Path any more. If the insight is strong, there may be only one more life-time. If the insight is weak, it can be seven more life-times. Having seen Nibbana for oneself once, one loses some of the difficulties one had before. The most drastic hindrance that one loses is the idea that this person we call "I" is a separate entity. The wrong view of self is lost. But that doesn't mean that a *sotapanna* is constantly aware of no-self. The wrong view is lost. But the right view has to be reinforced again and again and experienced again and again through that reinforcement.

Such a person no longer has any great interest, and certainly no belief, in rites and rituals. They may still be performed because they are traditional or that are customary, but such a person no longer believes they can bring about any kind of liberation (if they ever believed that before). And then a very interesting thing is lost: skeptical doubt. Skeptical doubt is lost because one has seen for oneself that what the Buddha taught was actually so. Until that time skeptical doubt will have to arise again and again because one can easily think: "Well, maybe. Maybe it's so, but how can I be sure?" One can only be sure through one's own experience. Then, of course, there is no skeptical doubt left because one has seen exactly that which has been described, and having seen it, one's own heart and mind gives an understanding which makes it possible to see everything else.

Dhamma must have as its base the understanding that there is no special entity. There is continuity, but there is no special entity. And that continuity is what makes it so difficult for us to see that there really isn't anybody inside the body making things happen. Things are happening anyway. So the first instance of having seen a glimpse of freedom, called stream-entry, makes changes within us. It certainly does not uproot greed and hate — in fact, they are not even mentioned. But through the greater understanding such a person has, the greed and the hate lessen. They are not as strong anymore, and they do not manifest in gross ways, but do remain in subtle ways.

The next stages are the once-returner, then the non-returner, then the arahat. Once-returner, one more life in the five-sense world. Non-returner, no human life necessary, and arahat, fully enlightened. Sensual desire and hate only go with non-returners, and complete conceit of self, only with arahat.

So we can be quite accepting of the fact that since we are not arahats, we still have greed and hate. It isn't a matter of blaming oneself for having them: it's a matter of understanding where these come from. They come from the delusion of *me*. I want to protect this jewel which is *me*.That is how they arise. But with the continued practice of meditation, the mind can become clearer and clearer. It finally understands. And when it does understand, it can see transcendental reality. Even if seen for one thought-moment, the experience is of great impact and makes a marked change in our lives.

THE BENEFITS OF WALKING MEDITATION

At our meditation retreats, yogis practice mindfulness in four different postures. They practice mindfulness when walking, when standing, when sitting, and when lying down. They must sustain mindfulness at all times in whatever position they are in. The primary posture for mindfulness meditation is sitting with legs crossed, but because the human body cannot tolerate this position for many hours without changing, we alternate periods of sitting meditation with periods of walking meditation. Since walking meditation is very important, I would like to discuss its nature, its significance, and the benefits derived from its practice. The practice of mindfulness meditation can be compared to boiling water. If one wants to boil water, one puts the water in a kettle, puts the kettle on a stove, and then turns the heat on. But if the heat is turned off, even for an instant, the water will not boil, even though the heat is turned on again later. If one continues to turn the heat on and off again, the water will never boil. In the same way, if there are gaps between the moments of mindfulness, one cannot gain momentum, and so one cannot attain concentration. That is why yogis at our retreats are instructed to practice mindfulness all the time that they are awake, from the moment they wake up in the morning until they fall asleep at night. Consequently, walking meditation is integral to the continuous development of mindfulness.

Unfortunately, I have heard people criticize walking meditation, claiming that they cannot derive any benefits or good results from it. But it was the Buddha himself who first taught walking meditation. In the *Great Discourse on the Foundations of Mindfulness,* the Buddha taught walking meditation two times. In the section called "Postures," he said that a monk knows "I am walking" when he is walking, knows "I am standing" when he is standing, knows "I am sitting" when he is sitting, and knows "I am lying down" when he is lying down. In another section called "Clear Comprehension," the Buddha said, "A monk applies clear comprehension in going forward and in going back." *Clear comprehension* means the correct understanding of what one observes. To correctly understand what is observed, a yogi must gain concentration, and in order to gain concentration, he must apply mindfulness. Therefore, when the Buddha said, "Monks, apply clear comprehension," we must understood that not only clear comprehension must be applied, but also mindfulness and concentration. Thus the Buddha was instructing meditators to apply mindfulness, concentration, and clear comprehension while walking, while "going forward and back." Walking meditation is thus an important part of this process.

Although it is not recorded in this sutta that the Buddha gave detailed and specific instructions for walking meditation, we believe that he must have given such instructions at some time. Those instructions must have been learned by the Buddha's disciples and passed on through successive generations. In addition, teachers of ancient times must have formulated instructions based on their own practice. At the present time, we have a very detailed set of instructions on how to practice walking meditation.

Let us now talk specifically about the practice of walking meditation. If you are a complete beginner, the teacher may instruct you to be mindful of only one thing during walking meditation: to be mindful of the act of stepping while you make a note silently in the mind, "stepping, stepping, stepping," or "left, right, left, right." You may walk at a slower speed than normal during this practice.

After a few hours, or after a day or two of meditation, you may be instructed to be mindful of two occurrences: (i) stepping, and (ii) putting down the foot, while making the mental note "stepping, putting down." You will try to be mindful of two stages in the step: "stepping, putting down; stepping, putting down." Later, you may be instructed to be mindful of three stages: (i) lifting the foot; (ii) moving or pushing the foot forward; and (iii) putting the foot down. Still later, you would be instructed to be mindful of four stages in each step: (i) lifting the foot; (ii) moving it forward; (iii) putting it down; and (iv) touching or pressing the foot on the ground. You would be instructed to be completely mindful and to make a mental note of these four stages of the foot's movement: "lifting, moving forward, putting down, pressing the ground."

At first yogis may find it difficult to slow down, but as they are instructed to pay close attention to all of the movements involved, and as they actually pay closer and closer attention, they will automatically slow down. They do not have to slow down deliberately, but as they pay closer attention, slowing down comes to them automatically. When driving on the freeway, one may be driving at sixty or seventy or even eighty miles per hour. Driving at that speed, one will not be able to read some of the signs on the road. If one wants to read those signs, it is necessary to slow down. Nobody has to say, "Slow down!" but the driver will automatically slow down in order to see the signs. In the same way, if yogis want to pay closer attention to the movements of lifting, moving forward, putting down, and pressing the ground, they will automatically slow down. Only when they slow down can they be truly mindful and fully aware of these movements.

Although yogis pay close attention and slow down, they may not see all of the movements and stages clearly. The stages may not yet be well-defined in the mind, and they may seem to constitute only one continuous movement.

As concentration grows stronger, yogis will observe more and more clearly these different stages in one step; the four stages at least will be easier to distinguish. Yogis will know distinctly that the lifting movement is not mixed with the moving forward movement, and they will know that the moving forward movement is not mixed with either the lifting movement or the putting down movement. They will understand all movements clearly and distinctly. Whatever they are mindful and aware of will be very clear in their minds.

As yogis carry on the practice, they will observe much more. When they lift their foot, they will experience the lightness of the foot. When they push the foot forward, they will notice the movement from one place to another. When they put the foot down, they will feel the heaviness of the foot, because the foot becomes heavier and heavier as it descends. When they put the foot on the ground, they will feel the touch of the heel of the foot on the ground.

Therefore, along with observing lifting, moving forward, putting down, and pressing the ground, yogis will also perceive the lightness of the rising foot, the motion of the foot, the heaviness of the descending foot, and then the touching of the foot, which is the hardness or softness of the foot on the ground. When yogis perceive these processes, they are perceiving the four essential elements (in Pali, *dhatu).* The four essential elements are: the element of earth, the element of water, the element of fire, and the element of air. By paying close attention to these four stages of walking meditation, the four elements in their true essence are perceived, not merely as concepts, but as actual processes, as ultimate realities.

Let us go into a little more detail about the characteristics of the elements in walking meditation. In the first movement, that is, the lifting of the foot, yogis perceive lightness, and when they perceive lightness, they virtually perceive the fire element. One aspect of the fire element is that of making things lighter, and as things become lighter, they rise. In the perception of the lightness in the upward movement of the foot, yogis perceive the essence of the fire element. But in the lifting of the foot there is also, besides lightness, movement. Movement is one aspect of the air element. But lightness, the fire element, is dominant, so we can say that in the stage of lifting the fire element is primary, and the air element is secondary. These two elements are perceived by yogis when they pay close attention to the lifting of the foot.

The next stage is moving the foot forward. In moving the foot forward, the dominant element is the air element, because motion is one of the primary characteristics of the air element. So, when they pay close attention to the moving forward of the foot in walking meditation, yogis are virtually perceiving the essence of the air element.

The next stage is the movement of putting the foot down. When yogis put their foot down, there is a kind of heaviness in the foot. Heaviness is a characteristic of the water element, as is trickling and oozing. When liquid is heavy, it oozes. So when yogis perceive the heaviness of the foot, they virtually perceive the water element.

In pressing the foot on the ground, yogis will perceive the hardness or softness of the foot on the ground. This pertains to the nature of the earth element. By paying close attention to the pressing of the foot against the ground, yogis virtually perceive the nature of the earth element.

Thus we see that in just one step, yogis can perceive many processes. They can perceive the four elements and the nature of the four elements. Only those who practice can ever hope to see these things.

As yogis continue to practice walking meditation, they will come to realize that, with every movement, there is also the noting mind, the awareness of the movement. There is the lifting movement and also the mind that is aware of that lifting. In the next moment, there is the moving forward movement and also the mind that is aware of the movement. Moreover, yogis will realize that both the movement and the awareness arise and disappear in that moment. In the next moment, there is the putting down movement and so also the awareness of the movement, and both arise and disappear in that moment of putting the foot down on the ground. The same process occurs with the pressing of the foot: there is the pressing and the awareness of pressing. In this way, yogis understand that along with the movement of the foot, there are also the moments of awareness. The moments of awareness are called, in Pali, *nama,* mind, and the movement of the foot is called *rupa,* matter. So yogis will perceive mind and matter rising and disappearing at every moment. At one moment there is the lifting of the foot and the awareness of the lifting, and at the next moment there is the movement forward and the awareness of that movement, and so on. These can be understood as a pair, mind and matter, which arise and disappear at every moment. Thus yogis advance to the perception of the pairwise occurrence of mind and matter at every moment of observation, that is, if they pay close attention.

Another thing that yogis will discover is the role of intention in effecting each movement. They will realize that they lift their foot because they want to, move the foot forward because they want to, put it down because they want to, press the foot against the ground because they want to. That is, they realize that an intention precedes every movement. After the intention to lift, lifting occurs. They come to understand the conditionality of all of these occurrences — these movements never occur by themselves, without conditions. These movements are not created by any deity or any authority, and these movements never happen without a cause. There is a cause or condition for every movement, and that condition is the intention preceding each movement. This is another discovery yogis make when they pay close attention.

When yogis understand the conditionality of all movements, and that these movements are not created by any authority or any god, then they will understand that they are created by intention. They will understand that intention is the condition for the movement to occur. Thus the relationship of conditioning and conditioned, of cause and effect, is understood. On the basis of this understanding, yogis can remove doubt about *nama* and *rupa* by understanding that *nama*and *rupa* do not arise without conditions. With the clear understanding of the conditionality of things, and with the transcendence of doubt about *nama* and *rupa,* a yogi is said to reach the stage of a "lesser *sotapanna.* "

A *sotapanna* is a "stream-enterer," a person who has reached the first stage of enlightenment. A "lesser *sotapanna*" is not a true stream-enterer but is said to be assured of rebirth in a happy realm of existence, such as in the realms of human beings and *devas.* That is, a lesser *sotapanna*cannot be reborn in one of the four woeful states, in one of the hells or animal realms. This state of lesser *sotapanna* can be reached just by practicing walking meditation, just by paying close attention to the movements involved in a step. This is the great benefit of practicing walking meditation. This stage is not easy to reach, but once yogis reach it, they can be assured that they will be reborn in a happy state, unless, of course, they fall from that stage.

When yogis comprehend mind and matter arising and disappearing at every moment, then they will come to comprehend the impermanence of the processes of lifting the foot, and they will also comprehend the impermanence of the awareness of that lifting. The occurrence of disappearing after arising is a mark or characteristic by which we understand that something is impermanent. If we want to determine whether something is impermanent or permanent, we must try to see, through the power of meditation, whether or not that thing is subject to the process of coming into being and then disappearing. If our meditation is powerful enough to enable us to see the arising and disappearing of phenomena, then we can decide that the phenomena observed are impermanent. In this way, yogis observe that there is the lifting movement and awareness of that movement, and then that sequence disappears, giving way to the pushing forward movement and the awareness of pushing forward. These movements simply arise and disappear, arise and disappear, and this process yogis can comprehend by themselves — they do not have to accept this on trust from any external authority, nor do they have to believe in the report of another person.

When yogis comprehend that mind and matter arise and disappear, they understand that mind and matter are impermanent. When they see that they are impermanent, they next understand that they are unsatisfactory because they are always oppressed by constant arising and disappearing. After comprehending impermanence and the unsatisfactory nature of things, they observe that there can be no mastery over these things; that is, yogis realize that there is no self or soul within that can order them to be permanent. Things just arise and disappear according to natural law. By comprehending this, yogis comprehend the third characteristic of conditioned phenomena, the characteristic of *anatta,* the characteristic that things have no self. One of the meanings of *anatta*is no mastery — meaning that nothing, no entity, no soul, no power, has mastery over the nature of things. Thus, by this time, yogis have comprehended the three characteristics of all conditioned phenomena: impermanence, suffering, and the non-self nature of things — in Pali, *anicca,dukkha,* and *anatta.*

Yogis can comprehend these three characteristics by observing closely the mere lifting of the foot and the awareness of the lifting of the foot. By paying close attention to the movements, they see things arising and disappearing, and consequently they see for themselves the impermanent, unsatisfactory, and non-self nature of all conditioned phenomena.

Now let us examine in more detail the movements of walking meditation. Suppose one were to take a moving picture of the lifting of the foot. Suppose further that the lifting of the foot takes one second, and let us say that the camera can take thirty-six frames per second. After taking the picture, if we were to look at the separate frames, we would realize that within what we thought was one lifting movement, there are actually thirty-six movements. The image in each frame is slightly different from the images in the other frames, though the difference will usually be so slight that we can barely notice it. But what if the camera could take one thousand frames per second? Then there would be one thousand movements in just one lifting movement, although the movements would be almost impossible to differentiate. If the camera could take one million frames per second — which may be impossible now, but someday may happen — then there would be one million movements in what we thought to be only one movement.

Our effort in walking meditation is to see our movements as closely as the camera sees them, frame by frame. We also want to observe the awareness and intention preceding each movement. We can also appreciate the power of the Buddha's wisdom and insight, by which he actually saw all of the movements. When we use the word "see" or "observe" to refer to our own situation, we mean that we see directly and also by inference; we may not be able to see directly all of the millions of movements as did the Buddha.

Before yogis begin practicing walking meditation, they may have thought that a step is just one movement. After meditation on that movement, they observe that there are at least four movements, and if they go deeper, they will understand that even one of these four movements consists of millions of tiny movements. They see *nama* and *rupa,* mind and matter, arising and disappearing, as impermanent. By our ordinary perception, we are not able to see the impermanence of things because impermanence is hidden by the illusion of continuity. We think that we see only one continuous movement, but if we look closely we will see that the illusion of continuity can be broken. It can be broken by the direct observation of physical phenomena bit by bit, segment by segment, as they originate and disintegrate. The value of meditation lies in our ability to remove the cloak of continuity in order to discover the real nature of impermanence. Yogis can discover the nature of impermanence directly through their own effort.

After realizing that things are composed of segments, that they occur in bits, and after observing these segments one by one, yogis will realize that there is really nothing in this world to be attached to, nothing to crave for. If we see that something which we once thought beautiful has holes, that it is decaying and disintegrating, we will lose interest in it. For example, we may see a beautiful painting on a canvas. We think of the paint and canvas conceptually as a whole, solid thing. But if we were to put the painting under a powerful microscope, we would see that the picture is not solid — it has many holes and spaces. After seeing the picture as composed largely of spaces, we would lose interest in it and we would cease being attached to it. Modern physicists know this idea well. They have observed, with powerful instruments, that matter is just a vibration of particles and energy constantly changing — there is nothing substantial to it at all. By the realization of this endless impermanence, yogis understand that there is really nothing to crave for, nothing to hold on to in the entire world of phenomena.

Now we can understand the reasons for practicing meditation. We practice meditation because we want to remove attachment and craving for objects. It is by comprehending the three characteristics of existence — impermanence, suffering, and the non-self nature of things — that we remove craving. We want to remove craving because we do not want to suffer. As long as there is craving and attachment, there will always be suffering. If we do not want to suffer, we must remove craving and attachment. We must comprehend that all things are just mind and matter arising and disappearing, that things are insubstantial. Once we realize this, we will be able to remove attachment to things. As long as we do not realize this, however much we read books or attend talks or talk about removing attachment, we will not be able to get rid of attachment. It is necessary to have the direct experience that all conditioned things are marked by the three characteristics.

Hence we must pay close attention when we are walking, just as we do when we are sitting or lying down. I am not trying to say that walking meditation alone can give us ultimate realization and the ability to remove attachment entirely, but it is nevertheless as valid a practice as sitting meditation or any other kind of *vipassana* (insight) meditation. Walking meditation is conducive to spiritual development. It is as powerful as mindfulness of breathing or mindfulness of the rising and falling of the abdomen. It is an efficient tool to help us remove mental defilements. Walking meditation can help us gain insight into the nature of things, and we should practice it as diligently as we practice sitting meditation or any other kind of meditation. By the practice of *vipassana*meditation in all postures, including the walking posture, may you and all yogis be able to attain total purification in this very life!

THE FIVE MENTAL HINDRANCES AND THEIR CONQUEST

Abbreviations:
AN ..... Anguttara Nikaya
MN ..... Majjhima Nikaya
SN ..... Samyutta Nikaya
Vism ..... Visuddhimagga

Unshakable deliverance of the mind is the highest goal in the Buddha's doctrine. Here, deliverance means: the freeing of the mind from all limitations, fetters, and bonds that tie it to the Wheel of Suffering, to the Circle of Rebirth. It means: the cleansing of the mind of all defilements that mar its purity; the removing of all obstacles that bar its progress from the mundane *(lokiya)*to the supramundane consciousness *(lokuttara-citta),* that is, to Arahatship.

Many are the obstacles which block the road to spiritual progress, but there are five in particular which, under the name of hindrances *(nivarana),* are often mentioned in the Buddhist scriptures:

1. Sensual desire *(kamacchanda),*
2. Ill-will *(byapada),*
3. Sloth and torpor *(thina-middha),*
4. Restlessness and remorse *(uddhacca-kukkucca),*
5. Sceptical doubt *(vicikiccha).*

They are called "hindrances" because they hinder and envelop the mind in many ways, obstructing its development *(bhavana).* According to the Buddhist teachings, spiritual development is twofold: through tranquillity *(samatha-bhavana)* and through insight *(vipassana-bhavana).* Tranquillity is gained by complete concentration of the mind during the meditative absorptions *(jhana).* For achieving these absorptions, the overcoming of the five hindrances, at least temporarily, is a preliminary condition. It is especially in the context of achieving the absorptions that the Buddha often mentions the five hindrances in his discourses.

There are five mental constituents which are chiefly representative of the first meditative absorption, and are therefore called the factors of absorption *(jhananga)*. For each of these there is, according to Buddhist commentarial tradition, one of the five hindrances that is specifically harmful for it and excludes its higher development and refinement to the degree required for jhana; and on the other hand, the cultivation of these five factors beyond their average level will be an antidote against the hindrances, preparing the road to jhana. The relationship between these two groups of five is indicated in this anthology, under the heading of the respective hindrance.

Not only the meditative absorptions but also lesser degrees of mental concentration are impeded by these five hindrances. So is the "neighborhood" (or "access") concentration*(upacarasamadhi)*, being the preliminary stage for the fully absorbed concentration *(appana)*reached in jhana. Likewise excluded by the presence of the hindrances is the momentary concentration *(khanikasamadhi)* which has the strength of neighborhood concentration and is required for mature insight *(vipassana)*. But apart from these higher stages of mental development, any earnest attempt at clear thinking and pure living will be seriously affected by the presence of these five hindrances.

This widespread harmful influence of the five hindrances shows the urgent necessity of breaking down their power by constant effort. One should not believe it sufficient to turn one's attention to the hindrances only at the moment when one sits down for meditation. Such last-minute effort in suppressing the hindrances will rarely be successful unless helped by previous endeavour during one's ordinary life.

One who earnestly aspires to the unshakable deliverance of the mind should, therefore, select a definite "working-ground" of a direct and practical import: a kammatthana[1] in its widest sense, on which the structure of his entire life should be based. Holding fast to that "working-ground," never losing sight of it for long, even this alone will be a considerable and encouraging progress in the control and development of the mind, because in that way the directive and purposive energies of mind will be strengthened considerably. One who has chosen the conquest of the five hindrances for a "working-ground" should examine which of the five are strongest in one's personal case. Then one should carefully observe how, and on which occasions, they usually appear. One should further know the positive forces within one's own mind by which each of these hindrances can best be countered and, finally, conquered; and one should also examine one's life for any opportunity of developing these qualities which, in the following pages, have been indicated under the headings of the spiritual faculties *(indriya),* the factors of absorption*(jhananga),* and the factors of enlightenment *(bojjhanga).* In some cases, subjects of meditation have been added which will be helpful in overcoming the respective hindrances.

By the "worldling" *(puthujjana),*[2] however, only a temporary suspension and partial weakening of the hindrances can be attained. Their final and complete eradication takes place on the stages of sanctity *(ariyamagga):*

Doubt is eliminated on the first stage, the path of stream-entry *(sotapatti-magga).*

Sensual desire, ill will and remorse are eliminated on the third stage, the path of non-returner *(anagami-magga)*

Sloth and torpor and restlessness are eradicated on the path of Arahatship*(arahatta-magga).*

Hence the reward of the fight against the hindrances is not only the limited one of making possible a shorter or longer spell of meditation, but every step in weakening these hindrances takes us nearer to the stages of sanctity where deliverance from these hindrances is unshakable.

Though most of the following texts, translated from the Discourses of the Buddha and the commentaries, are addressed to monks, they are likewise valid for those living the worldly life. As the Old Masters say: "The monk *(bhikkhu)* is mentioned here as an example of those dedicated to the practice of the Teaching. Whosoever undertakes that practice is here included in the term 'monk.' "

THE FIVE HINDRANCES

I. General Texts

There are five impediments and hindrances, overgrowths of the mind that stultify insight. What five?

Sensual desire is an impediment and hindrance, an overgrowth of the mind that stultifies insight. Ill-will ... Sloth and torpor ... Restlessness and remorse ... Sceptical doubt are impediments and hindrances, overgrowths of the mind that stultify insight.

Without having overcome these five, it is impossible for a monk whose insight thus lacks strength and power, to know his own true good, the good of others, and the good of both; nor will he be capable of realizing that superhuman state of distinctive achievement, the knowledge and vision enabling the attainment of sanctity.

But if a monk has overcome these five impediments and hindrances, these overgrowths of the mind that stultify insight, then it is possible that, with his strong insight, he can know his own true good, the good of others, and the good of both; and he will be capable of realizing that superhuman state of distinctive achievement, the knowledge and vision enabling the attainment of sanctity.

AN 5:51

One whose heart is overwhelmed by unrestrained covetousness will do what he should not do and neglect what he ought to do. And through that, his good name and his happiness will come to ruin.

One whose heart is overwhelmed by ill-will ... by sloth and torpor ... by restlessness and remorse ... by sceptical doubt will do what he should not do and neglect what he ought to do. And through that, his good name and his happiness will come to ruin.

But if a noble disciple has seen these five as defilements of the mind, he will give them up. And doing so, he is regarded as one of great wisdom, of abundant wisdom, clear-visioned, well endowed with wisdom. This is called "endowment with wisdom."

AN 4:61

There are five impurities of gold impaired by which it is not pliant and wieldy, lacks radiance, is brittle and cannot be wrought well. What are these five impurities? Iron, copper, tin, lead and silver.

But if the gold has been freed from these five impurities, then it will be plaint and wieldy, radiant and firm, and can be wrought well. Whatever ornaments one wishes to make from it, be it a diadem, earrings, a necklace or a golden chain, it will serve that purpose.

Similarly, there are five impurities of the mind impaired by which the mind is not pliant and wieldy, lacks radiant lucidity and firmness, and cannot concentrate well upon the eradication of the taints *(asava).* What are these five impurities? They are: sensual desire, ill-will, sloth and torpor, restlessness and remorse, and sceptical doubt.

But if the mind is freed of these five impurities, it will be pliant and wieldy, will have radiant lucidity and firmness, and will concentrate well upon the eradication of the taints. Whatever state realizable by the higher mental faculties one may direct the mind to, one will in each case acquire the capacity of realization, if the (other) conditions are fulfilled.

AN 5:23

How does a monk practise mind-object contemplation on the mental objects of the five hindrances?

Herein, monks, when sensual desire is present in him the monk knows, "There is sensual desire in me," or when sensual desire is absent he knows, "There is no sensual desire in me." He knows how the arising of non-arisen sensual desire comes to be; he knows how the rejection of the arisen sensual desire comes to be; and he knows how the non-arising in the future of the rejected sensual desire comes to be.

When ill-will is present in him, the monk knows, "There is ill-will in me," or when ill-will is absent he knows, "There is no ill-will in me." He knows how the arising of non-arisen ill-will comes to be; he knows how the rejection of the arisen ill-will comes to be; and he knows how the non-arising in the future of the rejected ill-will comes to be.

When sloth and torpor are present in him, the monk knows, "There is sloth and torpor in me," or when sloth and torpor are absent he knows, "There is no sloth and torpor in me." He knows how the arising of non-arisen sloth and torpor comes to be; he knows how the rejection of the arisen sloth and torpor comes to be; and he knows how the non-arising in the future of the rejected sloth and torpor comes to be.

When restlessness and remorse are present in him, the monk knows, "There are restlessness and remorse in me," or when agitation and remorse are absent he knows, "There are no restlessness and remorse in me." He knows how the arising of non-arisen restlessness and remorse comes to be; he knows how the rejection of the arisen restlessness and remorse comes to be; and he knows how the non-arising in the future of the rejected restlessness and remorse comes to be.

When sceptical doubt is present in him, the monk knows, "There is sceptical doubt in me," or when sceptical doubt is absent he knows, "There is no sceptical doubt in me." He knows how the arising of non-arisen sceptical doubt comes to be; he knows how the rejection of the arisen sceptical doubt comes to be; and he knows how the non-arising in the future of the rejected sceptical doubt comes to be.

MN 10 (Satipatthana Sutta)

To note mindfully, and immediately, the arising of one of the hindrances, as recommended in the preceding text, is a simple but very effective method of countering these and any other defilements of the mind. By doing so, a brake is applied against the uninhibited continuance of unwholesome thoughts, and the watchfulness of mind against their recurrence is strengthened. This method is based on a simple psychological fact which is expressed by the commentators as follows: "A good and an evil thought cannot occur in combination. Therefore, at the time of knowing the sense desire (that arose in the preceding moment), that sense desire no longer exists (but only the act of knowing)."

II. The Hindrances Individually

Just as, monks, this body lives on nourishment, lives dependent on nourishment, does not live without nourishment — in the same way, monks, the five hindrances live on nourishment, depend on nourishment, do not live without nourishment.

SN 46:2

1. Sensual Desire

A. Nourishment of Sensual Desire

There are beautiful objects; frequently giving unwise attention to them — this is the nourishment for the arising of sensual desire that has not arisen, and the nourishment for the increase and strengthening of sensual desire that has already arisen.

SN 46:51

B. Denourishing of Sensual Desire

There are impure objects (used for meditation); frequently giving wise attention to them — this is the denourishing of the arising of sensual desire that has not yet arisen, and the denourishing of the increase and strengthening of sensual desire that has already arisen.

SN 46:51

Six things are conducive to the abandonment of sensual desire:

1. Learning how to meditate on impure objects;
2. Devoting oneself to the meditation on the impure;
3. Guarding the sense doors;
4. Moderation in eating;
5. Noble friendship;
6. Suitable conversation.

Commentary to the Satipatthana Sutta:

1. Learning how to meditate about impure objects
2. Devoting oneself to the meditation on the impure

(a) Impure objects

In him who is devoted to the meditation about impure objects, repulsion towards beautiful objects is firmly established. This is the result.

AN 5:36

"Impure object" refers, in particular, to the cemetery

meditations as given in the Satipatthana Sutta and explained in the Visuddhimagga; but it refers also to the repulsive aspects of sense objects in general.

(b) The loathsomeness of the body

Herein, monks, a monk reflects on just this body, confined within the skin and full of manifold impurities from the soles upward and from the top of the hair down: "There is in this body: hair of the head, hair of the body, nails, teeth, skin, flesh, sinews, bones, marrow, kidneys, heart, liver, pleura, spleen, lungs, intestines, bowels, stomach, excrement, bile, phlegm, pus, blood, sweat, fat, tears, lymph, saliva, mucus, fluid of the joints, urine (and the brain in the skull)."

MN 10

By bones and sinews knit,
With flesh and tissue smeared,
And hidden by the skin, the body
Does not appear as it really is....
The fool thinks it beautiful,
His ignorance misguiding him ...

Sutta Nipata, v.194,199

(c) Various contemplations

Sense objects give little enjoyment, but much pain and much despair; the danger in them prevails.

MN 14

The unpleasant overwhelms a thoughtless man in the guise of the pleasant, the disagreeable overwhelms him in the guise of the agreeable, the painful in the guise of pleasure.

Udana, 2:8

3. Guarding the sense doors

How does one guard the sense doors? Herein, a monk, having seen a form, does not seize upon its (delusive) appearance as a whole, nor on its details. If his sense of sight were uncontrolled, covetousness, grief and other evil, unwholesome states would flow into him. Therefore he practices for the sake of its control, he watches over the sense of sight, he enters upon its control.

Having heard a sound ... smelt an odour ... tasted a taste ... felt a touch ... cognized a mental object, he does not seize upon its (delusive) appearance as a whole ... he enters upon its control.

SN 35:120

There are forms perceptible by the eye, which are desirable, lovely, pleasing, agreeable, associated with desire, arousing lust. If the monk does not delight in them, is not attached to them, does not welcome them, then in him thus not delighting in them, not being attached to them and not welcoming them, delight (in these forms) ceases; if delight is absent, there is no bondage. There are sounds perceptible by the ear ... odours perceptible by the mind ... if delight is absent, there is no bondage.

SN 35:63

4. Moderation in eating

How is he moderate in eating? Herein a monk takes his food after wise consideration: not for the purpose of enjoyment, of pride, of beautifying the body or adorning it (with muscles); but only for the sake of maintaining and sustaining this body, to avoid harm and to support the holy life, thinking: "Thus I shall destroy the old painful feeling and shall not let a new one rise. Long life will be mine, blamelessness and well-being."

MN 2; MN 39

5. Noble friendship

Reference is here, in particular, to such friends who have experience and can be a model and help in overcoming sensual desire, especially in meditating on impurity. But it applies also to noble friendship in general.

The same twofold explanation holds true also for the other hindrances, with due alterations.

The entire holy life, Ananda, is noble friendship, noble companionship, noble association. Of a monk, Ananda, who has a noble friend, a noble companion, a noble associate, it is to be expected that he will cultivate and practise the Noble Eightfold Path.

SN 45:2

6. Suitable conversation

Reference is here in particular to conversation about the overcoming of sensual desire, especially about meditating on impurity. But it applies also to every conversation which is suitable to advance one's progress on the path. With due alterations this explanation holds true also for the other hindrances.

If the mind of a monk is bent on speaking, he (should remember this): "Talk which is low, coarse, worldly, not noble, not salutary, not leading to detachment, not to freedom from passion, not to cessation, not to tranquillity, not to higher knowledge, not to enlightenment, not to Nibbana, namely, talk about kings, robbers and ministers, talk about armies, dangers and war, about food and drink, clothes, couches, garlands, perfumes, relatives, cars, villages, towns, cities, and provinces, about women and wine, gossip of the street and of the well, talk about the ancestors, about various trifles, tales about the origin of the world and the ocean, talk about what happened and what did not happen — such and similar talk I shall not entertain." Thus he is clearly conscious about it.

But talk about austere life, talk suitable for the unfolding of the mind, talk which is conducive to complete detachment, to freedom from passion, to cessation, tranquillity, higher knowledge, enlightenment and to Nibbana, namely, talk about a life of frugality, about contentedness, solitude, aloofness from society, about rousing one's energy, talk about virtue, concentration, wisdom, deliverance, about the vision and knowledge of deliverance — such talk I shall entertain." Thus he is clearly conscious about it.

MN 122

These things, too, are helpful in conquering sensual desire:

One-pointedness of mind, of the factors of absorption *(jhananga);*

Mindfulness, of the spiritual faculties *(indriya);*

Mindfulness, of the factors of enlightenment *(bojjhanga).*

C. Simile

If there is water in a pot mixed with red, yellow, blue or orange colour, a man with a normal faculty of sight, looking into it, could not properly recognize and see the image of his own face. In the same way, when one's mind is possessed by sensual desire, overpowered by sensual desire, one cannot properly see the escape from sensual desire which has arisen; then one does not properly understand and see one's own welfare, nor that of another, nor that of both; and also texts memorized a long time ago do not come into one's mind, not to speak of those not memorized.

SN 46:55

2. Ill-Will

A. Nourishment of Ill-Will

There are objects causing aversion; frequently giving unwise attention to them — this is the nourishment for the arising of ill-will that has not yet arisen, and for the increase and strengthening of ill-will that has already arisen.

SN 46:51

B. Denourishing of Ill-Will

There is the liberation of the heart by lovingkindness; frequently giving wise attention to it — this is the denourishing of the arising of ill-will that has not yet arisen, and of the increase and strengthening of ill-will that has already arisen.

SN 46:51

Cultivate the meditation on lovingkindness! For by cultivating the meditation on lovingkindness, ill-will disappears.

Cultivate the meditation on compassion! For by cultivating the meditation on compassion, cruelty disappears.

Cultivate the meditation on sympathetic joy! For by cultivating the meditation on sympathetic joy, listlessness disappears.

Cultivate the meditation on equanimity! For by cultivating the meditation on equanimity, anger disappears.

MN 62

Six things are helpful in conquering ill-will:

1. Learning how to meditate on lovingkindness;
2. Devoting oneself to the meditation of lovingkindness;

3. Considering that one is the owner and heir of one's actions *(kamma);*
4. Frequent reflection on it (in the following way):

   Thus one should consider: "Being angry with another person, what can you do to him? Can you destroy his virtue and his other good qualities? Have you not come to your present state by your own actions, and will also go hence according to your own actions? Anger towards another is just as if someone wishing to hit another person takes hold of glowing coals, or a heated iron-rod, or of excrement. And, in the same way, if the other person is angry with you, what can he do to you? Can he destroy your virtue and your other good qualities? He too has come to his present state by his own actions and will go hence according to his own actions. Like an unaccepted gift or like a handful of dirt thrown against the wind, his anger will fall back on his own head."
5. Noble friendship;
6. Suitable conversation.

Commentary to Satipatthana Sutta

These things, too, are helpful in conquering ill-will:

Rapture, of the factors of absorption *(jhananga);*

Faith, of the spiritual faculties *(indriya);*

Rapture and equanimity, of the factors of enlightenment *(bojjhanga).*

C. Simile

If there is a pot of water heated on the fire, the water seething and boiling, a man with a normal faculty of sight, looking into it, could not properly recognize and see the image of his own face. In the same way, when one's mind is possessed by ill-will, overpowered by ill-will, one cannot properly see the escape from the ill-will which has arisen; then one does not properly understand and see one's own welfare, nor that of another, nor that of both; and also texts memorized a long time ago do not come into one's mind, not to speak of those not memorized.

SN 46:55

3. Sloth and Torpor

A. Nourishment of Sloth and Torpor

There arises listlessness, lassitude, lazy stretching of the body, drowsiness after meals, mental sluggishness; frequently giving unwise attention to it — this is the nourishment for the arising of sloth and torpor that have not yet arisen and for the increase and strengthening of sloth and torpor that have already arisen.

SN 46:51

B. Denourishing of Sloth and Torpor

There is the element of rousing one's energy, the element of exertion, the element of continuous exertion; frequently giving wise attention to it — this is the denourishing of the arising of sloth and torpor that have not yet arisen and of the increase and strengthening of sloth and torpor that have already arisen.

SN 46:51

"May nothing remain but skin and sinews and bones; may flesh and blood dry up in the body! Not before having achieved what can be achieved by manly strength, manly energy, manly exertion shall my energy subside!"

MN 70

Six things are conducive to the abandonment of sloth and torpor:

1. Knowing that overeating is a cause of it;
2. Changing the bodily posture;
3. Thinking of the perception of light;
4. Staying in the open air;
5. Noble friendship;
6. Suitable conversation.

These things, too, are helpful in conquering sloth and torpor:

1. The recollection of Death

To-day the effort should be made,
Who knows if tomorrow Death will come?

MN 131

2. *Perceiving the suffering in impermanence*

In a monk who is accustomed to see the suffering in impermanence and who is frequently engaged in this contemplation, there will be established in him such a keen sense of the danger of laziness, idleness, lassitude, indolence and thoughtlessness, as if he were threatened by a murderer with drawn sword.

AN 7:46

3. *Sympathetic joy*

Cultivate the meditation on sympathetic joy! For by cultivating it, listlessness will disappear.

MN 62

4. *Contemplation of the spiritual journey*

"I have to tread that path which the Buddhas, the Paccekabuddhas and the Great Disciples have gone; but by an indolent person that path cannot be trodden."

Vism. IV,55

5. *Contemplation of the Master's greatness*

"Full application of energy was praised by my Master, and he is unsurpassed in his injunctions and a great help to us. He is honoured by practising his Dhamma, not otherwise."

Ibid.

6. *Contemplation on the greatness of the Heritage*

"I have to take possession of the Great Heritage, called the Good Dhamma. But one who is indolent cannot take possession of it."

Ibid.

7. *How to stimulate the mind*

How does one stimulate the mind at a time when it needs stimulation? If due to slowness in the application of wisdom or due to non-attainment of the happiness of tranquillity, one's mind is dull, then one should rouse it through reflecting on the eight stirring objects. These eight are: birth, decay, disease and death; the suffering in the worlds of misery; the suffering of the past rooted in the round of existence; the suffering of the future rooted in the round of existence; the suffering of the present rooted in the search for food.

Vism. IV,63

8. *How to overcome sleepiness*

Once the Exalted One spoke to the Venerable Maha-Moggallana thus: "Are you drowsy, Moggallana? Are you drowsy, Moggallana?" — "Yes, venerable sir."

(1) "Well then, Moggallana, at whatever thought torpor has befallen you, to that thought you should not give attention, you should not dwell on it frequently. Then it is possible that, by so doing, torpor will disappear.

(2) "But if, by so doing, that torpor does not disappear, you should think and reflect within your mind about the Dhamma as you have heard and learnt it, and you should mentally review it. Then it is possible that, by so doing, torpor will disappear.

(3) "But if, by so doing, that torpor does not disappear, you should learn by heart the Dhamma in its fullness, as you have heard and learnt it. Then it is possible ...

(4) "But if, by so doing, that torpor does not disappear, you should shake your ears, and rub your limbs with the palm of your hand. Then it is possible ...

(5) "But if, by so doing, that torpor does not disappear, you should get up from your seat, and after washing your eyes with water, you should look around in all directions and look upwards to the stars in the sky. Then it is possible ...

(6) "But if, by so doing, that torpor does not disappear, you should firmly establish the (inner) perception of light: as it is by day, so also by night; as it is by night, so also by day. Thus with a mind clear and unobstructed, you should develop a consciousness which is full of brightness. Then it is possible ...

(7) "But if, by so doing, that torpor does not disappear, you should, conscious of that which is before and behind, walk up and

down, with your senses turned inwards, with your mind not going outwards. Then it is possible ...

(8) "But if, by so doing, that torpor does not disappear, you may lie down on your right side, taking up the lion's posture, covering foot with foot — mindful, clearly conscious, keeping in mind the thought of rising. Having awakened again, you should quickly rise, thinking: 'I won't indulge in the enjoyment of lying down and reclining, in the enjoyment of sleep!'

"Thus, Moggallana, you should train yourself!"

AN 7:58

9. The five threatening dangers

If, monks, a monk perceives these five threatening dangers, it is enough for him to live heedful, zealous, with a heart resolute to achieve the unachieved, to attain the unattained, to realize the unrealized. Which are these five dangers?

(1) Here, monks, a monk reflects thus: "I am now young, a youth, young in age, black-haired, in the prime of youth, in the first phase of life. But a time will come when this body will be in the grip of old age. But one who is overpowered by old age cannot easily contemplate on the Teachings of the Buddha; it is not easy for him to live in the wilderness or a forest or jungle, or in secluded dwellings. Before this undesirable condition, so unpleasant and disagreeable, approaches me, prior to that, let me muster my energy for achieving the unachieved, for attaining the unattained, for realizing the unrealized, so that, in the possession of that state, I shall live happily even in old age."

(2) And further, monks, a monk reflects thus: "I am now free from sickness, free from disease, my digestive power functions smoothly, my constitution is not too cool and not too hot, it is balanced and fit for making effort. But a time will come when this body will be in the grip of sickness. And one who is sick cannot easily contemplate upon the Teachings of the Buddha; it is not easy for him, to live in the wilderness or a forest or jungle, or in secluded

dwellings. Before this undesirable condition, so unpleasant and disagreeable, approaches me, prior to that, let me muster my energy for achieving the unachieved, for attaining the unattained, for realizing the unrealized, so that, in the possession of that state, I shall live happily even in sickness."

(3) And further, monks, a monk reflects thus: "Now there is an abundance of food, good harvests, easily obtainable is a meal of alms, it is easy to live on collected food and offerings. But a time will come when there will be a famine, a bad harvest, difficult to obtain will be a meal of alms, it will be difficult to live on collected food and offerings. And in a famine people migrate to places where food is ample, and there habitations will be thronged and crowded. But in habitations thronged and crowded one cannot easily contemplate upon the Teachings of the Buddha. Before this undesirable condition, so unpleasant and disagreeable, approaches me, prior to that, let me muster my energy for achieving the unachieved, for attaining the unattained, for realizing the unrealized, so that, in the possession of that state, I shall live happily even in a famine."

(4) And further, monks, a monk reflects thus: "Now people live in concord and amity, in friendly fellowship as mingled milk and water and look at each other with friendly eyes. But there will come a time of danger, of unrest among the jungle tribes when the country people mount their carts and drive away and fear-stricken people move to a place of safety, and there habitations will be thronged and crowded. But in habitations thronged and crowded one cannot easily contemplate upon the Teachings of the Buddha. Before this undesirable condition, so unpleasant and disagreeable, approaches me, prior to that, let me muster my energy for achieving the unachieved, for attaining the unattained, for realizing the unrealized, so that, in the possession of that state, I shall live happily even in time of danger."

(5) And further, monks, a monk reflects thus: "Now the Congregation of Monks lives in concord and amity, without

> quarrel, lives happily under one teaching. But a time will come when there will be a split in the Congregation. And when the Congregation is split, one cannot easily contemplate upon the Teachings of the Buddha; it is not easy to live in the wilderness or a forest or jungle, or in secluded dwellings. Before this undesirable condition, so unpleasant and disagreeable, approaches me, prior to that, let me muster my energy for achieving the unachieved, for attaining the unattained, for realizing the unrealized, so that, in the possession of that state, I shall live happily even when the Congregation is split."[3]
>
> AN 5:78

These things, too, are helpful in conquering sloth and torpor:

Applied thought, of the factors of absorptions *(jhananga);*

Energy, of the spiritual faculties *(indriya);*

Investigation of reality, energy and rapture, of the factors of enlightenment*(bojjhanga).*

When the mind is sluggish, it is not the proper time for cultivating the following factors of enlightenment: tranquillity, concentration and equanimity, because a sluggish mind can hardly be aroused by them.

When the mind is sluggish, it is the proper time for cultivating the following factors of enlightenment: investigation of reality, energy and rapture, because a sluggish mind can easily be aroused by them.

SN 46:53

C. Simile

If there is a pot of water, covered with moss and water plants, then a man with a normal faculty of sight looking into it could not properly recognize and see the image of his own face. In the same way, when one's mind is possessed by sloth and torpor, overpowered by sloth and torpor, one cannot properly see the escape from sloth and torpor that have arisen; then one does not properly understand one's own welfare, nor that of another, nor that of both; and also texts memorized a long time ago do not come into one's mind, not to speak of those not memorized.

SN 46:55

4. Restlessness and Remorse

A. Nourishment of Restlessness and Remorse

There is unrest of mind; frequently giving unwise attention to it — that is the nourishment for the arising of restlessness and remorse that have not yet arisen, and for the increase and strengthening of restlessness and remorse that have already arisen.

SN 46:51

B. Denourishing of Restlessness and Remorse

There is quietude of mind; frequently giving wise attention to it — that is the denourishing of the arising of restlessness and remorse that have not yet arisen, and of the increase and strengthening of restlessness and remorse that have already arisen.

SN 46:51

Six things are conducive to the abandonment of restlessness and remorse:

1. Knowledge of the Buddhist scriptures (Doctrine and Discipline);
2. Asking questions about them;
3. Familiarity with the Vinaya (the Code of Monastic Discipline, and for lay followers, with the principles of moral conduct);
4. Association with those mature in age and experience, who possess dignity, restraint and calm;
5. Noble friendship;
6. Suitable conversation.

These things, too, are helpful in conquering restlessness and remorse:

Rapture, of the factors of absorption *(jhananga);*

Concentration, of the spiritual faculties *(indriya);*

Tranquillity, concentration and equanimity, of the factors of enlightenment*(bojjhanga).*

When the mind is restless it is not the proper time for cultivating the following factors of enlightenment: investigation of the doctrine, energy and rapture, because an agitated mind can hardly be quietened by them.

When the mind is restless, it is the proper time for cultivating the following factors of enlightenment: tranquillity, concentration and equanimity, because an agitated mind can easily be quietened by them.

SN 46:53

C. Simile

If there is water in a pot, stirred by the wind, agitated, swaying and producing waves, a man with a normal faculty of sight could not properly recognize and see the image of his own face. In the same way, when one's mind is possessed by restlessness and remorse, overpowered by restlessness and remorse, one cannot properly see the escape from restlessness and remorse that have arisen; then one does not properly understand one's own welfare, nor that of another, nor that of both; and also texts memorized a long time ago do not come into one's mind, not to speak of those not memorized.

SN 46:55

5. Doubt

A. Nourishment of Doubt

There are things causing doubt; frequently giving unwise attention to them — that is the nourishment for the arising of doubt that has not yet arisen, and for the increase and strengthening of doubt that has already arisen.

SN 46:51

B. Denourishing of Doubt

There are things which are wholesome or unwholesome, blameless or blameworthy, noble or low, and (other) contrasts of dark and bright; frequently giving wise attention to them — that is the denourishing of the arising of doubt that has not yet arisen, and of the increase and strengthening of doubt that has already arisen.

Of the six things conducive to the abandonment of doubt, the first three and the last two are identical with those given for restlessness and remorse. The fourth is as follows:

Firm conviction concerning the Buddha, Dhamma and Sangha.

In addition, the following are helpful in conquering Doubt:

Reflection, of the factors of absorption *(jhananga);*

Wisdom, of the spiritual faculties *(indriya);*

Investigation of reality, of the factors of enlightenment *(bojjhanga).*

C. Simile

If there is a pot of water which is turbid, stirred up and muddy, and this pot is put into a dark place, then a man with a normal faculty of sight could not properly recognize and see the image of his own face. In the same way, when one's mind is possessed by doubt, overpowered by doubt, then one cannot properly see the escape from doubt which has arisen; then one does not properly understand one's own welfare, nor that of another, nor that of both; and also texts memorized a long time ago do not come into one's mind, not to speak of those not memorized.

SN 46:55

FROM THE SAMAÑÑAPHALA SUTTA

I. The Sutta (Digha Nikaya No. 2)

Being endowed with noble mindfulness and clear comprehension, and endowed with noble contentedness, the monk resorts to a lonely place: to a forest, the foot of a tree, a mountain, a cleft, a rock cave, a cemetery, a jungle, an open space, a heap of straw. After the meal, having returned from the alms-round, he sits down, crosslegged, keeping his body erect and his mindfulness alert. Having given up covetousness (= sensual desire) with regard to the world, he dwells with a heart free of covetousness, he cleanses his mind from covetousness. Having given up the blemish of ill-will, he dwells without ill-will; friendly and compassionate towards all living beings, he cleanses his mind from the blemish of ill-will. Having given up sloth and torpor, he dwells free from sloth and torpor, in the perception of light; mindful and clearly comprehending, he cleanses his mind from sloth and torpor. Having given up restlessness and remorse, he dwells without restlessness; his mind being calmed within, he cleanses it from restlessness and remorse. Having given up sceptical doubt, he dwells as one who has passed beyond doubt; being free from uncertainty about salutary things, he cleanses his mind from sceptical doubt.

Just as when a man taking a loan, engages in a trade, and his trade succeeds, he now not only disposes of his old debt but he has also, beyond that, a surplus for maintaining a wife. And at that he rejoices, is glad at heart....

Just as when a man is sick and in pain, suffering from a grave disease, his food does not agree with him, and he has no strength left in his body. But some time later he recovers from that sickness; he can again digest his food, and he regains his strength. And at that he rejoices, is glad at heart....

Just as when a man has been thrown into prison, but some time later he is released from prison; he is safe and without fears, and he did not suffer any loss of property. And at that he rejoices, is glad at heart.... Just as when a man is a slave, not independent, but dependent on others, unable to go where he likes, but some time later he is set free from slavery, is now independent, no longer dependent on others, a freeman who can go where he wants. And at that he rejoices, is glad at heart....

Just as when a man, rich and prosperous, travels through a wilderness where there is no food and much danger, but some time later he has crossed the desert, and gradually reaches safely the vicinity of a village, a place of safety, free from danger. And at that he rejoices, is glad at heart.:

Similarly, so long as these five hindrances are not abandoned in him, a monk considers himself as indebted, as ailing, as imprisoned, as enslaved, as travelling in a wilderness.

But when these five hindrances are abandoned, he considers himself as free from debt, rid of illness, emancipated from the prison's bondage, as a free man, and as one arrived at a place of safety.

And when he sees himself free of these five hindrances, joy arises; in him who is joyful, rapture arises; in him whose mind is enraptured, the body is stilled; the body being stilled, he feels happiness; and a happy mind finds concentration.

Then detached from sensual desires, detached from unwholesome states, he enters into and dwells in the first absorption which is accompanied by applied thought and reflection, born of detachment, and filled with joy and rapture. He enters into and dwells in the second ... third ... fourth absorption.

II. The Commentary

A. The Similes for the Hindrances

The text of the discourse says: "Similarly, so long as these five hindrances are not abandoned in him, a monk considers himself as indebted, as ailing, as imprisoned, as enslaved, as travelling in a wilderness."

Hereby the Blessed One shows the unabandoned hindrance of sensual desire as similar to being in debt; and the other hindrances as similar to being ill, and so on. These similes should be understood as follows:

1. Sensual Desire

There is a man who has incurred a debt but has become ruined. Now, if his creditors, when telling him to pay back the debt, speak roughly to him or harass and beat him, he is unable to retaliate but has to bear it all. It is his debt that causes this forbearance.

In the same way, if a man is filled with sensual desire for a certain person, he will, full of craving for that object of his desire, be attached to it. Even if spoken to roughly by that person, or harassed or beaten, he will bear it all. It is his sensual desire that causes this forbearance. In that way, sensual desire is like being in debt.

2. Ill-Will

If a man suffers from a bilious disease, and receives even honey and sugar, he will not enjoy its flavour, owing to his bile sickness; he will just vomit it, complaining, "It is bitter, bitter!" In the same way, if one of angry temperament is admonished even slightly by his teacher or preceptor who wishes his best, he does not accept their advice. Saying "You harass me too much!" he will leave the Order, or go away and roam about. Just as the bilious person does not enjoy the flavour of honey and sugar, so one who has the disease of anger will not enjoy the taste of the Buddha's Dispensation consisting in the happiness of the meditative absorptions, etc. In that way, ill-will resembles illness.

3. *Sloth and Torpor*

A person has been kept in jail during a festival day, and so could see neither the beginning nor the middle nor the end of the festivities. If he is released on the following day, and hears people saying: "Oh, how delightful was yesterday's festival! Oh, those dances and songs!" he will not give any reply. And why not? Because he did not enjoy the festival himself.

Similarly, even if a very eloquent sermon on the Dhamma is going on, a monk overcome by sloth and torpor will not know the beginning, middle or end. If after the sermon, he hears it praised: "How pleasant was it to listen to the Dhamma! How interesting was the topic and how good the similes!" he will not be able to say a word. And why not? Because, owing to his sloth and torpor, he did not enjoy the sermon. In that way, sloth and torpor are comparable to imprisonment.

4. *Restlessness and Remorse*

A slave who wants to enjoy himself at a festival is told by his master: "Go quickly to such and such a place! There is urgent work to do. If you don't go, I shall have your hands and feet cut off, or your ears and nose!" Hearing that, the slave will quickly go as ordered, and will not be able to enjoy any part of the festival. This is because of his dependence on others.

Similarly it is with a monk not well versed in the Vinaya (the Disciplinary Code), who has gone to the forest for the sake of solitude. If in any matter, down to the question of permissible meat (Sub-Cy: e.g. pork) he gets the idea that it was not permissible (taking it for bear's flesh), he has to interrupt his solitude and, to purify his conduct, has to go to one skilled in the Vinaya. Thus he will not be able to enjoy the happiness of solitude because of his being overcome by restlessness and remorse. In that way, restlessness and remorse are like slavery.

5. Sceptical Doubt

A man travelling through a desert, aware that travellers may be plundered or killed by robbers, will, at the mere sound of a twig or a bird, become anxious and fearful, thinking: "The robbers have come!" He will go a few steps, and then out of fear, he will stop, and continue in such a manner all the way; or he may even turn back. Stopping more frequently than walking, only with toil and difficulty will he reach a place of safety, or he may not even reach it.

It is similar with one in whom doubt has arisen in regard to one of the eight objects of doubt.[4] Doubting whether the Master is an Enlightened One or not, he cannot accept it in confidence, as a matter of trust. Unable to do so, he does not attain to the paths and fruits of sanctity.

Thus, as the traveller in the desert is uncertain whether robbers are there or not, he produces in his mind, again and again, a state of wavering and vacillation, a lack of decision, a state of anxiety; and thus he creates in himself an obstacle for reaching the safe ground of sanctity *(ariya-bhumi)*. In that way, sceptical doubt is like travelling in a desert.

B. The Abandonment of the Hindrances

The text of the Discourse says: "But when these five hindrances are abandoned, the monk considers himself as free from debt, rid of illness, emancipated from the prison's bondage, as a free man, and as one arrived at a place of safety."

1. The Abandonment of Sensual Desire

A man, having taken a loan, uses it for his business and comes to prosperity. He thinks: "This debt is a cause of vexation." He returns the loan together with the interest, and has the promissory note torn up. After that he neither sends a messenger nor a letter to his creditors; and even if he meets them it depends on his wish whether he will get up from his seat to greet them, or not. And why? He is no longer in debt to them or dependent of them.

Similarly a monk thinks: "Sensual desire is a cause of obstruction." He then cultivates the six things leading to its abandonment (see p.9), and removes the hindrance of sensual desire. Just as one who has freed himself of debt no longer feels fear or anxiety when meeting his former creditors, so one who has given up sensual desire is no longer attached and bound to the object of his desire; even if he sees divine forms, passions will not assail him.

Therefore the Blessed One compared the abandonment of sensual desire to freedom from debt.

2. *The Abandonment of Ill-Will*

Just as a person suffering from a bilious disease, having been cured by taking medicine, will regain his taste for honey and sugar, similarly a monk, thinking, "This ill-will causes much harm," develops the six things leading to its abandonment and removes the hindrance of ill-will. Just as the cured patient partaking of honey and sugar appreciates the taste, so also this monk receives with reverence the rules of training, and observes them with appreciation (of their value). Therefore the Blessed One compared the abandonment of ill-will to the recovery of health.

3. *The Abandonment of Sloth and Torpor*

There is a person that once had been in jail on a festival day. But when freed and celebrating the festival on a later occasion, he will think: "Formerly, through the fault of my heedlessness, I was in prison on that day and could not enjoy this festival. Now I shall be heedful." And he remains heedful of his conduct so that nothing detrimental finds entry into his mind. Having enjoyed the festival, he exclaims: "Oh, what a beautiful festival it was!"

Similarly a monk, perceiving that sloth and torpor do great harm, develops the six things opposed to them, and so removes the hindrance of sloth and torpor. Just as the man freed from prison enjoys the whole length of the festival, even for seven days, so this monk who has given up sloth and torpor is capable of enjoying the beginning, the middle and the consummation of the

Festival of the Dhamma *(dhamma-nakkhatta),* and finally attains to Arahatship together with the fourfold discriminating knowledge *(patisambhida)*

Therefore the Blessed One spoke of the abandonment of sloth and torpor as being comparable to release from imprisonment.

4. The Abandonment of Restlessness and Remorse

There is a slave who, with the help of a friend, pays money to his master, becomes a free man, and is henceforth able to do what he likes. Similarly a monk, perceiving the great obstruction caused by restlessness and remorse, cultivates the six things opposed to them, and thus gives up restlessness and remorse. And having given them up, he is like a truly free man, able to do as he wishes. Just as no one can forcibly stop a free man from doing what he likes, so can restlessness and remorse no longer stop that monk from walking the happy path of renunciation *(sukhanekkhamma-patipada).*

Therefore the Blessed One declared the abandonment of restlessness and remorse as being similar to winning freedom from slavery.

5. The Abandonment of Sceptical Doubt

There is a strong man who, with his luggage in hand and well armed, travels through a wilderness in company. If robbers see him even from afar, they will take flight. Crossing safely the wilderness and reaching a place of safety, he will rejoice in his safe arrival.

Similarly a monk, seeing that sceptical doubt is a cause of great harm, cultivates the six things that are its antidote, and gives up doubt.

Just as that strong man, armed and in company, taking as little account of the robbers as of the grass on the ground, will safely come out of the wilderness to a safe place; similarly a monk, having crossed the wilderness of evil conduct, will finally reach the state of highest security, the deathless realm of Nibbana. Therefore the Blessed One compared the abandonment of sceptical doubt to reaching a place of safety.

Notes

1. I.e., subject of meditation: literally "working-ground."
2. A "worldling," or puthujjana, who may be a monk or layman, is one who has not yet attained to the first stage of sanctity, the Path of Stream-entry *(sotapatti-magga).*
3. This Discourse is one of the seven canonical texts recommended by the emperor Asoka in the Second Bhairat Rock Edict; "Reverend Sirs, these passages of the Law, to wit:—...'Fears of what may happen *(anagata-bhayani)....*, spoken by the Venerable Buddha, — these, Reverend Sirs, I desire that many monks and nuns should frequently hear and meditate: and that likewise the laity, male and female, should do the same. (Vincent A. Smith, Asoka. 3rd ed., p. 54).
4. They are, according to the Vibhanga: doubt in regard to the Buddha, the Dhamma, the Sangha, the (threefold) training, the past, the future, both past and future, and the conditionality of phenomena dependently arisen.

3

Vipassana: It's Relevance to the Individual and Society

Modern life is moving at such a rapid pace that there is no time even to breathe. Our fiercely competitive world is like a rat-race where, in spite of all the technological and economic improvements and multifarious pleasures, people are still unhappy. Humankind has made tremendous progress in the fields of science, industry, and political systems, etc., resulting in materialistic development. Man is the promoter and consumer of these advancements, which aim at improving our standard of living and total well-being.

But does this really happen? Look at the so-called "developed countries" of the world, which try to ensure a high standard of living. Despite their advances in such fields as health, education and technology, they are experiencing an increased incidence of mental illness, delinquency, crime, drug addiction, alcoholism, and suicide, etc.

Every society is made up of individuals. The individual in a modern society is a victim of varying degrees of stresses and strains. His or her existence is full of constant conflict between the world within and the world outside. The materialistic world holds humans under a hypnotic spell. Engaged all the time in filling their stomachs by earning and spending money, people are slaves of their own cravings, euphemistically called ambition, aspiration, aims or ideals. These, alas, are seldom fulfilled, which causes deep distress, frustration and dissatisfaction, whether one belongs to the "Haves" or the "Havenots." Suffering, then, is a common problem of humanity. It is a universal disease, not the bane of any one nation, or persons of any particular colour or creed. So the remedy must also be universal.*Vipassana* offers such a remedy.

The basis of any healthy, harmonious society is always the healthy, harmonious individual. Only if each individual has a pure, peaceful mind can we expect peace and harmony in the society.*Vipassana* is a unique technique for obtaining peace and harmony within an individual at the experiential level.

The great sage of India, Gotama the Buddha, discovered, or rather rediscovered this technique through his deep meditation. He attained enlightenment through this technique and was liberated from all the defilements of the mind. Then with great compassion and love, he distributed it to the suffering mankind. He did not establish any "ism" or "cult." He taught *Vipassana,* a way to purify the mind of its negativities of craving and aversion.

WHAT IS *VIPASSANA*?

It is not a rite or ritual based on blind faith. There is no visualization of any god, goddess or any other object, or verbalization of any mantra or *japa*. Neither is it an intellectual nor philosophical entertainment. The word *vipassana* is derived from "*passa*" (to look, to observe) and "*vi*" (in a special way). It means "observing oneself in a special way". It is a technique that purifies the mind, deconditioning the negativities of anger, hatred, greed, selfishness etc. by self-observation and introspection. It is insight meditation. It is looking at things *as they are* and not through coloured glasses. It is an effort to change the deep habit-pattern of the mind, which dwells in the continuous blind reactions of craving and aversion.

Vipassana is taught in a basic ten-day residential course. The course is very demanding, requiring the student to observe noble silence and follow strict rules of discipline. The daily schedule requires, on an average, ten hours of meditation, with regular breaks. Instructions are given periodically throughout the day, and every evening there is a videotaped discourse by the Teacher, S.N. Goenka, that explains and clarifies the day's practice.

There are three steps to the training given in a *Vipassana* course. The first is the observance of five basic precepts of morality which, in practice, means abstention from violence, lying, theft, sexual misconduct and the use of alcohol and other intoxicants. In short, observance of these precepts means right action, right speech, and right livelihood. Whenever one violates these, one generates impurities in one's mind. These impurities are the root cause of the stresses and strains from which one tries to gain release.

When you start practising *Vipassana,* deep inside you understand that every time you break any one of these precepts, you have started harming yourself, even before you start harming others. When you generate anger, you cannot possibly experience peace and harmony since you feel so agitated, so miserable. This is the law of Nature. It is a universal truth.

The next step is to achieve some mastery over our unruly minds by focussing attention on the natural and normal breath (not controlled and regulated breath as in *(praa"naayaaama).* This is called *aanaapaana-sati,* which means "awareness of respiration." There is no verbalization or visualization, just observation of natural and normal breath! This concentration helps to sharpen the mind. This helps the meditator to take the next step of *Vipassana,* where he or she is required to observe the sensations that manifest in the entire body every moment, as a result of the constant and continuous interaction of mind and matter.

Our minds are constantly reacting to pleasant and unpleasant happenings in the world outside. But a deep investigation of the mind through *Vipassana* reveals that when we react, we are actually reacting to the body sensations that result from our contact with the outside world or our own thoughts. When a thought arises, it manifests as a sensation on the body-pleasant or unpleasant-and one starts to like or dislike it. This is a law of Nature. Soon those likes and dislikes begin to consolidate and develop into negativities of craving and aversion. One starts tying knots deep in the unconscious mind. We create misery for ourselves by continuously reacting to the sensations.

In this technique we train the mind to observe all the sensations with detachment and equanimity-that is, without developing craving for pleasant sensations or aversion towards unpleasant or painful ones. As one proceeds on this path, one experiences that all sensations, whether pleasant or unpleasant, are constantly changing. They are impermanent, (*anicca*) and essenceless (*anattaa*) without any substance. This is the inherent nature of everything that exists in the Universe, whether animate or inanimate. One begins to understand experientially, not merely from book knowledge.

When one begins to be non-reactively aware of the different sensations, pleasant or unpleasant, the entire mass of the mind gradually becomes conscious and aware. The barrier between the conscious and unconscious mind is broken, and one stops reacting blindly. The mental purification- cleaning, deconditioning-strikes at the root-level, that is, the unconscious mind, where our deep rooted defilements are stored like sleeping volcanoes which cause us so much misery when they erupt.

To attain a stage which is free from these sleeping volcanoes, one has to walk on the Path oneself. It does not happen overnight. One needs a long and sincere practice of *Vipassana* with a proper understanding of the technique. As you progress on the Path, you learn to observe more objectively your own impurities of anger, hatred, envy, pride, jealousy, etc. more objectively.

Vipassana is, therefore, a process of self-purification through self-observation and introspection. It is a technique of non-verbal, self-administered "psychoanalysis" in that it sets into motion the process of tension-release. One is able, as it were, to operate on one's own mind and observe it as a witness. There is, therefore, no "*gurudom*" in this technique. You have to tread the Path yourself. No one else can do it for you.

One does not become a seasoned practitioner by taking just one ten-day course. The ten-day course only gives you a framework. It should be followed by regular practise in daily life and by taking more ten-day courses as boosters to help one become established in the practice. It is only then that one reaps the real benefits and realizes the full potential of this technique. There are longer courses of twenty, thirty and forty-five days which enable students to get further established in the practice. Practising seriously over a period of time, the mind gradually gets liberated from the negative habits of craving and aversion and their offshoots such as jealousy, ill will, selfishness and greed. One becomes peaceful and harmonious and then distributes this peace and harmony to others.

How does *Vipassana* help in daily living?

The progress on the path of *Vipassana* is not measured by how many courses one has taken, or how many years one has been practising, but by how equanimous one has become in daily living. You reap the benefits of *Vipassana* here and now. The first attack is on the ego, which begins to melt progressively as the cleaning process starts.

One student reported that during his stormy adolescent years he had acute differences of opinion with his parents. He left his parental home in great anger, never to see them again. He had not seen them for, nearly ten years in spite of their several attempts to contact him. When he came for a *Vipassana* course, his ego began to dissolve and he began to perceive his own shortcomings. He felt extremely miserable, but was able to consider his parents' point of view. He was able to see the situation from different angles, and not only through his coloured glasses. He decided to write to his parents and tell them of his whereabouts, return home and talk it over with them.

Mere advice and counselling do not help. It is only when our perception begins to change that we are able to observe a situation in its totality. As the layers of mental impurities begin to peel off, through the practice of *Vipassana*, there is greater clarity of thinking. We begin to develop better judgment of people and situations. This, in turn, helps to improve our relationships with other people. We become less and less demanding of people: family members, children, neighbours, colleagues, subordinates, etc. With greater clarity of thinking our decision-making ability, both in private and work life, becomes more appropriate and effective.

Another student who was a nurse reported how *Vipassana* helped reduce her nervousness. She was attached to the Crisis Department of a hospital. The sight of blood and mauled bodies of accident cases would simply paralyze her. She could have asked for a transfer from the department, but she decided to face the problem and not run away from it. With regular practice of *Vipassana*, she gradually became more stable and balanced. This greatly impressed the doctors and her colleagues. Her work in the service of her patients was now more effective.

When our minds undergo a cleaning process, our capacity to work increases many-fold. The energy that was being consumed in our struggle with tensions, emotional blocks, and a narrow-minded egocentred way of living-this now gets channelled more profitably. Our work efficiency increases both qualitatively and quantitatively.

A commonly expressed doubt is: Does this technique with its emphasis on equanimity make one inactive? No, it does not. A responsible person in society has to be full of action. What goes away is the habit of blind reaction. We learn to take proper action with positive feeling.

Apart from the purification of the mind, which is the primary goal of the technique, the meditator also experiences gains at the physical, and psychological level. Many common ailments such as hypertension, headaches, ulcers, acidity, etc., are very often psychosomatic. These are automatically cured as a by-product of the cleansing process of *Vipassana*. Many drug addicts and alcoholics have found a total cure as a result of regular practice of *Vipassana*. Many students who practise *Vipassana* regularly, keep reporting that their concentration, memory and ability to grasp the material they read has improved tremendously. One student who had given up his college studies midway and was on tranquillizers is now free of pills. He went back to his studies and has now completed them.

All these gains are only by-products of the cleansing process of *Vipassana*. They should never be the motive for the practice of *Vipassana*, as this is a devaluation of this exalted technique, which takes human beings to such great heights in liberating the mind of its impurities.

Vipassana, if practised correctly and with proper understanding, progressively makes one a better individual. This, in turn, enables one to make a positive and constructive contribution to, the society in which one lives. One learns the art of constructive social living, which promotes positive social interaction.

Vipassana is a technique which has a very practical approach. It not only helps us to pass through the vicissitudes of life in a detached way, but it also promotes social well-being. It is, therefore, a science, not only of self-development but also of social development. It is an art of living, whereby we learn to live in peace and harmony with our own selves and with others.

To summarize, the characteristic features of Vipassana are:

1. It is a universal technique which can be practised by anyone belonging to any country, caste or creed.
2. It strikes at the roots of our defilements in the unconscious mind and breaks the barrier between the conscious and unconscious layers of the mind.
3. There is no place for imagination in this technique, no verbalization of any mantra or visualization of any god or goddess, or any other object. The practice starts from experience of the apparent truth of body and mind and proceeds towards realization of the subtle and absolute Truth.
4. It is a highly individualistic and experiential method of meditation. Man must walk on the Path himself. No one else can make the effort for him or liberate him from the impurities of the mind. Hence there is no "*gurudom*" in this technique.
5. One reaps the benefits of this technique here and now, as one progressively becomes a better individual.

HOLISTIC EDUCATION AND *VIPASSANA*

Education, said Albert Einstein, is that which remains when everything that is learnt in school is forgotten. If we evaluate modem education by this definition, its chief outcomes can easily be identified as aggressive competition, pride and envy. At its best, the modem educational system imparts some professional knowledge and skills, but it lacks any cultivation of heart. The result is only to make the students conceited materialists.

Consequently, at an age when children should be dreaming of beauty, greatness and perfection, they now dream about sensory titillation and wealth, and spend time worrying about how to cam money [1]. No wonder that our society today is being devoured by the twin devils of acquisitiveness and unabashed consumerism, with the resultant serious social problems of corruption, strife and violence; and ecological problems such as environmental pollution and the rapid depletion of resources which threaten the very survival of humankind on this planet. Thinkers and philosophers of all hues [14], whether in India or abroad, agree that a complete revamping of the educational system is a prerequisite for the solution to these serious maladies besieging mankind. For, unless human beings become harmonized within themselves, through a fundamental change in their animal instincts-which should be the most important purpose of education-all changes in their outer circumstances will ultimately be overwhelmed by their instinctual, animal brutality.

A Vision of Holistic Education

Education should be concerned with the totality of life and not with immediate responses to immediate challenges [1]. Broadly speaking, four different but inter-related aspects of human life can generally be recognized: viz., the physical, emotional, intellectual and spiritual. Holistic education should cultivate all these aspects in full measure. For example, physical education should include not only the performance of physical exercises to keep the body fit, but also the training to use the senses and physical framework wisely.

Similarly, emotional education should emphasize the type of training of mind that develops the positive human emotions of universal love, compassion, forbearance, humility, equanimity, etc., and eradicates the baser instincts such as greed, envy, pride, aggressiveness, etc. In this way, one can establish a healthy relationship with society.

Intellectual education should require not only the development of the ability to think, but also the ability to act independently, rationally and logically on the basis of a deep understanding of the various phenomena of nature.

Finally, spiritual education should cultivate a refinement of the mind, to manifest that elusive "fourth dimension" of the human personality from which springs forth an intuitive understanding of the very purpose of our existence, and a clarity of what ought to be done to achieve it. It is quite clear that the modern educational system completely sidesteps the emotional and spiritual aspects of the human personality, and caters only to physical and intellectual growth-and this, too, only in a superficial manner. It is not as if the educationists and education planners have not been aware of this deficiency, for as early as 1966, the Kothari Commission recognized the need for inculcating social, moral and spiritual values through education [5]. But the way to achieve this in a composite society like India, where the notions of caste, creed and religion are very strongly entrenched, has defied a universally acceptable solution. There have, of course, been many attempts to impart moral education indirectly through various means such as prayers, discussions and contemplation sessions, etc. Even direct attempts have been made through meditation methods, lectures and discourses in various institutions such as Christian missionary schools; Islamic schools; Anglo-vedic schools; schools associated with the Ramakrishna Mission; ISKCON; Maharishi Mahesh Yogi centers; the Krishnamurti Foundation; and the Saibaba Trust, etc. However, these approaches have not been able to gain wide acceptance.

There exists in India and many other countries today, a scientific method of control and purification of mind which, if properly integrated with the educational process, has the potential of becoming a universally acceptable technique for nourishing the emotional and spiritual dimensions of human personality. This technique, an ancient science of mind and matter, is called *Vipassana*meditation. Following is a brief description of the technique and how it can be integrated into modern education.

Vipassana Meditation: Viewed from the perspective of holistic education, *Vipassana* meditation can be described as a technique of purifying the mind of its baser instincts so that one begins to manifest the truly human qualities of universal goodwill, kindness,- sympathy, tolerance, humility, equanimity, etc., and simultaneously gains an insight into the true nature and purpose of human existence. This is achieved in a very scientific manner through a systematic cultivation of Right Mindfulness coupled with non-reactivity; that is to say, development of the habit of paying penetrating attention to whatever is happening in our total organism-the body with its five senses and the mind which operates in and through it-without any admixture of subjective judgments or reactions. The quality which purifies the mind at the deepest level is the mental factor of objectivity, or equanimity, which develops from the constant, thorough understanding of the impermanence of all components of the mind-body phenomenon (ref. [8], p.258).

An important prerequisite for the systematic practice of *Vipassana* is scrupulous observance of five basic moral precepts-viz., abstention from killing, stealing, false speech, sexual misconduct, and intoxicants-since any willful violation of these precepts causes violent mental agitation which makes it impossible to observe the mind objectively. Of course, *Vipassana* practice also helps one to gain the mental strength needed to observe the moral precepts in day-to-day life. While the complete details of this systematic practice are best learnt in a meditation camp under the careful guidance of a teacher, some salient features of the technique and its theoretical basis are explained here.

The foundation stone in the cultivation of Right Mindfulness (or Awareness) consists of paying attention to the body (ref. 8, pp. 2542591. The practice of systematic self-observation begins by focussing attention on the respiration (ref. 9, p.5), the breath coming in and going out of the body. This practice-called *Anapana*-is an exercise in cultivation of, right awareness, not regulation or control of the breath (such as *praa.naayaama* or other breathing exercises). There is just a silent "bare observation" of the natural flow of respiration, with a firm and steady attention free from any strain. One observes the length of the breath, short or long. To aid the development of concentration, the student is advised to focus the attention on finer details, such as which nostril the breath is coming in and going out, or where the breath is touching in the area around the nostrils.

The whole exercise is one of observing the reality as it is, without any preferences or reactions. It is quite natural that in the beginning it will not be possible to focus the attention continuously on the breath, even for a minute or two. The habitual tendency of the mind to wander away from the assigned task comes to the fore very quickly, allowing the student to experience for him or herself the turbulent nature of the mind. The student learns to observe this fact itself dispassionately without feeling dejected about the repeated "running away" of the mind-and once again focuses one's attention on the breath.

With the systematic practice of *Anapana* for a few days, the concentration increases, and a natural calming and equalizing of the breath takes place. As the breath is very intimately related to the mind, this leads simultaneously to a tranquilizing of the mind-in fact, of the entire life-rhythm [61. The mind also becomes sharp enough to observe subtler realities of the body-mind complex, e.g., the sensations occurring in the area around the nostrils where attention is focused during the practice of mindfulness of breathing.

This leads us to the next step in the cultivation of Right Mindfulness, viz., awareness of the bodily sensations (ref. 9, p.21). The object of meditation now is body sensation. Sensations occur on the body, but they are felt by the mind. When one is investigating the internal experience of one's sensations, one is actually observing the interaction of mind and matter *(Vedanaa-samosara.naa sabbe dhamma:* Everything that arises in the mind is accompanied by sensation) (ref. 8, p. 253). Moreover, sensations *(vedana)* provide the crucial link between the impact *(phassa)* upon the six sense doors and the resultant reaction of craving and aversion *(ta"nhaa)* which is the root cause of all suffering [7; 8, p.2551. This profound discovery is, in fact, one of the most fundamental aspects of the teaching of the master scientist of mind and matter, Gotama Buddha.

The practice of *Vipassana* consists of "feeling" the sensations throughout the body without any reaction or evaluation whatsoever, thus developing equanimity at a very deep level. This is of course more easily said than done, because our subconscious mind, which is constantly "feeling" the body sensations, has the stubborn, recalcitrant habit of reacting to these sensations in a particular manner. It habitually reacts to pleasant sensations with craving and to unpleasant sensations with aversion, thus strengthening the mind's conditioned tendency to run after sensory pleasure and to run away from pain.

The exercise of awareness and equanimity in the face of the entire spectrum of sensations acts to gently break this habit pattern. One repeatedly observes the sensations as they actually are: constantly changing-arising, staying for some time, fading away, and giving rise to other sensations. Through this repeated practice, the habit of reaction is replaced by an experience of the truth of *anicca* or impermanence. The student is trained to focus one's attention on the changeful nature of the sensations, thereby gradually correcting the conditioned habit of evaluating them as pleasant or unpleasant. This scientific method of observing the sensations as they really are-without any evaluation based on past conditioning-is what is described by the word*vipassana. Vipassana,* a Pali word, literally means "to see things as they really are"-in their true nature, their true characteristic of impermanence *(anicca).*

One can thus gradually train the mind to observe the bodily sensations in an objective manner-without any notion of their being G4my sensations"-in the same way as one would dispassionately observe the waves arising and disappearing in the sea. With the practice of this objective observation, the attitude of "enjoyership"-one of the chief manifestations of ego-is thus enfeebled.

The attitude of remaining equanimous towards all internal phenomena arising from the interaction of mind and body is simultaneously strengthened, as the student repeatedly observes the fact of the evanescent nature *(anicca)* of the mind-body process.

The systematic practice of mindfulness of sensations integrates within itself other important aspects of the cultivation of Right Mindfulness, viz., the mindfulness of the state of mind and the contents of the thought at any given moment (ref. [91, p.25). As the alertness and objectiveness of the meditator increase (by the. continual practice of non-reactive observation of sensations), he or she can quickly become aware of the mental reactions which keep arising from time to time. As an adjunct to the main practice of mindfulness of body sensations, a student practises from time to time the bare registering of one's state of mind. One observes the various mental states without self-justification or self-condemnation. This practice reveals the changing nature of the mental states, and thereby strengthens the meditator's conviction about the *anicca* of all body-mind phenomena.

The most significant consequence of *Vipassana* practice is that it gives the mind a natural slant towards the goal of full enlightenment, the complete liberation from all bondages. Simultaneously, one develops the steadfast confidence that all hindrances on the Path can be overcome.

Role of *Vipassana* in Education

We can now understand how *Vipassana* can fill that vital gap in modern education-viz., the training of mind, leading to a balanced, harmonious and purposeful life., *Vipassana* meditation imparts a way to observe all the phenomena of this sensory world objectively and impersonally under the penetrating gaze of an equanimous mind. The multifold benefits which accrue from this practice are being discussed at length in this seminar and have formed the basis for research conducted by the *Vipassana* Research Institute (Igatpuri, India) in many areas of human activity. Here, only those aspects related to the field of education are being discussed.

The attitude of "bare attention" (bestowed by a mind at once aware and non-reactive) slows down the transition from thought to action, allowing the practitioner more time-those crucial few moments needed to come to a mature decision. The tendency of the base, animal instincts to overpower the faculty of human reason can thus be effectively checked, leading to a gradual reduction in negative traits such as rashness, intolerance, intemperance and aggressive behaviour which characterize modem youth. This emotional education should naturally lead to a marked improvement in the student-teacher relationship, which has been constantly deteriorating over the years due to the corroding influence of a materialistic world view coupled with the negative traits mentioned above.

On the positive side, this training of non-reactive observation of facts, coupled with the insight of*anicca* enhances one's ability to face the vicissitudes of life squarely and equanimously without taking recourse to such escapist alternatives as smoking, alcohol and drugs, which have become the bane of modern society. This attitude of equanimity also reduces the obsessive preoccupation with indulgence in unending materialistic desires, thereby allowing space for the manifestation of the so-called "higher needs"-the self-actualization needs of meaningfulness, justice, truthfulness, service, love, compassion, etc., which modem psychology recognizes as essential components of basic human needs [10]. Recent research has shown that people able to manifest these "higher needs" are generally much more creative and innovative, because self-actualization needs provide "a more durable fuel for creativity" than the drive for sensual gratification [11].

The observation of mental contents is also a powerful tool of self-education because it reveals to the meditator a very clear picture of his weak points and strong points without doing damage to his self-esteem. The habitual attitude of hurriedly glossing over one's weaknesses, or blowing one's strengths out of proportion, is thus checked. One gradually gains the inner strength needed to overcome one's weaknesses without a need to exercise a violent exertion of will or forceful repression, both of which are harmful in the long run. This candid self-examination promotes honesty towards oneself, increases one's tolerance of others' faults, assists in the development of humility and compassion, and reduces vanity.

The attitude of Right Awareness coupled with equanimity closely corresponds to the disposition of the true scientist and scholar, which is characterized by clear definition of the subject, unprejudiced receptivity for the facts, exclusion of the subjective factor in judgment, and deferring judgment until a careful examination of the facts has been made (ref. [6], p.39). This practice should therefore be of great help in augmenting the scientific temper.

Vipassana meditation reinforces the scientific outlook in another much more direct way. Every meditator, after some length of practice of mindfulness of sensations, reaches a state where he experiences the whole body as a mass of vibrations. This experience is in line with the quantum-relativistic description of matter [12]. This direct experience provides much more clarity about the nature of matter than the scores of mathematical formulae produced by classroom descriptions.

Another important benefit of the systematic practice-especially of mindfulness of breath, which is of crucial significance in education-is improvement in one's ability to concentrate on a task. As explained earlier, the essence of the practice is to train the mind to keep the attention continuously on an object (viz., the breath), and to minimize the drifting of the mind into futile daydreams, which are the chief obstacle to concentration. The training of observing the mental states also comes in handy. Once such daydreams have arisen (whether during meditation or during normal activity), if one briefly makes these daydreams themselves an object of close observation, their power of distraction is drastically curtailed and they get quickly dispersed. This results in a quick retrieval of concentration.

The attitude of impersonal non-reactive observation is of profound value in the ultimate deliverance of the mind from all bondages, which is the true purpose of spiritual education. To quote Venerable Nyanponika Thera (ref. [6], p.43): "The inner distance from things ... as obtained temporarily and partially by bare attention, shows us, by our own experience, the possibility of winning perfect detachment and the happiness resulting from it. It bestows upon us the confidence that such temporary setting aside may well become one day a complete stepping out of this world of suffering. It gives a kind of foretaste, or at least an idea, of the highest liberty, the 'holiness during lifetime' that has been alluded to by the words 'in the world but not of the world.' "

To achieve this objective, the principal requirement is to develop an insight into the basic characteristics of life. Impermanence (*anicca*) is the fundamental characteristic with which a *Vipassana* student is continually confronted. As this experience becomes ingrained, realization of the other characteristics-viz., of suffering *(dukkha) and* egolessness (*anattaa*)-automatically develops, leading one to a clear understanding of the purpose of life and the way to achieve it-the very acme of spiritual education.

It should be evident from the preceding brief description that *Vipassana* meditation is a purely scientific technique, a universal culture of mind, which does not subscribe to any sectarian beliefs, dogmas or rituals. It should be universally acceptable, therefore, as an integral part of education. Its benefits have been corroborated by thousands of practitioners-both young and old belonging to diverse castes, creeds, countries and religious beliefs. Vivekanańda's dream of evolving a "man-making education" [2] could be fulfilled by the integration of *Vipassana* into modern education. It is high time that an action plan in the field of education be drawn, at least on an experimental scale, to scientifically validate the efficacy of *Vipassana* over an extended period. Some of the crucial issues which need to be addressed include:

1. How to motivate the students, teachers and management of schools and colleges to introduce*Anapana* and *Vipassana*, and reduce resistance from unwilling students and teachers?
2. The extent of training needed before authorizing educational staff members to teach meditation in schools and colleges.
3. The format and minimum duration of in-house camps organized to initiate young students to*Anapana* meditation, keeping in view the practical constraints (especially of overnight stay).
4. How to maintain continuity of practice within the tight schedule of schools and colleges?
5. Should there be a formal course on meditation in the curricula of schools and colleges?
6. How to assess the beneficial influence of *Vipassana* on teachers, students and the teaching-learning process?
7. How to integrate *Vipassana* with the student counselling services in the schools and colleges?

A properly thought out action plan if sincerely implemented should ultimately pave the way for the formation of institutions, which can impart truly holistic education. Such institutions would make a crucial contribution to developing wholesome individuals and a harmonious society.

THE EFFECT OF VIPASSANA ON THE WORK ENVIRONMENT

To study the effect of Vipassana on the work environment, we interviewed people who had attended a ten-day Vipassana course. A questionnaire was given to them. Their colleagues were also interviewed to find out their views about the results of Vipassana.

In general, everyone experienced a positive change in the behaviour of Vipassana students and a consequent improvement in the work environment. There was a new dimension of trust, commitment and cooperation with others, and a remarkable rise in goodwill. There was a decrease in hatred or strong dislike towards others, short-temperedness, mental fatigue, jealousy, negative feelings towards others, and confrontation because of jealousy, ego, guilt-feelings, etc.

Now let us look at the interviews of Vipassana students in detail:

Mr. Balle, Manager (R&D) has been practising Vipassana for the last ten years. He said that his anger and short-temperedness have greatly lessened and he has cooled down considerably. He thinks twice or before answering now, and does not give harsh replies to either seniors or juniors. His subordinates feel free to approach him and the atmosphere has become cordial both in the office and at home.

His trust in people has increased. He feels comfortable with all types of people. For example, while others were having difficulty in dealing with one person in the factory, Mr. Balle was comfortable with him and in due course they became friends. Because Mr. Balle benefited from Vipassana, he recommended it to his friend, who was clever but short-tempered. After the friend attended a Vipassana course his shorttemperedness was reduced remarkably-even his family members were surprised. Later his friend sent another two or three doctor friends for a Vipassana course.

As Mr. Balle has become less angry and more trusting of his subordinates, the commitment of his subordinates to work has increased. During work on a project, normally a direction of work is selected and work is started accordingly. Previously, projects used to reach a lot of ends, with new lines of action being chosen and work re-started. A lot of fline was wasted. Now after learning Vipassana, Mr. Balle chooses the direction of work in consultation with his colleagues so that the risk of selecting a wrong direction is reduced and time is saved. The result is a direct increase in productivity, i.e., more output in less time.

All Vipassana students and their colleagues agree that there has been a positive improvement in the atmosphere of the workplace. Different reasons have been mentioned by them. For example, Mr. Kulkarni (Executive) says that previously he had very high expectations of results from his subordinates. If these expectations were not fulfilled then it gave rise to anger and tension. Now after he has learrit Vipassana, he looks at the 65 mistakes of subordinates objectively and gives guidance to them to correct those mistakes. His concentration and peace of mind have increased and tension has lessened, which has resulted in more work output each day.

Colleagues of a Vipassana student have reported that after a Vipassana course, he is more co-operative at work and less aggressive. Now, before replying to them, he thinks first and then takes action or not, as appropriate. They say that are now more comfortable with him.

Mr. B. Sitharam (GM) attended his second ten-day course in January 1993. After his first course he stopped using tobacco, paan and alcohol. He practises Vipassana every day for one hour. His wife attended a ten-day course in November 1993.

Mr. N.P. Joshi (Assistant Manager) feels that after learning Vipassana he has become more polite and more considerate towards others. His wife attended a course in January 1994. Her outlook towards life has changed. Now his nine-year-old son is also planning to attend a course in May 1994.

Mr. P.J. Shah (Purchase Officer) practises Vipassana daily for one hour. He says that even if his mind is upset, it becomes fresh and sharp after meditating. His shorttemperedness has been reduced. His working efficiency and decision making power have improved and he feels more confident. Mr. Pathak, a Stores Officer, has practised Vipassana since July 1992. Before that, he used to sleep during lunchtime; now it is not required since his mind is more fresh. He works more quickly and therefore completes most of his work before the end of the day. As a result he can give attention to other areas, like housekeeping. His subordinates report that Mr. Pathak has cooled down, and is less angry and tense. His colleague, the Purchase Officer, focussed on the term, "reliability". He said that the answers given by Mr. Pathak are more reliable. This shows that his work is more efficient and accurate.

A general observation of all employees is that those who are practising Vipassana are clearing paperwork daily, with less pending work, showing that they have better concentration and work faster. They have given up the habit of cigarette and tobacco smoking.

Increased trust and co-operativeness have strengthened the attitude of teamwork which is essential for the success of the organization. If we widen this concept of co-operation with people and team spirit, we can see that it will also greatly benefit the society at large.

In a nutshell, we can conclude confidently that Vipassana has a very positive effect on productivity and the work environment.

The Relevance of Vipassana for the Environmental Crisis

Environmental pollution is a great threat to the survival of humankind on this planet. If effective measures are not taken immediately, a catastrophe which is similar in destructive capacity to that caused by nuclear war is imminent as a result of environmental pollution and increased exposure to U.V. radiation through ozone depletion. The rate of pollution caused by human beings far exceeds nature's ability to purify and rejuvenate its life-sustaining air and water. We understand the problem that we now face, hence the search for development with sustainability. But it is our contention that a radical solution has not yet been looked for, let alone found, and that man is only trying to grapple with this enormous global problem with patchwork technological remedies.

From the point of view of the Buddha's teaching, environmental pollution is but the external manifestation of man's internal moral pollution, which has assumed alarming proportions and reached a crisis. A number of *suttas* in the Pali Canon such as the *Agga~n~na* (*Digha*. III. 80),*Cakkavattisiihanaada* (*Digha* III 58) and some in the *A"nguttaranikaaya* (I. 160; II. 75) express that when moral degeneration becomes rampant in society, it causes adverse changes in the human body and in our environment. The legend in the *Agga~n~na Sutta* states that moral degeneration causes the loss of beauty in the human personality and depletion of natural food resources in the external world. These adverse repercussions are proportionate to the extent of moral degradation.

Crime also increases in society and, grappling with these problems, people try to organize appropriate social institutions to make life more tolerable, peaceful and comfortable for one and all, to the best of their ability.

Thus Buddhism believes that moral consciousness/the human mind, the human body, the external world consisting of fauna and flora, and society are intricately interconnected through an all-embracing network of cause and effect, to make one whole psychologically sensitive and responsive ecosystem. It is this fact that the Buddha succinctly summarizes in the stanza:

Cittena niyyati loko cittena parikissatiCittassa ekadhammassa sabbeva vasa"m anvaguu ti.

The world is led by the mind, it is dragged hither and thither by the mind.

The mind is one reality under the power of which everything goes.(Sa"myutta-nikaaya, I. 39)

If we loosely translate the phrase *cittena niyyati loko* as "the world operates through human ideas," we can see at a practical level how the face of the earth has been changed with advancing human ideas/knowledge during the course of history. At the dawn of civilization when man was hunting and gathering food, nature remained almost undisturbed. During the age of settled agricultural life, irrigation schemes were developed and the face of nature was modified to a certain extent. The industrial revolution brought about further changes with excessive exploitation of natural resources and mass production. The twentieth century, which boasts of 90% of the scientists the world has ever produced, has ushered in the Nuclear Age and the Space Age.

Thus we see how human ideas have brought about vast changes in nature, to such an extent that Nature's purifying, rejuvenating and replenishing capacities have been outstripped by man's activity of exploitation, causing unprecedented pollution and impoverishment. According to Buddhist interpretation, the root cause that is responsible for this crisis is man's greed for luxury, wealth and power. The human brain has developed without keeping pace with the human heart and moral responsibility. Intellectually, modem man may be a giant, but emotionally he is a dwarf suffering with spiritual bankruptcy. One sociologist observes that modem man has one leg strapped to a jet plane and the other leg tied to a bullock cart.

Thus man is tom apart with conflicting desires and practical realities. Further, man's intellect is limited; he lacks the vision to see how far-reaching his behaviour and activities are, and how they affect negatively or positively his own well-being, and unsuspected aspects of the physical activities of Nature.

The Buddha's theory of *pa.ticcasamuppaada* too maintains the same principle, that mind and matter, man and nature are interconnected and interdependent. Man depends on nature for sustenance, for, it is said: *Sabbe sataa aahaara.t.tthitikaa.* In search of food and also clothing, shelter and medicine, humans change their environments according to their technological skills. For example, modem men use chemical fertilizers, insecticides, and herbicides in agriculture for better harvests. These destroy the natural bacterial balance, which gives rise to adverse chain reactions, which in turn affect human health and well-being.

Further, the same truth of dependence of man and Nature is reiterated in the commentaries through the theory of the five cosmic laws, *pa"nca niyaama dhamma.* The five are as follows: physical laws *(utuniyaama,* lit. season law), biological laws *(biijaniyaama,* lit. seed law), psychological laws *(cittaniyaama,* lit. mind law), moral laws *(kammaniyaama,* lit. action law) and causal laws *(dhammaniyaama,* lit. reality law). *(Sa"mlyuttanikaaya* 1125 states as synonyms *dhamma.t.thitataa dhammaniyaamataa idappaccayataa).* Causal laws operate within the first four spheres as well as among them.

Thus all cosmic laws, physical, biological, psychological and moral, interact with one another, and man experiences weal or woe, happiness or unhappiness according to the nature of moral energy he generates. If wholesome moral energy is widespread, there is peace in society and life is comparatively happy and comfortable. If unwholesome moral energy is widespread, strife in society is similarly rampant and life becomes more and more troublesome.

The sixth and fifth Centuries B.C. can be cited as an exceptionally fortunate era when morally wholesome energy was poured out through the teachings of spiritual giants such as the Buddha, Jina Mahavira, Zoroastra, Confucius and Socrates, from different quarters of the world. The twentieth century seems to be the direct opposite of that era. Crime, terrorism and war reign supreme in the world today. Famine, starvation and malnutrition have engulfed many of the third world countries. AIDS and other luxuryrelated deadly diseases are rampant in affluent countries. This state of affairs reminds us of a commentarial statement regarding the fate of mankind in a morally bankrupt world. According to that, when mankind comes under the grip of greed, hatred and delusion, its downfall is brought about by famine, fire/ weapons, and disease respectively (*Diighanikaaya A.t.thakathaa* III. 854). The situation in the modern world is such that all three morally unwholesome motivational roots seem to be active and man is receiving three-pronged retribution for his own immoral actions.

Another important point raised in the *Agga~n~na Sutta* is that man is a creature with a strong tendency for imitation *(di.t.thaanugati"m aapajjamaanaa).* Therefore new ideas, actions and behaviour on the part of a few, quickly become new trends in society, especially when they are pleasure-oriented and economically attractive. Aided by modem mass media and commercial propaganda, sensualism, aggressiveness, hunger for wealth, status and power have become social trends in the modern world. According to our thinking, this imitative tendency is not the only cause responsible for these current trends, as they seem to be aided by the collective consciousness of mankind (called *dhammadhaatu* in Pali) which envelops the whole world. We therefore tend to argue that *terra firma* is covered over by a biosphere and an atmosphere into which is absorbed what we prefer to be called the psychosphere. Our argument for putting forward this idea is as follows:

The *Saama~n~naphalasutta (Diigha,nikaaya* I.76) states that the mind is interwoven with the body, and that it can be seen to be so by one who has developed the *fourth jhaana,* like a coloured thread that passes through a transparent gem. It can be surmised that the mind is associated with the air element in the body because the breathing pattern changes with emotional changes, e.g., we sigh when we are sad, we yawn when we are lazy, we snort when angry and gasp in pain.

These changes can be accepted as conclusive proof that the mind and breath are fused together. It is scientifically known that the carbon dioxide level of the exhaled breath increases under negative emotional stress. This may be because the breath has absorbed from the bloodstream toxic chemical properties added to the blood from the endocrine glandular secretions when the mind is charged with negative emotions such as anger and fear. When large masses of people pour out such psychogenic venom with each exhalation, the atmosphere gets polluted in a subtle way, and it is very probable that sentient beings and even vegetation are sensitive to this type of pollution. It is experimentally known that plants thrive much better in an environment of peace and love, but they tend to get stunted or they wither away when harshly treated with violent abusive words even though both groups are equally well provided with water, manure, sunlight and horticultural care.

According to scientific thinking air pollution with increased carbon dioxide is due to fossil fuel burning which in the long run would contribute to global warming with catastrophic effects on human well-being. It is now conjectured that the disappearance of the dinosaurs from the face of the earth is due to reduction of oxygen level and increase of carbon dioxide in the atmosphere. The present situation of environmental pollution is far more grave than that which caused the extinction of those enormous beasts, as carbon dioxide is produced by machines unknown during the dinosaur age. While metal machines physically pollute the atmosphere, billions of human machines also add psychogenic toxins to the carbon dioxide they breathe out. Therefore we venture to argue that pollution in the psychosphere is a crucial factor in the environmental crisis man is faced with today. Even the physical pollution caused by emissions from machinery and over-cxploitation of natural resources is the result of man's greed for luxury, wealth and power. It is therefore possible to conclude that the environmental pollution is really the external manifestation of the internal moral pollution of modern man.

As man's moral disposition has a direct deep-rooted relationship with the cnvironmental crisis Vipassana meditation offers a relevant practical method to effect a wholesome attitudinal change in man to give him a sense of direction and goal in life, and also help him restore the sustainability of nature.

Taking a phrase from Erich Fromm we can say that man has to change his attitude from the 'having mode' to the 'being mode' of life. Man motivated by the 'having mode' tries to satisfy his greed extracting as much as possible from nature, thus leading to cxcessive exploitation bringing in its wake all the ills of pollution and depletion. Man inspired by the being mode on the other hand utilizes nature's resources to satisfy his needs and this attitude leads to conservation and sustainability of nature. It is interesting to note that ancient Indian Languages such as Sanskrit and Pali do not even have a verbal root 'to have'. The idea of having has to be expressed periphrastically. If one wishes to say 'I have sons and wealth' in Pali one must say *Puttaa me atthi dhana"m atthi,* which literally means 'to me there are sons, there is wealth'. Thus the being mode had been so ingrained in the human heart of ancient Indian culture even language lacked a verbal root 'to have'.

Vipassana meditation teaches man to lead a simple life satisfying his needs. *Appicchataa,* the ability to be satisfied with little is methodically cultivated as a virtue of great value. If it is cultivated collectively by mankind, giving up the present trend of consumerism, much of the sting of the eco-crisis can be mitigated. All the ills of large-scale deforestation such as soil erosion, landslides, changes in weather-pattern, drought, etc. are fundamentally related to consumerism. Without changing to a simple life style an effective solution to these life threatening problems cannot be worked out.

Metta forms a part and parcel of the meditative life. If one practises *mattaa* one would refrain from over-exploitation and over consumption out of sympathy for future generations too as non-renewable natural resources are fast diminishing due to demands made by the present consumerist life style.

Practising *mettaa* man would also have sympathy for other species and forms of life which are threatened by extinction today. It is strategically important to remember that natural bio-diversity is extremely valuable for a healthy balanced eco-system.

Vipassana meditation cleanses man of his psychological impurities. Nature can cope with the biological impurities produced by man, but nature cannot help nor cope with the psychological pollution produced by man. Hence the spread of crime, terrorism and war like an epidemic in society, pollution related diseases threatening human life, and the imminence of large scale destruction through ecological imbalance and pollution.

Let us come back to the Buddha's statement: *cittena niyyati loko,* that the world operates through the human mind. So long as the human mind is motivated by morally wholesome intentions, man can lead a comparatively happy life and nature would be manageably hospitable. When the motivational roots are evil, man experiences misery as is maintained by the first two verses in the *Dhammapada*. Now it appears that evil is so widespread that even nature has been adversely affected, rendering it more inhospitable. The environmental crisis has to be treated as the result of a moral crisis. Man has to cultivate a morally wholesome attitude and lifestyle for a change for the better and this has to be accepted as a survival imperative.

VIPASSANA AND BUSINESS MANAGEMENT

Business Management

With the growing complexities of business especially industrial business-the use of meditation techniques has become popular during the last few years. However, they have been used mainly as stress relieving techniques for executives subjected to the tensions of achieving targets.

Management of a medium scale industrial business requires organization, quality control, production, purchasing, marketing, fund flow, administration, etc. Each of these operations requires clear thinking, planning, coordination, execution, cost accounting, and profitability projections. There are presently several colleges which teach this type of management. There are special techniques of management for large organizations with turnovers of three hundred crores rupees (one hundred million U.S. dollars) and over. Research and development methods are also available for upgrading the technology of these business.

Need for Meditation

Where exactly does meditation come into the picture? To get an answer, we have to look to more industrialized countries such as the United States and Germany. The nature of the societies produced by advanced industrialization has been characterized by heavy alcohol, drug and cigarette consumption; pandemic divorces and broken families; economic recession and job insecurities; and strong feelings of competition and frustration leading to heart attacks, suicide and so on.

Fragmented Society

People who become business managers come from this fragmented society. Business schools teach them to work for more profits and higher salaries, and the stress involved leads to greater consumption of drugs and alcohol, and various health problems such as hyper-tension. The level of equanimity in such societies deteriorates. The business owners, executives and managers develop feelings of pride, prejudice, jealousy and arrogance and experience their concomitants: depression, anxiety, stress and other harmful effects.

Positive Transformation

The *Vipassana* meditation technique improves the lives of executives and business managers by transforming their attitudes. Prejudice is replaced by compassion; jealousy changes into joy at the success of others; greed and arrogance are replaced by generosity and humility, and so on.

This transformation of attitude results in stress reduction, and mental equanimity and balance. It is a creative force capable of inducing a dynamic work approach in subordinate staff. The positive change is brought about by a change in the attitude and actions of the executive-to polite and compassionate behaviour, gentle speech, and a mind full of love and friendliness. This positive change in consciousness is the aim of genuine meditation practice, and it forms a new and advanced basis for business and industrial management.

Present Scene

Business management is presently judged by profits or "money-making" ability. Managers are evaluated by their ability to make more money by increasing product turnover, developing new technologies with better payoffs, or decreasing costs through new inventions. In return, they want higher salaries and more requisites. Although there is nothing inherently wrong with generating profits and an increase in incomes, the real aim of an economic venture is to create a wealth which combines money with health and happiness. Vipassana makes a significant contribution towards improving the mental health and happiness of individuals-vital components of wealth.

HUMAN RESOURCE DEVELOPMENT

Many companies currently have human resource development departments, popularly known as HRD. HR13 is a welcome new concept because human beings working in business or industry should not be taken for granted. They need to be developed. One of the parameters in this process is the development of mutual respect, which naturally improves interpersonal relations. Meditation will also help to achieve this, enabling us to overcome the hostility towards fellow human beings- colleagues, subordinates, superiors, government officers and others. This hostility manifests as anger, arrogance, jealousy, vengeance, selfishness, greed, prejudice and ill will. Lectures, seminars, books, discussions and so on give some understanding of these subjects. Nevertheless, more than 95% of the negative material in the human mind remains unaffected despite an intellectual understanding of the value of overcoming hostility, negativity and selfishness. This statement stems from my own experience, as well as interviews with more than one hundred business executives during the last ten years.

Right Livelihood

The practice of Right Livelihood is an important aspect of Vipassana meditation. It can become the foundation for business management practice, upon which can be based traditional management techniques of using statistical data such as of cash-flow projections, return on capital, GNP, the turnover of profits, and so on. These parameters are useful if they are based on the concept of Right Livelihood.

Briefly, the application of this concept means that income, whether of a business corporation or an individual, should not only be ethical, but the consciousness of the individuals producing this income should be reasonably clean, i.e., free from the negativities mentioned above. A mental climate free of negativities automatically becomes pure and exhibits the characteristics of genuine love, respect, co-operation, compassion and equanimity. Wealth produced by a group consciousness of this nature not only produces money, but also the mental health and happiness resulting from a stress-free mind.

Subconscious Mind

Without going into the details of Vipassana meditation, I will touch upon an important aspect of the transformation of consciousness: the subconscious mind. Very little is known about this mind which is filled with negativities which are counter-productive to wealth in its totality. While it is possible to recognize and experience these negativities, it is not possible to empty the mind of these defilements without a proper technique.

Most meditation techniques are unable to reach the subconscious mind, they are not colourless and can therefore "taint" the mind which further complicates the situation. Vipassana bases every step on "reality-as it is." Vipassana allows a meditator to experience moments of "no nutriment to the mind. This starts the process of "detoxifying" the mind of its impurities.

Industrial Sickness

A mind which does not meditate and develops impurity causes grave consequences. When the minds of industry leaders are impure, the ramifications are pervasive and serious. This phenomenon is exemplified by the classic example of the management failure at the Bombay Textile Mills. Twenty years ago, it was a viable, profit-making unit; however ' the greed for quick money caused a financial tragedy. The incoming cash, which could have been used for modernizing the plant and machinery, or for financing working capital was syphoned out for the personal gain of the directors. Their livelihood was not "right livelihood". The defilement of greed killed the best interests of the directors and caused widespread misery to a large section of Bombay's workforce and economic system.

Vipassana meditation is a surgical operation of the mind. When practised properly the pace of purification can be dramatically increased. The technique frees one's mind from greed. A healthy mind is alert and capable of meeting the demands of a situation. It naturally comes out of addictions and indulgences. The practice of Vipassana results in the diminishment 'of craving. A business conducted with the base of such a mind would have resulted in the growth of the textile industry rather than creating sick production units.

An analysis of the increasing industrial sickness and the failure of business manage merit reveals a pattern. In many cases, over anxiety for export or expansion causes the working capital to be diverted into the generation of fixed assets. The result is an acute shortage of working capital and excessive borrowing-clearly dangerous avenues for business practice. With a mind made mature by meditation, these kinds of desire-driven actions are checked by the calm and cool temper of equanimity, which reduces the possibility of making such mistakes.

Pure Mind: The Basis of Management

The Vipassana technique does not create by itself a new technology of management. It contributes to the improvement of management by correcting the root of the problem-impurity of mind-so that a business is continually nourished by the pure food of right thoughts and action. It is excessive craving and greed which poison the minds of managers; this impurity is corrected by meditation.

Attitude towards Competition

Vipassana also changes one's attitude towards competitors. When a business cuts out a competitor, there is a chain reaction: a vicious cycle starts. Many businesses have been ruined by this attitude. Vipassana purifies the mind and fills it with wisdom which enables the practitioner to appreciate that there is room for everyone to coexist. The purification resulting from Vipassana practice results, as it were, in fertile soil where seeds of healthy business management are nurtured. The soil of healthy minds brings forth management practices where the primary aim is to generate peace and happiness in the society, with the secondary aim of generating money as a means for buying goods and services, and attaining economic emancipation and a higher quality of life.

Conclusion

I have had detailed discussions with more than a dozen business executives who are small-scale entrepreneurs, after their Vipassana courses. These discussions have confirmed that, after a Vipassana course, they are able to work 20% faster than before, and the quality of their work has the improved value of being performed by a subtle mind. They report that qualities of greed, anger, arrogance, and prejudice have decreased and there is less friction in dealing with staff members. Very healthy and cordial interpersonal relations have resulted, and the wealth of their enterprises has steadily increased as a result of these positive changes.

VIPASSANA AND BUSINESS

Vipassana helps in breaking the barrier between the conscious and unconscious mind. Through the process of observing without reacting, the mind is cleansed of its negativities. With the technique of Vipassana, one reaches deep down to the unconscious level of the mind and experiences sensations within the framework of the body without reacting to them. The law of nature is such that whatever actions we perform are stored in the form of its effect in the unconscious part of the mind. The collection of such impressions *(saizkhari7)* is not only from this life but also from earlier lives. This storehouse is the guide to our reactions to the outside environment.

At the experiential level, the major benefits derived are:

1. As more of the mind becomes conscious, one becomes more perceptive and better able to understand a wide variety of situations. In my personal experience, I have found solutions to many difficult problems by meditating.
2. By reducing craving and aversion, one is able to face situations in life more objectively, and thus improve the process of decision-making. It reduces irritation and disappointments under situations which would otherwise create pressure on the mind.
3. Business people, depending on the complexities of their work, generally have to face a lot of stress and strain. Such stress has an impact on physical health, and it is said that more than fifty percent of physical problems are psychosomatic in nature. As a side-effect of this meditation, physical health can be improved through the process of mind purification.
4. One often seeks power and position in business but is unable to enjoy them because of the negative effect they create through inflation of the ego. The ego stops us from

developing the human qualities of love, compassion, peace and equanimity. Vipassana is beneficial in business, but more importantly, it helps us experience true peace of mind and happiness through a reduction of the ego. This comes with the understanding of the impermanence of both mind and matter.

5. Continuous practice of Vipassana increases equanimity and thus one is able to live more harmoniously, without being much affected by the tensions of everyday life.
6. 'Business houses have tremendous strengths at their command-in finance, management and technology. Through development of a better value system, Vipassana induces us to work with the aim of serving humanity. In business, it improves the quality of products and services we produce for society, and encourages a greater service orientation to meet the larger needs of society. 1 was motivated to start the Lupin Rural Support Programme immediately after learning meditation. This programme has provided increased prosperity and happiness for roughly 200,000 people where we operate, and in turn much happiness to us. We are motivated to develop many more such experiments of human service, some of which we are working toward now. Vipassana leads to purification of the mind, and a purer mind will seek happiness through improved service to society.

It is said that Vipassana is the oldest science of India. Its rediscovery by Gotama Buddha allowed him to realize the ultimate truth, and he taught this technique for the benefit of humanity. Later on, Emperor Ashoka encouraged the spread of this teaching for the benefit of his subjects, as indicated in the rock edicts. We are extremely grateful to Goenkaji for bringing this lost wisdom to our country. Because Vipassana goes beyond the barriers of caste, sect, communalism, and narrow nationalism, it brings improves morality so that along with material benefits there can be real happiness. Further, it can be an effective instrument in strengthening national integration and international understanding factors which are of great relevance in today's times.

VIPASSANA IN JAILS: A HISTORICAL REVIEW

The first course of *Vipassana* conducted by Goenkaji in a prison was in 1975 at the Central Jail Rajasthan. When I was the Home Secretary of that state, I had myself undertaken a *Vipassana*course, and experienced a profound change in myself. On the fourth day of my course, I felt that*Vipassana* was a technique which could solve not only individual problems but also problems of society, and could bring reform in government as well. On the evening of the fourth day I met Goenkaji and shared my reflections with him. I asked him whether this technique could be a tool to change the system in government. He agreed, and I immediately asked whether we could arrange to hold a course in a jail. He was very positive and told me he would come if I arranged it. This was a big challenge!

I set about talking to the authorities concerned-the Chief Minister, the Chief Secretary, the jail officials. Initially everybody was very skeptical, but finally a decision was taken to make an experiment!

The real difficulty came when Goenkaji arrived in Jaipur for the course. I had to tell him that it would not be possible for him to stay in the jail; he was to stay in a beautiful bungalow outside the jail instead. He said he had to stay inside the jail twenty-four hours a day, because *Vipassana* is a deep operation, and he is like the surgeon.

The difficulty was the jail manual. Only those who had been sentenced to imprisonment or those under trial or members of the jail staff could stay in the jail. I posed the problem to Goenkaji and he said, "Sentence me!" I was aghast, shocked; how could my Teacher be sentenced to imprisonment? The legal department was consulted and it seemed there was no solution. We issued administrative instructions and resolved the problem.

Goenkaji was allowed to stay in the jail, in a makeshift room in the jail dispensary. Another problem came when the course was just about to start. At that time ankle locks and handcuffs were used for hardened criminals. Four such prisoners were brought into the meditation hall bound in these iron handcuffs and ankle locks. Goenkaji was walking nearby and when he saw this, he was amazed. He asked me what was going on. I told him these were hardened criminals. He exclaimed, "How can people in chains be put before me? This cannot happen. Remove the chains!"

But the Inspector General of Prisons (IG) said that the security in the jail was his responsibility, and he could not remove the ankle chains or the handcuffs. However, Goenkaji was firm. He said he could not give *Dhamma* with people sitting before him in chains-he had come to remove the chains. The IG told him he could remove the chains from within, but not the outside chains! Goenkaji insisted that those who were meditating must not be in chains. This was a big dilemma, a big problem!

The IG was a very experienced officer. He asked me not to force him to relax security requirements for those prisoners. He said any one of them might try to be a hero, and strangle me or Goenkaji to death in a split second. We discussed the problem and finally came to an agreement to remove the chains and fetters. An armed guard would be kept ready at a strategic point to shoot the criminal if he started to advance menacingly. I told the IG to ensure that any mishap or panic shooting did not take place.

The chains and locks were removed. Goenkaji was pleased. The course started. I sat close by. The IG stayed out of the hall but remained very close. My eyes were fixed on the "Four", heart throbbing and deep anxiety within! But every passing moment was a relief unbounded. As Goenkaji started chanting, his loving kindness (*mettaa*) was flowing profusely. The red-hot eyes of the criminals who were the cause of so much turmoil changed and their faces beamed; tears streamed down their cheeks. Tears rolled down my face also; it was a rare moment filled with joy after such high tension. The efficacy of *Vipassana* was established! Goenkaji's narration of Angulimala's story flashed in my mind.

There was another event which was deeply moving. There were two condemned prisoners awaiting execution of the death sentence. They couldn't be accepted in the course. During his morning round, Goenkaji passed through their cells and decided that they could be given*Anapana* and *Vipassana* in the cells by loudspeaker from the hall and we agreed. They started meditation, made great progress, and felt happy. They listened to the discourses in the cells, as did many others. We had arranged the relay of the discourses throughout the entire jail campus.

After the course was over, one of the condemned prisoners sent me a message that he had decided to withdraw his mercy petition to the President of India. He was ready to die. He now had *Dhamma* and felt totally fearless of his impending death! In the meantime his petition had been rejected, and the day of execution by hanging had been fixed. I was invited to witness the sad event. The prisoner came out of the cell smiling and in high spirits. He thanked the jail staff and went to the gallows with a cheerfulness never witnessed before.

In 1976 a course was held in the Police Academy at Jaipur for the police officials, where personnel right from the deputy IG to the constables sat. We had a second course in the Jaipur Central Jail in 1977. These were very successful courses. Then I was transferred to another post. My successor in the office felt that meditation courses might dilute the deterrent impact of punishment, so the programme did not continue. I had a great longing that *Vipassana* would come there again. I asked Goenkaji about it, and he said that the seed of *Vipassana* had been planted and it would sprout again some day. Every year I would go and talk to him, expressing regret that this valuable experience was not being repeated. Goenkaji told me not to worry, the time would come.

The time did come. The seed sprouted, and sprouted so well. In 1990 another course was arranged in the Jaipur Central Jail. My colleague Mr. Tandon conducted that course. It went very smoothly and a big transformation took place. I was very happy. Then the Gujarat Government was approached, but they had a lot of misgivings. I was told by the Home Department of Gujarat that if I conducted the course they would not have any objection. I welcomed the offer. We had the first course in a Gujarat jail in I99I, at the famous Sabarmati Jail, Ahmedabad. Then the courses started in Central Jail, Baroda. Dr. B.G. SavIa led the first course. To date there have been five courses. The Superintendent of Baroda Jail, Mr. R. Vora, has written a book in Gujarati about these courses, entitled *"Diwaloṇ Mein Diwyat"* (Divinity Within Walls). It is an inspiring story. Baroda Jail is now a house of reforms.

Then came the courses at Tihar Jail, in the capital city of India, New Delhi. With eight to nine thousand prisoners, Tihar is one of the largest jails in the world and, until recently, one of the most infamous. Bringing *Vipassana* to Tihar was also a difficult journey. I will begin with a brief mention about the first course, which was held in late November 1993.

In July 1993 Mr. M.L. Melita, Additional Secretary in the Ministry of Home Affairs, Government of India, wrote to me asking if I could organize a *Vipassana* course in the Central Jail, Tihar. He knew about the benefits of the Rajasthan experiment in the central Jail, Jaipur. Soon an urgent telephone message came from Ms. Kiran Bedi, Inspector General Prison, Tihar Jail, urging me to arrange the course. It took some time to make preparations, such as training of jail staff, selection of the Ward and course venue, precourse orientation etc., for which we made a few visits to Tihar jail and met Ms. Bedi and her team of dedicated officers and staff.

I was amazed at the enthusiasm and team work at Tiliar under the dynamic leadership of Kiran Bedi. She accorded a high priority to reform measures such as a sustained literacy drive, vocational training, a de-addiction programme, yoga and all those steps that could lead to the alleviation of suffering. Later when Goenkaji led a Vipassana course in Tihar in April, he publicly mentioned that he would like to call her "Karuna" Bedi, for her deep compassion. Once I mentioned that she has kindled the light "Kiran" in the darkness of jail. She blushed.

So the hour struck for the first *Vipassana* course in Ward I0 of Jail 2. The ward housed convicts of serious crimes and a few high security persons awaiting trials and court hearings. Ninety-six inmates were selected, most of them convicts, and also twenty-three jail officials of different ranks.

When my two colleagues, Professor Dhar and Mr. Chaddha, and I arrived for the course, we found that Kiran Bedi had given a directive that we should have a good room and good food. But she also said that special food would not be given to the course participants because there were about 9,000 prisoners in the jail, and if she gave milk and fruit and such things to only some of them, there would be a big revolt.

Now, what was the prison food? In the morning there was a *parotha* or bread *pakoda;* for lunch, there was *roti* (flat bread) and *dal*, or *roti* and *subji* (vegetables); in the evening there was*khichri* (mixed rice/*dal*), a little milk, and sometimes *kheer* (rice pudding). Evening *khichri* was a real treat, but the food was very tough-chillies, *pakoras* and dark tea.

When I found that we were to live in a good room and take good food while the prisoners were deprived of this, I felt that this could not be. So we decided that we would live as the prisoners live. We would not stay in the special room, and we would eat the same food as the prisoners.

The course started. The first night was a very difficult night for me and for my colleagues. The cell in Tihar Jail is a unique structure with two rooms. The first room, with an outside *verandah,* is open to the sky, with bars across the top and high walls to prevent escape. The inside room has three compartments: space for a bed-a raised platform of stone or concrete about 3 ft by 6 ft, an open water pool for bathing and washing clothes, and a toilet, all close together. It was winter, which in Northern India is very cold. For reasons of hygiene and health, I advised my colleagues to stay in the outside room because the inner room was close to the toilet, and there was a pool of water.

I discovered in the early morning that they had gone to the inner room due to the severe cold. But I remained in the outer room which was open to the sky. The ceiling bars had been covered with blankets, but around eleven o'clock a shrill and icy wind swiftly blew the blankets away. I was shivering, badly shivering, even though the jail authorities had provided sufficient new blankets an

I had my own blanket. It was a very difficult night, and then in the morning came the jail breakfast! I have stomach problems and at my home I am very fussy about food, having boiled vegetables and no chillies, etc. But those ten days I took the prison food, and I can say that nothing happened-no constipation, no burning in the stomach. As the days passed, each one of us felt that we had never eaten such delicious food! In fact, when I returned to my home, I asked my wife to cook the *dal* I ate in jail! The cook who prepared the food was a convicted prisoner but he was very kind and compassionate. We all felt convinced that his good volition added to the taste.

The Jail "lunger" where food is prepared is an institution in itself. It is very neat, clean, efficiently run and managed by the convicts, an ideal community kitchen.

On the second day I discovered to my great distress that out of one hundred and nineteen students, about thirty were smoking, and many were talking. They broke the rules of silence and*sila* [precepts] with impunity. I was alarmed, and called a meeting with them to ask why they were doing this. They said I couldn't stop them from smoking. They also said they would talk, whether there was a course or not.

My colleagues and I discussed what we should do in these circumstances. We called another meeting with the inmates, who argued that they had been told that smoking or talking was not permitted in the "*shivir*" (which they interpreted as the *Dhamma* hall) and was therefore allowed in their rooms, which they called "*chakkies*." [This term refers to the grinding stone used for the arduous work of grinding corn, a reminder of enforced hard labour in prisons.] We were very firm and said we would not compromise on this; if they did not observe this *sila,* they would not be allowed to continue in the course.

As a result of this discussion some agreed to abide by the rules, but still there were others who were very adamant. We decided to separate those who were unwilling to follow the discipline. I told them they would be segregated; they could attend the discourse, but not the rest of the course. The next morning, some of them came and said that we had made them outcasts! They wanted to join those who were meditating and I made them promise not to smoke or talk. I implored them not to betray us. The course proceeded and they kept their promise. Many threw away their *bidis* [cigarettes], and one person who had smack (heroin) also threw that away. Seeing all this was a wonderful experience and made us very happy. Man could fall to any depth but he could rise to any height also.

On the sixth day, another volcano erupted. There was one hardened criminal on the course. Even the jail staff feared him. After the evening discourse, he said to a jail official, "What kind of meditation is this? Observe the breath, observe the breath. This is not meditation." He continued: "In the discourses, the Teacher is critical of our beliefs and tradition. I'll break this TV set, and teach a lesson to these teachers! They will run away from here!" The jail official came running to me and said that the situation was very bad, and asked me what to do. I became a little anxious, but I was confident. I said that nothing would happen and he should not worry.

During the night, something else happened: loud shouting started coming from the cells. Some prisoners were chanting: "Jay sia Ram, Jay sia Ram, Jay sia Rarn." I called the ward-in-charge. He said this was an alarm signal and anything might happen. He said our lives might be in danger, because these fellows could do anything. He advised us to remain in our cells and offered to lock them, then escort us to the Dhamma hall when necessary. I said that he should not worry and that we would face the situation. I told him not to report this matter to the Superintendent or the IG.

At about midnight, after much deliberation, Professor Dhar and I decided that in the morning we would go together to meet the man who was threatening us. But I thought, Professor Dhar is a young man with family responsibilities, and I am an old man-so I should go first.

So while Professor Dhar was taking his bath, I went to the cell of the hostile convict. He stared at me, and I looked at him. He looked down; I also looked down. Again he stared at me, and I looked at him. Then he said, "Why have you come? What do you want?" I said, "I have just come to see you, to see how you live and what you do." Then he said, "Be free of care! I will protect this jail and we will act according to your instructions. We will not smoke. If anybody smokes, I will take care of him. So be assured, nothing will happen. And don't depend on these jail officials. They will not protect you. We will protect you." After hearing these words, I felt deeply relieved. I made a round of the wards, then Professor Dhar came running! After assuring him that everything was fine, we together made two more rounds and talked to the prisoners. Most of them were calm-no anger, hatred or disappointment.

A big change came in the whole environment. I and my two colleagues felt we were working with familiar people. They were good human beings! They worked sincerely and worked hard. Many inmates were suffering acutely and felt full of revenge. Some said they had previously decided to kill those people who were responsible for sending them to jail. But when they finished the course, they said, "Now we have no hatred against those who implicated us. We are so grateful to have had this opportunity. If we had not come to jail, we never would have had this experience. When we are released from this jail, we will be messengers of *Vipassana*." I found that about twenty to twenty five of the inmates reached a very subtle stage of meditation. We could discern a deep calm within them, glow and hope on their faces. Real change took place.

On *metta* day [the tenth day when silence is broken], arrangements were made for some press people and *Doordarshan* [national TV] to come. The IG and some officers from the Home Ministry also came, including Mr. Mehta. Students-both inmates and jail staff-shared their experiences. These were very inspiring expressions from people who had undergone a deep transformation.

On the morning of the eleventh day, Kiran Bedi asked the prisoners if they had any request. They asked her not to let us leave, as they wanted more courses for their colleagues. Many said that they wanted to sit the next course. The IG asked us for a response to their request. I said it was not possible as no assistant teachers were available and so much planning is always needed. She insisted that we give our assurance to the prisoners! So I told the prisoners that we would arrange more courses. They said, "No, we will not let you go!" After much discussion I said that very soon we would have four simultaneous courses. I was confident that Goenkaji would agree and send experienced teachers there, which he did. Our departure from Jail No. 2 and it's grateful inmates was tearful and moving.

The next four courses were from January 1 to 12, 1994, held in Jails No.A, No. 3 and No 4, for a total of about three hundred students. So, we fulfilled our promise to have more courses soon, and the courses went smoothly. Separate arrangements were made for the assistant teachers' stay and the jail menu was greatly improved for all.

However, Kiran Bedi would not rest; with 9,000 people in the jail, she said we had to proceed faster for change to come. She argued that she might be sent to another post! She wanted all in Tihar to learn Vipassana. I said politely that we could not go faster. She asked us to make it possible! She wanted a course for at least 1,000 people. Then I recalled Sayagyi U Ba Khin's prediction that one day Goenkaji would teach Dhamma to 1,000 people. I thought the time had come.

Goenkaji agreed. The historic course for 1,004 male prisoners was held at Tihar Jail No. 4 from April 4 to 15, 1994. Goenkaji and Mataffi conducted the course, assisted by 15 male assistant teachers. Two female assistants conducted a simultaneous separate course for forty-nine women in Jail No. I.

This may well have been the largest *Vipassana* course ever held in the world. The congregation of over one thousand prisoners under a *shamiana* [a large tent] was unique and implied serious security risks as well. The participants came from all the four jails of the prison complex: under-trials and convicts involved in major crimes including terrorist activities. They came from different backgrounds and religious groups, and there were also some foreigners. No coercive vigil was kept in or around the *shamiana.*

The course started smoothly and the group responded well to the training given to the Master Teacher himself. They were, indeed, a privileged group. As the training progressed, they felt deeply relaxed, their tension and anguish greatly mitigated. On the *metta* day we witnessed an overwhelming expression of joy and gratitude by the participants. Most of them felt assured that through the practice of *Vipassana,* they could emerge from the life of crime and lead a happy life. Some said that on release from jail they would dedicate their lives to the propagation of*Vipassana* and the redemption of society from crime and terrorism.

On day eleven, a permanent *Vipassana* centre was inaugurated in Jail No. 4 by Goenkaji, in the presence of the IG, jail officials, the prisoners who took the course, and guests from the international press and the governments of India, Thailand, Sri Lanka and Nepal. Two courses will be held at the new centre every month. A one-day course for old students will be held on the eleventh day of each course. Goenkaji named the new centre "Dhamma Tihar." The historic course was a profoundly rewarding experience.

There are now about thirty jail officials who have learnt Vipassana. They will be a great source of support and assistance. Also, some of the inmates who were students in the first course served as*Dhamma* workers in the next courses. My colleagues' comments were that these prisoners were the best *Dhamma* workers they had ever had. They had done only one course; moreover, they were persons condemned by society who had committed murders and other serious crimes. Through *Vipassana,* they had become gentle, calm, kind and compassionate. They served so well. It was a pleasure to see them working so wholeheartedly and with so much devotion.

This is a brief historical review of how *Vipassana* came to jails. I wish to make one more comment about prisons in the larger context. The system of incarcerating people started in antiquity, long, long back-we can't say when exactly. Very unfortunately, all societies, ancient and modem, have committed human degradation in prisons.

Times are changing. There is a new trend in India and many parts of the world, with the realization that the role of prisons is not to inflict punishment but instead to confine the wrong-doer to prevent further mischief and to reform him. More and more, prisons are being viewed as institutions of reform and rehabilitation rather than places of humiliation and punishment.

Following the success of courses at Tihar in January, the Ministry of Home Affairs, Government of India, called a meeting of the Inspectors General of Prisons from all over India, and a proposal was adopted to introduce *Vipassana* as a reform measure in all the prisons in India.

This is a very significant development. The initiative Mr. M.L. Mehta took in getting *Vipassana*to Tihar Jail and the success of the experiment heralds a new era of reform and rehabilitation for those who fall to crime. *Vipassana* provides an effective way to liberate them, not only from the life of crime but also from all suffering and misery. I am confident that the inmates not only of jails in India, but of all jails in the world, will get the benefit of *Vipassana.*

References

[1]. *Krishnamurti on Education,* Krishnamurti Foundation, 1992.

[2]. *Swami Vivekananda on Education,* compiled by T.S. Avinashilingam, Sri Ramakrishna Mission Vidyalaya, Coimbatore, 1993.

[3]. "A New Education," *All India Magazine,* Sri Aurobindo Society, Oct. 1990; and On Education, All India Magazine, Sri Aurobindo Society, Nov. 1990.

[4]. P.L. Dhar and R.R. Gaur: "Appropriate Engineering Education," paper presented at National Workshop on Technology Assessment, a Futuristic Viewpoint, 1IT, Delhi, 1988.

[5]. *Report of Education Commission* (1964-66): Education and National Development, Ministry of Education, Govt. of India, 1966.

[6]. Venerable Nyanaponika Thera., *The Heart of Buddhist Meditation,* Rider, London 1962.

[7]. Amadeo Sole-Leris., *Tranquillity and Insight,* Shambala, Boston 1986.

[8]. Sayagyi U Ba *Khin Journal,* Vipassana Research Institute, Igatpuri, India, 1991.

[9]. *Mahaavatipa.t.thaana Sutta"m,* Vipassana Research Publications, Igatpuri, India, 1993.

[10]. A. Maslow. *Motivation and Personality,* New York; Harper Press, 1954.

[11]. Pradeep N. Khandwala, "Fourth Eye: Excellence Through Creativity;" A.H. Wheeler an 0.1 Allahabad, 1984.

[12]. P.L. Dhar and R.R. Gaur., *Science and Humanism-Towards a Unified World View,* Common Wealth Publishers, New Delhi, 1992.

4

Vipassana Meditation: A Positive Mental Health Measure

INTRODUCTION

Health, as defined by the World Health Organization, is a state of complete physical, mental and social well-being and not merely an absence of disease or infirmity. This is considered to be an idealistic goal, setting out the standard of positive health, with due emphasis on the promotion and protection of health. "Health for All by 2000 A.D." is the main social target set the by the 30th World Health Assembly [14]. Health, therefore, is a dynamic concept and can be described as a multidimensional process involving the well being of an individual in the context of his or her environment.

This presentation shall deal primarily with the mental dimension of health since it is the "mind" which is the central directing force of one's entire life and activity, and also because every health disorder is affected directly or indirectly by psychological factors. It is truly said that mind matters most.

In Indian parlance, health is a positive concept: "*swasthya*" means being oneself. Indian introspectionists over millennia have produced a rich harvest of profound psychological insights, which needs to be reinterpreted in the contemporary context and the currently familiar idiom; for example, *nibbaana* or "*nirvana*" by Gotama Buddha as the burning out of passions or mental impurities; "*moksha*" by Lord Krishna as freedom from conditioning and constraints of all kinds; "*sahaja*" by Guru Nanak as one's nature: literally born along with oneself [7]. Various austerity and self-control measures and meditative approaches have been detailed in their treatises, to enable one to attain the desired goal of self-realization or self-liberation, called in modern parlance a higher psychic state or transpersonal consciousness.

Abraham Maslow [6], generally regarded as the modern founder of transpersonal psychology, postulated the concept of "self-actualization", which emphasizes the importance of maximal growth and development of human potential. It has also been equated with such terms as self-realization, optimal functioning, psychological health and individual autonomy. All these imply the highest stage of personality development or the optimal personality functioning and positive mental health. Shostrom [8] describes self-actualization as an ongoing process of growth towards experiencing one's potential in terms of creative expression, interpersonal effectiveness and fulfilment in living. Vipassana is a way and means to such self-actualization or self-realization.

Vipassana Meditation [11]

Also known as Insight Awareness or Mindfulness Meditation, Vipassana is a very ancient meditation technique of India, laudatory references to which are found even in the Rigveda. Long lost to humanity, it was rediscovered twenty-five centuries ago by Gotama Buddha. Although Vipassana contains the core of what was later called Buddhism, it is not an organized religion, requires no conversion and is open to students of any faith, nationality, colour or background.

To learn Vipassana, one is required to take a ten-day residential course under a qualified authorized teacher. Meditation teacher Shri S.N. Goenka and about two hundred assistant teachers trained by him ' hailing from various parts of the world and practically all walks of life, are discharging this onerous responsibility voluntarily and selflessly.

There are in all thirty-one permanent Vipassana Centres across the globe in countries like India (14), Nepal (2), Sri Lanka (1), Myanmar (1), Thailand (1), Japan (1), the United States (4),Australia

(4), New Zealand (1), France (1) and the United Kingdom (1). The main Centre is the Vipassana International Academy, located at Dhamma Giri, on the outskirts of the town of lgatpuri in the Nasik district, about 135 kilometres from Bombay.

Vipassana is a Pali term and it means insight, to see things as they really are. It is a scientific technique to explore the laws of nature (called Dhamma), within the framework of one's own mind and body. During the training period of ten days, the participants follow a basic code of morality, which includes celibacy and abstention from all intoxicants. For the first three and a half days, one is trained to focus one's attention on breathing (Anapana) and thereafter, one learns to examine the reality pertaining to oneself, systematically and dispassionately. One realizes, by direct experience, the scientific laws that operate on one's thoughts, feelings, judgements and sensations. One also learns to live in conformity with these laws, a life full of peace and harmony, a really healthy and happy life.

PSYCHIATRY AND MEDITATION

Both the words "psychiatry" and "meditation" carry mystical auras. In fact, psychiatry is a very young science, barely a century old, while many meditation techniques derive from the ancient past. Nevertheless, sometimes the claim is made that meditation is not scientific. Actually, meditation is a science, a methodology practised and perfected centuries ago by the scientists of mind and matter, by the Rishis, Munis, and Buddhas. After all, what is science? Science is objective observation and analysis of data, and their application. Science seeks to know the truth. We will see later in this article how, even by modem criteria, Vipassana meditation is a perfect science.

People think of psychiatry as a science dealing with abnormal minds. But it would be more accurate if the word "behaviour" were substituted for "minds" in this definition, for, indeed, this is what psychiatry is' It is the study of abnormal behaviour. Now, to define normality is a difficult task. Normality generally means "average." Behaviour refers to vocal or physical actions, i.e., vocal or physical behaviour. In psychiatry and psychology, mental behaviour is studied only by inference after it manifests in vocal and physical actions. The aim of these sciences is to bring the behaviour of an individual closer to normal (which most of the time means average).

We might use a more modern definition of psychiatry: an application of neuroscience to the problems of particular groups of patients. Initially the scope of psychiatry was not well defined. As a result, psychiatrists were dealing mostly with minor illnesses. During the 1960s and 1970s, many psychiatrists in the West were practising psychoanalysis. Their subjects were often people with minor psychiatric problems; very rarely were they psychotic. During this period an impression was created in some quarters that psychiatry can deal with all the problems of humanity. But the reality was that psychiatry was not contributing to peace in the general society in any significant way, except for helping a small number of patients.

Reasonable psychiatrists gradually realized that the boundaries of psychiatry are not coextensive with those of all human mental activity. This realization is of immense significance, since it helps both the psychiatrist and the common man to define the scope of psychiatry. Failure on the part of the ordinary person to understand the scope of psychiatry has led to various problems. For example, at times a psychiatrist is called upon to help when the problem is not actually psychiatric, stemming from the unreasonable faith and expectation that the psychiatrist knows everything about the mind. In contrast to this LWeption of the psychiatrist's omniscience, there is the other side of the coin: a lack of M. in the whole specialty, even on the part of some health professionals, with the result that psychiatric help is not sought even when it is appropriate and beneficial.

In recent times psychiatry has emerged as a branch of medicine with more focus on major psychiatric illnesses. This has redefined the role of psychiatry as a biological science, and pychiatrists are now playing the more appropriate role of specialists treating biological disorders which are accompanied by behavioural disturbances. This certainly does not mean that the psychiatrist's role is limited to prescribing medicine; he or she uses various other modalities of therapy as well. But more and more, psychiatrists have started restricting themselves to their proper domain: the treatment of major psychiatric disorders. These conditions are ones which psychiatrists

are better equipped and better qualified to treat. Psychiatrists are trained to deal with "abnormal" behaviour. In cases which are closer to normal (or average) behaviour, the difference in effectiveness between psychiatric treatment and other treatment modalities rapidly decreases.

The World Health Organization is constantly trying to improve its diagnostic criteria for psychiatric disorders. The new International Classification of Diseases (ICD-10) is an Important step in that direction. Many efforts are currently being taken to systematically demarcate the field of psychiatry. This is to help psychiatrists concentrate on a specific sub-population, to assist researchers in seeking to find remedies for various disorders, and to protect people from improperly being labelled as psychiatric patients. However, the boundaries remain fuzzy. Even a competent psychiatrist at times finds it difficult to decide whether to try treat a particular individual, or to conclude that the person is not in need of psychiatric treatment.

Everyone suffers from various kinds of misery. When confronted with problems in business, one person might become angry very easily, while another person is inclined to sadness. In such instances, the individual may well not have a psychiatric disorder. He or she might benefit as much from the advice and support of a friend or relative as from psychiatric intervention. Even so, everyone's life is bound to have challenges, and suffering occurs again and again.

What does any person do when faced with life's problems? Every individual encounters the suffering that results when unwanted things happen, when wanted things do not happen; when one gets what one does not like, or loses what he likes. Where should one look for the solution?

Mind is the principal factor. We have to study it-probe it to its depths in order to master it-in order to solve our problems. This is precisely what the science of meditation is all about. Meditation is the science of exploring the entire phenomenon of mind and matter. Psychiatry studies mind only indirectly and only to the extent that it renders itself observable by its manifestation in vocal and physical actions. In the science of meditation, the mind is studied directly. This science has been extensively practised in India since ancient times.

It is true that all actions have their origin in the mind. But not everything that arises in the mind manifests as a vocal or physical action. Physical actions which appear to be similar might originate from quite different mental volitions. For example, a person who freezes when he sees a snake might have two entirely different reasons for this action. He may be extremely frightened; or he may be very calm and is staying immobile so as not to frighten the snake, or so as to observe the snake. Similarly, a person who gives a coin to a beggar may be giving it out of compassion; just to get rid of a nuisance; or because others are watching him and he does not want to appear to be a stingy person.

So the first problem with the psychiatric approach is that it is very difficult to derive conclusions about the mind from vocal and physical behaviour. The mind must be studied directly. Another problem results from what is known as "Cartesian dualism," the arbitrary separation of mind and matter. For a long time the specialized medical profession studied the body but excluded study of the mind. And when psychiatrists started studying the mind, in whatever manner, they ignored the body. Today the importance of a holistic approach is widely accepted. But there is neither a satisfactory method of enquiry, nor proper understanding of the interaction of mind and matter, with the result that there are many theories, but few facts. The mind-matter phenomenon is not being properly studied.

These problems are solved through the proper understanding of meditation. The term "meditation" has a variety of meanings. In English, the term is loosely used to refer to thinking about something. Dictionaries define it as "contemplation": to exercise the mind in contemplation, to focus on a subject of contemplation; to ponder, muse, or ruminate. When we refer to meditation here, we are not using the term in this pedestrian sense.

The Enlightened One, Gotama Buddha, used the word *bhavana* to describe practices of mental development. This word can be translated roughly as meditation. It refers to specific mental exercises, precise techniques for focusing and purifying the mind. When we use the word "meditation" here, we use it in this technical sense. Almost all Indian languages have specific words for different meditation practices because India has a rich tradition of these disciplines. Such words as *dhyana, japa, traa.taka, saadhandaa, vipassanaa, (vidarshanaa), bhaavanaa,* etc., refer to different kinds of mental practices. Broadly speaking, meditation is an exercise in the concentration

of mind on various objects. Since concentration of mind is the prerequisite for any task, it is a very important factor in the exploration of the mind-matter phenomenon. There are many possible objects of concentration: visual, auditory, imaginations, verbalizations, etc.

The Enlightened One gave us a wonderful object of concentration, our own natural respiration. Unlike other objects which are either external or do not have any direct relation to our mind and body, this is an object which has many advantages. It is internal, and constantly present from birth to death. It is a tangible reality, even if a gross one. It is both conscious and unconscious, intentional and unintentional. Its rhythm is so intimately connected with the mental state that any defilement arising in mind, even the slightest agitation, disturbs the rhythm of the respiration. We cannot find any other object of concentration which is so intimately connected with the mind-matter phenomenon and yet renders itself so easily to observation.

But concentration is not the goal of meditation; it is only a tool. A tool for what?

Here we encounter the third problem of the modern scientific approach, that of defining the problem itself. The four Noble Truths of suffering are very simple, logical and universal: suffering exists; it has a cause; this cause can be eradicated; there is a Path to its eradication. Yet these universal truths are not appreciated by many modern psychiatrists because psychiatry focuses more on the "why" than on the "how." This attitude of searching for meaning while ignoring fundamental mechanisms of reality serves to obscure, rather than enhance, the study of the problems of the human mind.

The Enlightened One was a true scientist, the greatest scientist of mind and matter. He not only explored the mind and matter phenomenon himself in its entirety, but he showed the way to do it so that other people could come out of their misery. He taught a method to observe how the mind works, how mind and matter interact. He taught Vipassana.

Vipassana means to see, to see in a special way, to observe inside. It is objective observation of the internal reality. It is development of insight into one's own nature. It involves no assumptions; rather, mere observation. It is a practical way of understanding our problem of suffering and solving it. In the same way as the problem is universal, the remedy also is universal. In Vipassana we learn to observe our sensations objectively. Sensations are the meeting point of the intimate mind-matter interaction. Though sensations arise in the body, they are felt by the mind. While observing the sensations, we start understanding how the mind works. Each of us becomes a scientist of mind and matter. We get direct knowledge. The Enlightened One described four fundamental processes of mind: consciousness, perception, sensations, and conditionings. No one need accept these processes intellectually; they become clear once we start experiencing the truth within.

As we learn to observe the sensations inside, it becomes experientially clear that it is towards these very sensations that we keep continuously reacting. The sensations are the basis on which the old conditionings, the patterns of reaction-craving and aversion-develop. This profound discovery was the kingpin upon which the liberation of the Enlightened One rested. It is our conditioning which makes us suffer again and again, and this conditioning can be eradicated by the practice of objective observation of the sensations. By practising Vipassana we learn not to develop new conditionings of craving and aversion towards the sensations; and as a consequence, we start to eradicate the old conditionings. The practice is a process of gradual eradication of mental defilements. Hence, it is a process of eradication of misery.

This non-sectarian scientific technique is useful in enabling one and all to live better lives, happy lives, peaceful lives. For many who undergo a ten-day Vipassana course under the supervision of a competent instructor, the course is a life-transforming experience. The practice of exploring mind and matter at the deepest level is not easy. It requires a certain mental and physical stability. A sincere seeker who wishes to undergo the training in Vipassana meditation needs to have a minimum mental and physical health. Generally all but those with severe psychiatric problems are fit to undertake a course. (It is advisable to contact the management of the Vipassana course in advance if an applicant's mental suitability is in question.)

Vipassana is the universal remedy to the universal malady of misery. But this does not mean that psychiatry has no role to play in helping the suffering humanity. For those who are so deranged as to be incapable of taking up the delicate task of Vipassana meditation, psychiatrists have an important role to play. Psychiatrists can help in alleviating suffering of people with mental illness. Except from the small section of the population with severe psychiatric disorders, Vipassana is useful to one and all.

The scope of psychiatry is limited to a small population. Vipassana meditation is universal in scope because it encompasses all aspects of human mental activity. Psychology purports to study the entirety of human mental activity, but as we have already discussed, it is the "science of behaviour," and therefore, limited. Behaviour in this context is defined as anything a person does that can be observed in some way. The contention is that behaviour, unlike mind, thoughts or feelings, can be observed and studied. The catch here is that the observer is always an outsider, another person. Modem psychologists believe that behaviour is the only avenue through which internal mental events can be studied.

Any person who takes a ten-day course in Vipassana can easily see the fallacy in this approach of modem psychology. He knows from his own experience that internal mental events can be observed directly. Every Vipassana meditator becomes a true psychologist unto himself. And through this pure science of self-observation, he starts coming out of misery. May more and more people walk on the Path shown by the Enlightened One. May more and more people learn to observe the reality within. May all beings be happy, may all beings be peaceful.

MECHANISM AND PSYCHOLOGICAL EFFECTS

The teachings of the Buddha embody "Abhidhamma", a very systematic and intricately laid out psychology, which presents a set of concepts for understanding mental activity and methods for healing mental disorder. It differs markedly from the contemporary psychotherapeutic outlook. In this model of mental activity, every mental state is composed of a set of properties of mental factors, which gives it its distinctive characteristics. There are 52 basic perceptual, cognitive and affective categories of these properties. The basic dichotomy in this analysis of mental factors is between pure, wholesome or healthy and impure, unwholesome or unhealthy mental properties; healthy mental states are antagonistic to unhealthy ones, inhibiting them. Vipassana meditation aims to eradicate these unhealthy properties from the mind; the operational definition of mental health is their complete absence, as in the case of an *arahanta* (saint) [4].

"Everything that arises in the mind is accompanied by a concomitant physical sensation", said the Buddha. This interrelationship is the key to the practice of Vipassana meditation. Vipassana trains the concentrated attention to follow the mechanics of mental processing with the base of physical sensations, in a detached fashion. This perspective of an observer allows the controlled release of mental contents such as craving and aversion, past and future, in a seemingly endless stream of memories, wishes, thoughts, conversations, scenes, desires, dreads and lusts. Thousands and thousands of emotionally-driven pictures of every kind rise to the surface of the mind and pass away without provoking a reaction, while simultaneously anchoring one in concrete, contemporary reality.[1]

The mind is deconditioned with meditation altering the process of conditioning per se, so that it is no longer a prime determinant of future acts [4]. A refinement of awareness occurs and one responds consciously to life situations thereby becoming free from limitations, which were forged by mere reactions to them. One's life becomes characterized by increased awareness, reality-orientation, nondelusion; self-control and peace.[1] Such a person is able to make quick decisions, correct and sound judgement and concerted effort-mental capabilities which definitely contribute to success in contemporary life.[10]

Vipassana is not merely an exercise to be performed in the special environment of a meditation retreat. When a ten-day course is over, meditators take the tool home with them. The path of Vipassana is a continuous, disciplined pursuit of this experiential gnosis throughout life; it is a human capacity and a personal choice. Through Vipassana, one can transcend body-mind or even East-West dualism and shake hands with ethical rootedness, cultivated mindfulness and wisdom in all its enduring forms.[2]

VIPASSANA, HEALTH AND HEALERS: A REVIEW

Considerable data is available, documenting the various biopsychosocial benefits that accrue from the practice of Vipassana meditation. It indicates the vast th rapeutic potential that Vipassana has. For instance, many case report studies have been recorded on the positive effects of Vipassana in different psychosomatic disorders such as chronic pain, headaches, bronchial asthma, hypertension, peptic ulcer, psoriasis, etc., and so also in different disorders including alcoholism and drug addiction. Beneficial aspects of Vipassana have also been studied in special population groups such as students, prisoners and police personnel, besides individuals suffering from chronic pain and various mental disorders.[11,12,13].

However healing-not disease cure, but the essential healing of human suffering-is the purpose of Vipassana. Suffering springs from ignorance of one's true nature. Insight, truth experiential truth-alone frees one.[2] "Know thyself" all wise persons have advised. Vipassana is a practical way to examine the reality of one's own mind and body to uncover and solve whatever problems lie hidden there, to develop unused potential and to channel it for one's own good and the good of others.[5]

All people need healing, most particularly healers. "Physician heal thyself" is a well-known phrase. Freud and Jung insisted that analysts be analysed. The very vulnerability and compassion that sets the healer on a lifelong journey to heal, coupled to the constant exposure to human suffering, requires a treatment of its own. Vipassana is acceptable and relevant to healers of diverse disciplines because it is free of dogma, experientially based and focussed on human suffering and relief. With its practice, healers are able to deepen their autonomy and self-knowledge, at the same time augmenting their ability to be a professional anchor to others in the tumult of their lives. Vipassana is verily the path of all-healing, including self-healing and other-healing.[2]

A Model for Clinical Application

The clinical utility of Vipassana is more likely to be in terms of providing a general psychological pattern of positive mental states rather than a response to any particular problem. Generally, the conventional psychotherapies are generated as treatments for the latter. Many therapists [11,12,13], who are themselves meditators, teach "Anapana"-a preparatory step in the training of Vipassana, to their clients. The clients may be suffering from various neurotic, psychosomatic and personality disorders including addictions, and Anapana is taught as a supplementary form of treatment, with a good clinical response.

Before commencing the formal training in Anapana, the therapist explains to the patient its potential benefits, particularly relaxation. This helps reduce the patient's apprehension and enables him or her to cooperate and participate actively in the treatment. In addition, it is necessary to ensure that the physical environment is one that will facilitate relaxation; the room should be quiet and free from interruptions and the patient's couch should be reasonably comfortable.

The patient is asked to lie comfortably on the couch, close his eyes and observe, that is, cultivate awareness, of his respiration at the entrance of his nostrils-whether in-breath or out-breath, deep or shallow, fast or slow; natural breath, bare breath and only breath. When his mind wanders, the patient is asked to passively disregard the intrusion and repeatedly focus his attention on his breath, without getting upset or disturbed about the drift of his mind.

Two things happen. One-his mind gets concentrated on the flow of respiration. Two-he becomes aware of the relationship between his mental states and the flow of the respiration; that whenever there is agitation in the mind-anger, hatred, fear, passion, etc.-the natural flow of respiration gets affected and disturbed. He thus learns to simply observe and remain alert, vigilant and equanimous.

The patient is advised to continue practising the technique on his own, twice daily-in the morning and in the evening, each session lasting f6r about thirty minutes. The therapist reviews the progress of his patient from time to time, simultaneously counselling and motivating him to undertake a regular ten-day Vipassana meditation course. The patient is thus encouraged to continue to strive for his personal autonomy9, that is, to take personal responsibility of his own health and well-being.

Conclusion

Vipassana's ability to tranquillize the human mind, changing its turbulence to calmness with increased vitality, makes it a positive mental health measure and an excellent human potential development method. The meditator becomes free to live for higher values, richer goals: loving-kindness, compassion, sympathetic joy and peacefulness. Vipassana thus leads people from narcissism to mature, social love, to a life of altruiSM3 and this personal transformation becomes the catalyst for social change and development.

More scientific research needs to be pursued on the role of Vipassana, both as a self-regulation strategy for specific psychotherapeutic and psycho-physiological aims and as a discipline and way of life for deep self-exploration and transformation. The various psycho-physiological changes with Vipassana ought to be studied with the aid of modern sophisticated instruments. Also, long term prospective studies on meditators, besides multicentred controlled clinical trials of this technique, need to be conducted to clarify which individual types and health disorders respond to and benefit from the practice of Vipassana. Such endeavours will make "Health for AW' a more realistic proposition.

References

[1]. Fleischman P.R., "The Therapeutic Action of Vipassand' and "Why I Sit," Buddhist Publication Society, Kandy, Sri Lanka, 1986.

[2]. Fleischman P.R., "Vipassana Meditation: Healing the Healee' and "The Experience of Impermanence," Vipassana Research Institute, lgatpuri, India, 1991, 3-15.

[3]. Goenka, S.N., "Altruism: Quintessence of Religion," in *Issues of Biomedical Ethics - Proceedings of the Festival of Life International Congress,* December 1988, Bombay; Editors: Vas C1 & de Souza E1, McMillan India Ltd., Delhi, 1990, 95-102.

[4]. Goleman D., "Meditation and Consciousness: An Asian Approach to Mental Health,"*American Journal of Psychotherapy,* 1977, 30: 41-54.

[5]. Hart W., "The Art of Living"in *Vipassana Meditation as taught by S.N. Goenka,* Harper and Row, New York, 1987.

[6]. Maslow A.H., *Motivation and Personality,* Harper and Row, New York, 1954

[7]. Neki J.S., "Psychotherapy in India," *Indian Journal Psychiatry,* 1977, 19(2): 1-10.

[8]. Shostrom E.L., "Comments on Test Review: The Personal Orientation Inventory," *Journal of Counselling Psychology,* 1973, 20: 479-491

[9]. Surya N.C., "Personal Autonomy and Instrumental Accuracy," in: *Psychotherapeutic Processes,* Editors: Kapur M., Murthy VX, Sathyavathi K., & Kapur R.L., N.I.M.H.A.N.S., Bangalore, India, 1979, 1-19.

[10]. Thray Sithu Sayagyi U Ba Khin, *The Real Values of True Buddhist Meditation,* Buddha Sasana Council Press, Yegu, Rangoon, Bunna, 1962.

[11]. "Vipassana Research Institute: A Reader International Seminar on Vipassana Meditation,"*December 1986,* Igatpuri, India, 1986.

[12]. "Vipassana Research Institute: A Reader: Seminar on Vipassana Meditation, Relief from Addictions, Better Health," *November 1989,* Igatpuri, India, 1990.

[13]. "Vipassana Research Institute: A Reader: International Seminar on Vipassana Meditation and Health," *November 1990,* Igatpuri, India, 1990.

[14]. World Health Organization, *"Health for All,"* Sr. No. 1, Geneva, 1978.

5

Practical Advice for Meditators

TWO STREAMS IN MEDITATION

Two apparently distinct streams of Buddhist meditation may be discerned, though when meditation is established, these are seen to be complementary.It may be profitable for some people whose minds are very active and who suffer from distraction, to follow with mindfulness the mad monkey-mind's acrobatics. As the mind is really a series of mental events which arise and pass away with incredible rapidity, each of which is a mind complete with supporting mental factors, so at the beginning this kind of mindfulness is really one "mindful" mind watching other "minds" (which are all within one's own mental continuity of course).

One thereby develops the ability to look into the mind and to see where it has gone to. Has it gone to the past, present or future? Has it gone to materiality, or to feelings, or perhaps to cognitions, to volitional activities, or has it gone to consciousness? By this method of "Where has it gone?", the distracted mind slowly comes under the surveillance of the mindful mind, until mindfulness forms a strong foundation for further development. Considerable, though mundane, brilliance of mind is both needed and developed by this practice, which however should be balanced by the tranquility of the absorptions. When the mind has become calm, one should start to practice for the absorptions *(jhana)*, which will in their turn be the basis for the arising of real insight. This method is called "wisdom leading to calm." Other methods suited to those whose minds are less disturbed initially, include the classic forty subjects of meditation (see Appendix); and these, together with more developed types of meditation practice, involve the use of a definite object for concentration. This may be one's own body or a part of it, a colour or a picture, a word or a phrase, or abstract contemplation and so forth. All these methods involve some firm but gentle discipline of the mind, in that each time it strays away, it must be gently brought back again (by mindfulness, of course) to concentrate again on the chosen subject.

Some people have the quite mistaken idea that practice of this sort must necessarily lead to tranquility almost at once. They may be surprised when beginning to practice themselves, since they actually experience more troubles than they had previously. This is firstly, because they never before really looked into their mind to know the state it has always been in; and secondly, because having taken up a discipline of the mind, it is as though one stirs up with a stick a stagnant pond, or pokes with a stick a fire smoldering under ashes. The wild elephant of the mind, long accustomed to roam in the jungle of desires, does not take readily to taming, or to being tied to the post of practice with the thongs of mindfulness. However, diligence and heedfulness will eventually win for one the fruits of tranquility.

All these forty subjects are of this second type in which the calm gained from practice is then used for the arousing of wisdom. They are for this reason called "calm-leading-to-wisdom" methods, and are very important in the present distracted age. For their full explanation one should consult the *Path of Purification (Visuddhi-magga,* translation), although even the great learning in that book cannot replace the personal contact with a teacher.

Practical Advice for Meditators

Turning from the psychological to the practical aspect, meditation for laypeople may be divided into two categories: that which is done intensively, and that which one practices while going about one's daily life. The meditation practiced intensively is also of two sorts: regular daily sitting, and occasional retreat practice.

Regular Daily Sitting

We shall first discuss the regular daily period of intensive sitting which should, where possible, be made every day at the same time. One should guard against its becoming a ritual by earnestness and by being intensely aware of why one had undertaken it. The following suggestions may be found helpful as well.

As to material considerations, the place for meditation should be fairly quiet. If one has a small room which can be used for this purpose, so much the better, and in any case, it is better to meditate alone, unless other members of the household also practice. Where this latter is the case one should make sure that one's mind is pure also in relation to others, for otherwise greed, hatred, and the rest of the robber gang are sure to steal away the fruits of meditation.

Quietness is best obtained by getting up early before others rise; and this is also the time when the mind is clear and the body untired. The sincere meditator therefore keeps regular hours, for he knows how much depends on having just enough sleep to feel refreshed.

After rising and washing one should sit down in clean loose clothing in the meditation place. One may have a small shrine with Buddhist symbols, but this is not essential. Some people find it useful to begin by making the offerings of flowers, incense, and light, carefully reflecting while doing so. It is very common in Buddhist countries to preface one's silent meditation by chanting softly to oneself, "Namo tassa bhagavato arahato samma-sambuddhassa," with the Refuges and Precepts. If one knows the Pali passages in praise of the Buddha, Dhamma and Sangha, these may also be used at this time.[1]

Another useful preliminary is a reflection, a discursive recitation, of some truths of the Dhamma, such as the passage suggested below:

"Having this precious opportunity of human birth, I have two responsibilities in the Dhamma: the benefit of myself and the benefit of others. All other beings, whether they be human or non-human, visible or invisible, great or small, far or near, all these beings I shall treat with gentleness and wish that they may dwell in peace. May they be happy . . . May they be happy . . . May they be happy . . . ! I shall help them when they experience suffering, and be glad with them when they are happy. May I develop as well the incomparable equanimity, the mind in perfect balance that can never be upset!

"In looking to the welfare of others, I shall not forget my own progress on the path of Dhamma. May I indeed come to know how, driven here and there by the winds of kamma, I have suffered an infinity of lives in all the realms of existence! I must also turn my mind to consider how short and fleeting is this life. How mind and body are ever changing, arising and declining from moment to moment. How neither mind nor body belongs to me, neither of them is mine. I must also turn this mind to consider how beset by troubles is this brief life. Having been sired by craving and born out of ignorance, I must realize that death is inescapable, that old age and disease are natural to my condition. I must make efforts to realize for my own good and the good of others that this person called 'myself' is a complex of mentality and materiality wherein no abiding entity such as a soul or self is found.

"May I through this practice experience insight into impermanence, ill and no-self! May I be one who dwells in the Void! And having realized this sublime truth may I show the way to others!"

When sitting, care should be taken that the body is kept erect, yet relaxed. There should be no strain, but neither should the head droop, nor the lumbar region sag. The body should feel poised and balanced upright. Although the cross-legged positions (such as the lotus posture) are best when the meditator is seated on a fairly soft mat, a chair may be used by those unaccustomed to the lotus posture or else unable to train themselves to sit in that way. Sitting in lotus posture or half-lotus posture will be found much easier if a rather hard cushion is placed so as to raise the buttocks. The knees will then tend to touch the ground and a firm three pointed sitting (two knees and buttocks) is then attained.

One should sit for the same length of time every day until, as one becomes more proficient in collecting the mind, automatically one will feel like extending the practice. One widely used method for measuring the meditation period is sitting for the length of time taken for a stick of incense to burn down. Having placed the hands in meditation posture relaxed in the lap, the eyes may be closed or left slightly open according to which is found most comfortable.

Methods used for helping to concentrate the mind are many, and the two main streams in classical meditation have been briefly reviewed in the section above. Other helpful methods include the repetition of a word or phrase and perhaps with it the use of a rosary. If one practices mindfulness of breathing, one may find the use of a word such as "Buddho," or "Araham" good for quietening the mind. The first syllable is silently repeated when breathing in, and one concentrates on the second during the out-breathing. Also the counting of breath (up to ten, but generally not over this number to prevent the mind wandering) is used as an aid for concentration. But any such aids should be dropped when concentration improves. When the meditation is on a phrase only, a rosary may be used in conjunction, each repetition being marked by one bead.

One's meditation goes well if one finds the mind increasingly absorbed on the chosen meditation subject, but one should not assume that meditation is useless just because for a period, longer or shorter, not much more than sleepiness or distraction is experienced. These hindrances have to be faced; and if they are met, not by irritation or despair, but by quietly observant mindfulness, they can and will be overcome. For success, great persistence and evenness of effort are necessary.

The meditation period may close with some chanting, the usual subject being the well being of others and the distribution of merits to them. A translation, or the original Pali, of the Metta Sutta*(Discourse on Lovingkindness)*[2] may be chanted at this time and, as it is not long, can be easily memorized. As methods of chanting vary, it is very helpful if one can obtain recordings, perhaps on tape, of the passages one wishes to learn, recorded by bhikkhus.

While on the subject of chanting, it is very useful to know a few discourses of Lord Buddha in one of the Buddhist classical languages, and to use these for collecting the mind if there should be an occasion when no concentration at all can be obtained. At such a time a meditator should not feel depressed but should continue sitting and chant softly to himself. This is what Buddhist monks do twice a day as part of their mental development, and it is useful as well for fostering a more devotional approach necessary as balance with intellectual characters. Another useful method for the overcoming of distraction is walking-practice, which may be done in any passage of the house or in a secluded walk in the garden. A length of twenty or thirty paces will be sufficient, for if longer the mind tends to wander, and if shorter, distraction may be increased. One should walk at the speed one feels to be natural, with the hands clasped the left in the right, and arms relaxed in front of the body. At the ends of the walk one should turn in a clockwise direction.[3]

Perhaps a few words on devotion would not be out of place here, for this is very important in meditation practice. No one who is not a devoted Buddhist takes up *Buddhist* meditation, for the simple reason that he does not have the Buddhist ideals in his heart. The taking to heart of the Triple Refuge and the understanding of the Triple Gem are closely linked with Buddhist meditation. A really devoted Buddhist, who puts his whole life into the Dhamma, will have no insurmountable difficulties in meditation practice. Whatever obstacles he comes to, those he leaps over, sustained by devotion. He is prepared for the way to be long and hard because he realizes that he has made it like that. If he finds his way blocked, his meditation failing to progress and he himself without a teacher, he does not waver or falter on the way. He thinks, "I am now experiencing the results of intentional actions (kamma) made by me in the past." And he remembers Lord Buddha's last words: "Subject to breaking-up are all compounded things. With mindfulness strive on." All difficulties are compounded things and will eventually change; meanwhile much may be done with mindfulness, vigor and devotion.

If one is not too tired after work and if there is opportunity in the evening, another period of sitting can be undertaken then. In any case, before sleep, it is a wise practice to sit, if only for a few minutes, so as to purify the mind before lying down. One may consider thus: "When I lie down there is no certainty that I shall awake." One may, therefore, be lying down to die, and this is a good reflection to rouse skillful states of mind and banish sensual unskillful ones. If one practices this, "the lying-down to die," it will be a very good preparation for the real event, which is bound to take place at some time in the unknown future. It may even generate the right conditions for the arising of insight allowing one "to die," giving up the grasping at what does not belong to one, that is, the mind and body. At this time also, a Dhamma phrase or word may be used, repeating which one eventually falls to sleep. In this way one ends and begins the day with practice of Buddhist teachings. And apart from devotion of one's whole day to them, what could be better?

Retreats

Regarding the second division of intensive practice, that is, when undertaken in retreat, much will depend upon what facilities are available to the earnest student. There are now a few places in the West where meditation instruction can be sought. The most important thing is to have direct contact with an able meditation master (books serve at the beginning, while even a teacher is later found deficient in some way). After satisfying this one condition, only one other is necessary: one must strive with diligence to practice and realize his teachings. If these two conditions are fulfilled, then one is the most fortunate among human beings.

Many will be without access to a teacher and some may like to try a period of solitary meditation in some quiet part of the country. This should only be attempted if one has already developed a good power of mindfulness. Otherwise what was meant to foster meditation may become a very unprofitable time, perhaps accompanied by the seeming intensification of the mental defilements.

Daily Life

As to the other sort of meditation practice, which is performed in daily life, though much may be written, the following few words may serve as a guide. First, one should not deceive oneself regarding concentration of the mind. It is of no use pretending to oneself or to others that one's daily life *is* meditation — unless of course one has already great powers of concentration. Only the real adept, often one who has sat for many years keeping the monastic discipline, can really perceive ordinary life as meditation; and such a one would be most unlikely to tell others of this fact. Refusing to allow pride an opportunity to distort the real state of mental affairs, one should take stock with fairness and admit one's limitations. This is already a great step forward. The layman who thinks of himself as an Arahat already, has blocked off very effectively all real progress; while the honest man has at least the wisdom to be humble.

Much may be accomplished with mindfulness, while without it there is no hope for meditation in daily life. How are quite ordinary events capable of being made into meditation? By mindfulness, which to begin with, may be defined as, *awareness of the present work in hand.* At first great effort has to be made in order to remain mindful of what one is supposed to be doing, nor can one pretend that such mindfulness is pleasant always. To escape from dull and unliked work and situations, we tend to turn either to fantasy worlds, hopes, or else to memories, which are respectively the delusive escapes into the present, future or past. But for one really interested in understanding himself, none of these courses is very rewarding, since they are compounded of delusion with various ingredients, such as fear, craving or ignorance. While in the practice of strict meditation, mindfulness may follow all the wanderings of the mind; in daily life it is better that the mind should be constantly returned to the job in hand. One should not "send" one's mind anywhere, neither to a dream-world nor to the past, nor to the future. Lord Buddha compared these periods of time thus:

"The past is like a dream,
The future as a mirage,
While the present is like clouds."

Such a simile may be useful as the mind darts about between dreams, mirages and clouds, all insubstantial, though the ever-changing present, so like the clouds in the sky, is the only aspect of time compared to things of greater reality. One may also consider meditation as the exercise of mindfulness which keeps the mind "inside" this body, that is, always focused upon some aspect of it. Of course only the most sincere meditator, who sees the advantage in this to be greater than any pleasure offered by the world, is likely to practice in this way, since this cuts off not only interest in outer objects but also the toying with pleasant or intriguing ideas.

Indeed, with work that is really interesting, the way of mindfulness is the only way to convert one's day into something worthwhile. Days pass and bring us nearer to death and an unknown rebirth, while it is *now* that one has the chance to practice Dhamma. Instead of reacting with aversion or deluded fantasies towards what one does not like (or in other situations indulging one's greed), the Way of Mindfulness constitutes the Middle Practice-Path transcending these ancient patterns of reaction. There is no need to be ruled either by greed or by hatred, nor to be dominated by delusion; but only mindfulness shows the way beyond these.

Constantly bringing the mind back and disengaging it from tangles is the basic practice in everyday life. It is also wise to take advantage of those odd times during work when one waits for something to do, to meet someone, for a bus or train, or any time when one is alone for a few minutes. Instead of turning to a newspaper for distraction, to the wireless, or to another person for gossip, it is more profitable to "retire inside" oneself. Disengaging attention from exterior objects, take up mindfulness of breathing, or the repetition of some phrase of Dhamma, or significant word such as "Buddho" or "Arahant," doing this until one has again to attend to work. Going inwards as often as possible will be found very useful, strengthening one's sitting practice just as the latter in turn strengthens the ability to turn within.

Mindfulness of breathing is especially good as a concentration method for use during travel and during the times when one is restlessly expecting a bus or a train. Why be agitated or impatient? A little mindful breathing is just the practice for these moments, since it calms the feverish workings of the mind and the restless movements of the body. One does not have to aimlessly stare out of windows while traveling! Why be a slave of the "eye-dominant" when a little useful practice could take its place? One does not have to listen to the idle chatter of others, so why be a slave to the "ear-dominant"? One cannot shut one's ears, but everyone can withdraw attention to some extent while practicing mindfulness.

It is mindfulness also which helps to bring into focus counteractive contemplations. Lust, for instance, is soon dissipated by thoughts of a decaying corpse. The looks which are bestowed on pretty girls (or handsome man) seem ridiculous when it is thought that old ladies and equally ancient men never attract such desire-filled attention. Only when one sees how lust burns up the one who indulges in it, only then does it seem worth relinquishing.

Similarly gluttony, even in a mild form, can be demolished by contemplating the bodily processes connected with food. Chewed food looks a good deal less palatable then when the same stuff before mixing with spittle was nicely laid out on plates. Vomit is just the same substances in the process of change but does not readily arouse greed. Excrement even if placed on the finest gold plate fails to become attractive — yet this is the remnants of the food so eagerly gorged! By the time that one has contemplated food in these three stages, greed has quite disappeared, and one may take food just as a medicine to preserve the body.

Mindfulness is also responsible for becoming sufficiently aware in a moment of anger to turn the mind to other subjects or persons. It is mindfulness that warns one of an approaching situation where anger may arise, and makes it possible to turn aside and dwell in equanimity, or where the Divine Abidings are well developed, in friendliness.

When envy rears its ugly head, mindfulness gives one presence of mind to know "envy has arisen," and if efforts to arouse gladness with others' joy fail, it is mindfulness that helps one dwell in equanimity, or if all else fails, helps turn attention to other objects.

Lord Buddha has truly said, "Mindfulness, I declare, is helpful everywhere."

The social implications of meditation should be obvious from the above. Those who have the strange delusion that Buddhism is a religion of meditative isolation, offering society no social benefits, should understand that a Buddhist believes society can only be changed for the better, and with some degree of permanence, by starting work on himself. Buddhist ideals of society are expressed in a number of important discourses addressed by Lord Buddha to lay people, and in them the developments of the individual is always stressed as a very necessary factor. The advantages of a society in which there are a large number of those dwelling at peace with themselves need hardly be stressed. The development of wisdom and compassion by one man has its effect in leavening the materialistic dough around him. The Buddhist call is therefore *first*to gain peace in one's own heart, when will *follow,* quite naturally, peace in the world. Trying to obtain peace the other way round will never be practical nor produce a lasting peace, for the roots of greed, hatred, and delusion have still a firm grip on the hearts of people. Impractical? Only for those who do not practice. Those who take up the cultivation of mindfulness find out for themselves how it helps to solve life's problems.

Although many journeys to remote and attractive places are now performed with ease, the way leading to Nibbana still needs effort. But if the way is sometimes drear, with mindfulness the only guiding light, at least from reflection one knows that the goal is glorious and of great worth, not only for oneself but for others as well.

Divine Abidings and their Perfection *(Brahma-vihara)*

The way to that goal leads through what are called the Divine Abidings,[4] which train the deep-rooted emotions from being unskillful into the skillful way of the Dhamma. As had already been emphasized above, the aim of oneself as of all beings, is to gain happiness-producing conditions. Therefore one must act in such a way that happiness will result from one's actions. One should, in this case, treat others as they would wish to be treated, for every living being is dear to itself, and wishes its own welfare and happiness. One cannot expect to have an isolated happiness arising from no cause or from itself, nor can happiness be expected if one maltreats other beings, human or otherwise. Every being desires life and is afraid of death, this being as true of ourselves as of other creatures. Only a man who constantly leads an upright and compassionate life is really dear to himself, for he does actions which are of great profit, of great happiness. Other people, although they think that they are dear to themselves, are really their own worst enemies, for they go about doing to themselves what only an enemy would wish for them.

Good conduct depends on a well-trained mind which has gradually been freed from the clutches of greed, hatred and delusion. To hold one's neighbor as dear as one should truly hold oneself, is easily said but with difficulty done. It is the particular merit of Lord Buddha's teachings that they always point out *how* a method is to be translated into experience, the method here being the mental training of the Divine Abidings. When we say "mental," this word should be understood not in the narrow sense of the intellectual processes, but rather to include the full range of the mind-and-heart, intellect and emotions.

There are four states of Divine Abidings: friendliness, compassion, gladness and equanimity. These, especially the first, are very popular meditations in Buddhist countries. What follows is a short explanation of each.

Friendliness (metta) is an unselfish love which can be extended to everyone. This becomes easy once one has gained the meditative absorptions, when the quality of friendliness becomes an integral part of one's character. In the normal way of things, people only "love" the few people to whom they are especially attached by ties of family, etc. Such is love with sensual attachment, a limited love, and those outside that love are either ignored or disliked. Sensual love, then, is not only linked to attachment (greed), but also to hatred and delusion, so that the person who is content with this love pays a heavy price for it. A love without attachment is scarcely conceivable to many people, but such love is much superior to the former; being without attachment it can become infinite and need not be confined to this or that group of beings. As it can be made infinite, leaving none outside it, there is no question of the three roots of unskill being linked with it.

Friendliness can be developed gradually in one's meditation period every day, *but if it is really effective* it must show in one's daily life. It makes life easier by turning persons whom one formerly disliked or hated into, at the beginning, those whom one disregards, and then as one's practice becomes stronger, into objects for the arising of loving-kindness. It is Lord Buddha's medicine for the disease of hatred and dislike. Finally, one is warned that it has two enemies: the "near" one is sensual attachment, often miscalled "love," while the "far" enemy to its development is hatred. In the development of friendliness one must beware of these two.

Compassion (karuna) is taking note of the sufferings of other beings in the world. It overcomes callous indifference to the plight of suffering beings, human or otherwise. Likewise, it must be reflected in one's life by a willingness to go out of one's way to give aid where possible, and to help those in distress. It has the advantage of reducing one's selfishness by understanding others' sorrows. It is Lord Buddha's medicine for cruelty, for how can one harm others when one has seen how much they have to suffer already? It has also two enemies: the "near" one is mere grief; while its "far" enemy is cruelty.

Gladness (mudita) is to rejoice with others over their success, gains happiness. It overcomes the grudging attitude to others, and the envy which may arise on hearing of others' joy. It must show in one's life as a spontaneous joy at the very time when one learns that other people have some gain or other, material or immaterial. It has the advantage of making one open-hearted towards others, and does away with secretiveness. A person who develops gladness attracts many friends who are devoted to him, and with them and others he lives in harmony. It is Lord Buddha's medicine for envy and jealousy, which it can inhibit completely. The two enemies of gladness are the merely personal happiness of reflecting on one's own gains — this is the "near" enemy; while the "far" one is aversion to, or boredom with, this gladness.

Equanimity (upekkha) is to be developed to deal with situations where one should admit that it is beyond one's powers to change them. It overcomes worry and useless distraction over affairs which either do not concern one or else cannot be changed by oneself. It is reflected in one's life by an ability to meet difficult situations with tranquility and undisturbed peace of mind. The advantage to be seen in its development is that it makes one's life more simple by disengaging from useless activity. It is Lord Buddha's medicine for distraction and worry, and its enemies are mere indifference, which is the "near" one; while greed, and its partner resentment, which involve one unskillfully in so many affairs, are its "far" enemies.

The mind well-practiced in these four virtues, and then well-trained by their use in daily life, has already gained very much.

Three of the perfections *(parami),* or qualities, practiced by many Buddhists who aspire to enlightenment may also be outlined here, as they too have an intimate bearing on the practice of meditation.

Patience and its Perfection *(Khanti-parami)*

Patience is an excellent quality much praised in Buddhist scriptures. It can be developed easily only if restlessness and hatred have already been subdued in the mind, as is done by meditation practice. Impermanence, which has the tendency to make one rush around and thus miss many good chances, results from the inability to sit still and let things sort themselves out — which sometimes they may do without one's meddling. The patient man has many a fruit fall into his lap which the go-getter misses. One of them is a quiet mind, for impatience churns the mind up and brings with it the familiar anxiety-diseases of the modern business world. Patience quietly endures — it is this quality which makes it so valuable in mental training and particularly in meditation. It is no good expecting instant enlightenment after five minutes practice. Coffee may be instant, but meditation is not, and only harm will come of trying to hurry it up. For ages the rubbish has accumulated, an enormous pile of mental refuse, and so when one comes along at first with a very tiny teaspoon and starts removing it, how fast can one expect it to disappear? Patience is the answer, and determined energy to go with it. The patient meditator really gets results of lasting value; the seeker after "quick methods" or "sudden enlightenment" is doomed by his own attitude to long disappointment.

Indeed, it must soon become apparent to anyone investigating the Dhamma, that these teachings are not for the impatient. A

Buddhist views his present life as a little span perhaps of eighty years or so, and the latest one so far of many such lives. Bearing this in mind, he determines to do as much in this life for the attainment of Enlightenment as possible. But he does not overestimate his capabilities; he just quietly and patiently gets on with *living* the Dhamma from day to day. Rushing headlong at Enlightenment (or what one thinks it is), like a bull in a china shop, is not likely to get one very far, that is unless one is a very exceptional character who can take such treatment, and most important, one who is devoted to a very skillful master of meditation.

With patience one will not bruise oneself, but will go carefully step by step along the way. We learn that a Bodhisatta is well aware of this, and that he cultures his mind with this perfection so that it is not disturbed by any of the untoward occurrences common in this world.

He decides that he will be patient with exterior conditions — not to be upset when the sun is too hot or the weather too cold. Not to be agitated by other beings which attack his body, such as bugs and mosquitoes. Neither will he be disturbed when people utter harsh words, lies or abuse about him, either to his face or behind his back. His patience is not broken even when his body is subjected to torment, blows, sticks and stones, tortures, and even death itself; he will endure these steadily, so unflinching is his patience. Buddhist monks also are advised to practice in the same way.

In Buddhist tradition the perfection of patience is rather better known than some of the others. This is because a quite outstanding Birth Story illustrates it. The Khantivadi (Teacher of Patience) Birth Story[5] should be read many times and made the object of deep and frequent reflections. Only an exceptionally noble person, in this case Gotama in a previous life, when he was called the Patience-teaching Rishi, can gently exhort a raging and drunk monarch, who out of his jealous anger, is slowly cutting that person's body to pieces. Such nobility did the Bodhisatta have and such nobility, steadfast endurance, and gentleness, is required of all who would try to reach the goal of Enlightenment.

Energy and its Perfection *(Viriya-parami)*

Just as Enlightenment is inconceivable unless a person has patience, so it is not attainable without effort being made. The Dhamma never encourages the doctrine of fatalism, and true Buddhists never think of events as being rigidly predetermined. Such fatalism is combated by mindfulness and by energy itself. This perfection is the counterpart of the previous one, and balanced by practice, they ensure that the sincere Buddhist neither passively accepts what he should combat nor rushes around to the disturbance of himself and others when he should have patience. By way of warning it may be mentioned here that in the Buddhist world can be found a number of "methods" which seem to promise the riches of Dhamma all in no time. One hears such remarks as, "What's the use of books and study?" Or even, "The development of calm is a waste of time! One should only develop insight." Such lop-sided approaches do not reflect the wisdom of Lord Buddha, who taught time and again the necessity of a *balanced* development of mind. Books and their study *are* useful to some people who wish to gain a good background of what Lord Buddha really said, before taking up more intensive practice. As for the other assertion, no real insight (only delusive ideas) will arise to the person whose mind has no experience of calm. Such views as these, which are usually based on some peculiar experience of those "teachers" who originate them, are apt to mislead many, since the craving for quick results coupled with the dislike of the necessary hard work, are easily stirred up. There must be patience to accept that the conditions required for success of meditation (as outlined here) have to be fulfilled, and the only result if failing to do so, is straying off the Way. The meditator applies himself steadily to whatever task he has in hand and, coming to the end of it, does not feel tired at all but straightaway takes up a new objective.

It is interesting in this respect that tiredness is of two kinds: that relating to physical exhaustion; and the other kind which is mentally induced and involves the unskillful factors of sloth and torpor. While the former is of course unavoidable, the latter occurs only when the unskillful root of delusion (or dullness) becomes predominant in the mind. This happens when there is a situation which is unpleasant to "me," unwanted, and from which "I" want to escape. People complain that they become much more tired sitting in meditation while practicing intensively than they do when, say, they do a bit of heavy reading. When the self feels threatened by a self-revealing event, then this self, rooted in unknowing, throws up a dense fog of torpor proceeding from the root of delusion. On the other hand, many who have practiced much meditation remark that they do not have to sleep so long as they did formerly, while energy, when it becomes a perfection as practiced by the Bodhisatta, is quite natural and unforced.

This perfection is illustrated by the story of the caravan-leader who saved the merchants, men and animals entrusted to his care, by vigorous action. When others would have given themselves up to death since the caravan had taken a wrong course in the desert and all supplies were exhausted, their leader forced one of them to dig for water, which he found. In this way, in a previous life did Gotama, as the caravan-leader, make effort not only for his own life but also for the welfare of others. Monks are also referred to as "caravan-leaders" in several places in Pali scriptures, showing that it is not only Lord Buddha or a Bodhisatta who is able to guide others. If we deal energetically with our own training then we too have energy for the advancement of others. Many other stories like the above could be found in Buddhist works showing how necessary is energy, from which spring persistence and determination for the seeing of the truly real, Nibbana.

Collectedness and its Perfection *(Samadhi-parami)*

Bearing in mind the meanings of this word together with such specialized terms as (mind-) development *(bhavana)*, absorption *(jhana)*, insight *(vipassana)*, one-pointedness *(ekaggata)*,and meditaton exercise *(kammatthana)*, we may now examine what constitutes perfected collectedness. What especially marks off the good Buddhist's practice, whether he be a Bodhisatta or not, from that of an ordinary meditator (in any religion), is that the latter will most likely become firmly attached to the delights occurring in the upper reaches of the sensual realm, or to the pure joys of the realm of form and, as a result, come to birth in one of these heavenly states. If one gets oneself trapped in one of these bourns, where pleasures and joys are great and sufferings but little, then it is unlikely that one will be able to generate the energy necessary for the perfection of wisdom. Therefore, the good meditator tries to become proficient in the absorptions (so that he can enter them when he likes, and emerge when he likes), while not being attached to them. But one should note that this applies only to the skilled meditator who has already obtained the absorptions. If one has not reached to these levels, then ardent aspiration, not detachment, will be the correct attitude.

After these absorptions have been attained, they may be reviewed as impermanent, unsatisfactory and devoid of self or soul *(aniccam, dukkham, anatta),* at which time detachment from them will naturally arise and insight *(vipassana)* be experienced. The absorptions (and the powers which may arise in connection with them) are thus, in the Buddhist way of training, never an end in themselves but are always used to promote insight and wisdom, which arise when the collected mind is set the task of examining the mind and body in order to know completely their characteristics.

A story which brings out the meaning of this perfection is told of Kuddalamuni's life. His name means the Mattock sage and he was thus called because of the difficulty he experienced in freeing himself from attachment to his mattock. Several times leaving his house with intent to meditate in the forest, he was dragged back by the memory of his mattock and his old occupation of farming. One day, reflecting on the inconstancy with which he pursued meditation, he took his mattock and, whirling it round his head, sent it spinning into the depths of the nearby Ganges. Having done this, he burst out in a great cry of joy. The local rajah who was passing that way with his army, sent a man to enquire why this farmer was so joyful, to which the sage replied by relating his experience. The rajah and many others were much impressed by his reply, and some followed him to take up a meditative life in the forest; after which, we are told, all passed away to experience life in the realm of form. The Mattock-sage, who was none other than Gotama in a past life, exhibited even then another aspect of the perfection of meditation: the ability to train others in meditation after gaining proficiency in it oneself.

Finally, we may add brief notes on some of the dangers to meditation practice.

DANGERS TO MEDITATION

While the number of ways a meditator may go astray is legion, the few mentioned below deserve a special mention due to their common occurrence. First, a danger that cannot be stressed enough is the lack of right motivation for the practice of meditation. When the Eightfold Path is described, in its "wisdom" section, standing next to the (at first) intellectual right understanding, comes right motivation, thus emphasizing that the emotional roots underlying practice of the Way must be skillful ones: those connected with renunciation (non-greed), goodwill (non-hatred) and non-violence are mentioned. If one approaches Buddhist meditation with neither right understanding regarding *dukkha* and its cessation, nor with right motives, then one's meditation is liable to seriously astray.

There have, for instance, been those who took up meditation as a way to invest themselves with power, so that they could easily sway or hypnotize disciples. Others have seen it as a quick way to gain both disciples and riches. Fame may also be an unworthy motive. All these, as motives for playing with meditation, may easily lead the unwary into illness, and sometimes mental unbalance. There is nothing worse in Buddhist meditation, where a person's own sure experience is of paramount importance, than a half-baked disciple who sets himself up as a master.

This obviously leads on to a further danger — that of pride, of which there are several forms. One such is the pride of the person who has seen manifestations of light during meditation, and supposes this to be the sign preceding mental absorption. Then there is the pride of one who touches on a mental absorption if only for an instant and as a result assumes that he has become a Noble One, and this can be a very powerful factor in convincing himself if not others. Quite ordinary people who take up meditation may beware of the common "holier-than-thou" attitudes: "I make an effort, whereas you . . .," or, "*I* meditate every day, whereas you . . ." Pride is a great obstacle to any progress, and while it is only a Buddha or Arahat who is entirely rid of it, everyone should have the mindfulness to check it. Related to this is the danger for the person who always looks for so-called progress. He is sure that he is making "progress" because in meditation he sees lights, hears sounds, or feels strange sensations. He becomes more and more fascinated by these as time goes by, and gradually forgets that he started with the aspiration to find the way to Enlightenment. His "meditation" then degenerates into visions and strange happenings, leading him into the realms of occultism and magic. There is no surer way for a meditator to become entangled than this way. Fascinating though all such manifestations may be, they should be rigorously cut down by resorting to bare attention, never permitting discursive thought regarding them, and thus avoiding these distractions.

Among "visions" which one may see, whether they be internal (produced from one's own mind) or external (produced by other beings), there may be for some meditators an experience of the fearful, such as the sight of one's own body reduced to bones or inflated as a rotting corpse. If such an experience occurs, or others of a similar nature, one should withdraw the mind from the vision immediately, supposing that one has no teacher. Visions of the fearful variety which occur to some people may be very useful if rightly employed, but without a teacher's guidance they should be avoided.

Another danger is trying to meditate while one is still too emotionally insecure, unbalanced or immature. An understanding of the value of meritorious deeds or skillfulness will come in useful here. As merit purifies the mind, it will be an excellent basis for mind-development, and both the ease with which absorptions are gained and the ease with which insight arises are to some extent dependent upon merit. Meritorious deeds are not difficult to find in life. They are the core of a good Buddhist life: giving and generosity, undertaking the precepts, help and service to others, reverence, listening whole-heartedly to Dhamma, setting upright one's understanding of Dhamma — all these and more are meritorious deeds which bring happiness and emotional maturity. *Merit,* one should always remember, *opens doors everywhere.* It makes possible, it makes opportunities. To have a mind at all times set upon making merit, is to have a mind that may be trained to develop absorptions and insight.

Obviously it follows that to try to practice meditation while all the time retaining one's old cravings, likes and dislikes is, to say the least, making one's path difficult if not dangerous. Meditation implies renunciation, and no practice will be successful unless one is at least prepared to make efforts to restrain greed and hatred, check lust, and understand when delusion is clouding the heart. How far one carries renunciation and whether this involves outward changes (such as becoming a monk or nun), depends much on a person and his circumstances, but one thing is sure: inward renunciation, an attitude of giving-up with regard to both unskillful mental events and bodily indulgence, is absolutely essential.

Often connected with the above dangers is another, to be seen in cases where a man suddenly has an opportunity to undertake a longer period of meditation practice. He sits down with the firm resolve, "Now I shall meditate," but though his energy is ever so great and though he sits and sits and walks and walks, still his mind is disturbed and without peace. It may well be that his own strong effort has much to do with his distractions. Moreover, he has to learn that it is necessary to meditate knowing the imitations of his character. Just as any other worker who knows the limits of his strength and is careful not to exhaust himself, so is the able meditator careful. With mindfulness one should know what are the extremes, of laziness and of strain, to be avoided.

It is through straining or forcing meditation practice that many emotionally disturbed states arise. Sudden bursts of intense anger all over insignificant trifles, fierce cravings and lusts, strange delusions and even more peculiar fantasies can all be produced from unwisely arduous practice.

With all these dangers it is a skilled teacher who is most necessary to give advice, so that these and other wrong turnings are avoided and one keeps straight along the way to Nibbana. Those who are without a teacher should proceed with utmost caution, making sure that their development of mindfulness is very good indeed. If they are mindful and see that despite their efforts, their meditation practice is making no real difference to their lives in terms of greater internal peace, or externally in relation to others, then it should be apparent that something is wrong. Meditation may be laid aside for some time while making efforts to contact a genuine source of information, preferably a living meditation master, in the meantime giving due attention to unsolved moral problems, which until sorted out will not permit the mind to develop; and making a great effort to live one's life according to Buddhist standards. When quite basic matters of this sort are neglected, one cannot hope to make much progress upon the Middle Practice-Path.

Appendix 40 Meditation Exercises as listed in the *Path of Purification*

If one has no meditation teacher from whom one may request a meditation subject, then one has to rely upon one's knowledge of one's character in order to prescribe for oneself a suitable meditation. There are forty meditation exercises *(kammatthana)* noted by the great teacher Buddhaghosa as being suited to certain types of character. For the purposes of meditation, he considers six characters: faithful, intelligent, and speculative (in which the skillful roots of non-greed, non-hatred and non-delusion are variously dominant); and greedy, hating, and deluded (in which greed, hatred and delusion, the unskillful roots, are dominant). The trouble here is twofold: firstly, very few "pure" types can be found, most people being mixtures of two or more of them — and moreover ever-changing mixtures; and secondly, it is rather difficult to judge which class one's character belongs to since one's own delusion and pride are apt to blur one's judgements. This is but one small matter in which the value of the meditation teacher may be discerned very easily. One may learn much about oneself, however, by being mindful *at the time when some unexpected event takes place. At that time* one can spot one's reaction and the stains which are present in the mind. Later judgements are not worth very much, since by that time the mind has got round to self-justifications, and other kinds of distortions of the original event.

Below is given the list of the forty meditation exercises with some notes upon their practice, the characters which are benefited, and the types of stains combated by them. The most widely used meditation exercises are starred (*).

Ten Kasinas (spheres, lit: totalities)

1. earth
2. water
3. fire
4. air
5. blue
6. yellow
7. red
8. white
9. light *
10. limited space

5-8 recommended for the practice of *hate* characters because of their pure, pleasing colors.

Apart from the possible exception of 5-8, no special moral stain is counteracted by these ten kasinas. As they are to be developed through the eye, they will not be very suitable for anyone with weak sight (according to Buddhaghosa).

The only one of the ten kasinas which seems to be practiced much these days is that of light, which some people find arises quite naturally when they begin to concentrate the mind. While Acariya Buddhaghosa's explanations in *Path of Purification* tend to stress the importance of using exterior supports for practice (the making of the earth kasina is very minutely described), whenever the writer has heard of them being employed (in Thailand), they are always in the nature of visions *(nimitta)* arising internally and being developed from this basis. It appears that contemplations of an exterior earth, etc. kasina is unknown in Thailand.

Ten Kinds of Foulness *(asubha)*

11. the bloated (corpse) counteracting delight in beauty of proportions
12. the livid ... beauty of complexion
13. the festering ... scents and perfumes
14. the cut-up ... wholeness or compactness

15. the gnawed ... well-fleshed body
16. the scattered ... grace of limbs
17. the hacked and scattered ... grace of body as a whole
18. the bleeding ... ornaments and jewelry
19. the worm-infested ... ownership of the body
20. the skeleton ... having fine bones and teeth

11-20 recommended for *greed* characters.

These and similar lists in the Satipatthana Sutta reflect the time when disposal of corpses upon charnel-grounds was common. Now, however, even in Buddhist lands they are difficult to find, let alone in Western countries. Teachers in Thailand at the present time stress that *one's own body* is to be seen in these ways as a vision *(nimitta)* arising in the course of mind-development. As these can be fearful, one should have the instruction of a skilled teacher for dealing with such visions, when they can be of great advantage. It may be stressed here that there is nothing morbid in contemplating such sights, interior or exterior, as these. The body's decay is just something natural, but normally it is not seen because people do not like to admit this. Instead of facing bodily decay and bringing it out into the open, dead bodies are even made to look attractive by embalmers and cosmeticians; and where this cannot be done, they are stowed away in beautiful coffins with bright flowers, etc. Buddhist training makes one look squarely at those aspects of life which normally (that is, with craving) are not considered "nice," and makes one calmly face them in respect of one's own mind and body.

Ten Reflections *(anussati)*

21. upon the Buddha *
22. " the Dhamma
23. " the Sangha
24. " virtue *(sila)* ..... {counteracts the stain *(kilesa)* of bad conduct *(duccarita)*}
25. " generosity ..... {counteracts meanness *(macchariya)*}
26. " celestials ..... {counteracts scepticism *(vicikiccha)*}
27. " death ..... {counteracts laziness}
28. " body * ..... {counteracts lust & sensuality *(kama-raga)*}

29. " breathing * ..... {counteracts delusion, worry}

30. " peace ..... {counteracts disturbance}

21-26 recommended for *faith* characters

27 " " *intelligent* characters

28 " " *greedy* characters

29 " " *deluded/speculative* characters

30 " " *intelligent* characters

This group of ten has a more miscellaneous character than the previous two groups. In practicing the first three recollections (21-230 one recited the lists of qualities of each one of these.[6] Or if the mind does not become concentrated in this way, one chooses one particular quality and recites that silently and continuously (such as "Buddho" or "Araham"). Rosaries are used in some places in connection with practice of this sort. The recollections on virtue and generosity are specially good to cultivate in one's old age. One reviews all the meritorious deeds *(puñña)* made by one in the course of life, and recollecting them the mind becomes tranquil and happy, and having such a mental state at the time of death, one is sure to be reborn in very favorable surroundings. One cannot recollect the celestials *(deva)* except by hearsay unless one has seen them. This practice is suitable for those who have increased the range of their minds and so have made contact with other more subtle beings. Death may be recollected by *intelligent* characters since they will not be frightened at the prospects which this practice opens up. It is a great incentive to practice *now* when one does not know whether even one second from hence, one will be alive. The twenty-eighth recollection — on the body — is for *greedy* characters, who need to develop dispassion regarding the body. This is achieved by the analysis of the body into thirty-two unbeautiful parts, and then by selecting one or more of these and examining it. However, this practice comes to perfection when with insight the body is illuminated and its various components are clearly seen and their nature understood. The mindfulness of breathing is recommended for calming and clearing the mind, and a person of almost any temperament may practice it with benefit, though great care is needed in the subtler ranges of this exercise. The breathing is never forced but observed constantly with mindfulness, the point of concentration being usually the nose-tip or nostrils. However, teachers vary in their practice of it. The recollection of peace, says the great Acariya, is only of certain benefit to those who have already experienced Nibbana, such as stream-enterers; but others can gain some calm from contemplation of peacefulness. The peace spoken of here is really Nibbana, and as one cannot recollect what one has not known, if a worldling *(puthujjana),* this is a practice for the Noble Ones *(ariya).*

Four Divine Abidings *(Brahma-vihara)*

31. friendliness * ..... {counteracts the stain of hatred, dislike}
32. compassion ..... {counteracts callous indifference}
33. gladness (with others) ..... {counteracts envy}
34. equanimity ..... {counteracts worry}

31 recommended for *hate* characters

Four States of Formlessness *(arupa-bhava)*

35. sphere of infinite space
36. " " infinite consciousness
37. " " nothingness
38. " " neither-perception-nor-non-perception

These formless absorptions cannot be developed unless one has already perfected the four ordinary absorptions of form. It is said that this group of four may be explored on the basis of the fourth absorption *(jhana).* As few people are likely to have experienced this, we pass on to:

Perception of the Loathsomeness of Food

39. While it is essential for the bhikkhu who has to rely upon collected food (which is sometimes good and sometimes not), lay people can also benefit from this practice, which Acariya Buddhaghosa notes is for *intelligent* characters, and is designed to lessen, and lead to the destruction of, greed and gluttony.

One Defining of the Four Great Elements

40. These are earth (solidity), water (cohesion), fire (temperature), and air (movement), all of which characterize our physical bodies. These elements may be perceived by

an analysis based upon the use of mindfulness.[7] This practice is also said to be particularly fitted for the *intelligent* character.

Those practices not mentioned in connection with character are suited to anyone. As all of these practices are aimed at the lessening and eventual destruction of the stains *(kilesa),* one may appreciate how important they are thought in Buddhist training. Where the stains are present, there the darkness of unknowing holds sway; but where they are not found, there shines forth the wisdom and compassion of Enlightenment.

References:

1. See *The Mirror of the Dhamma,* WHEEL No. 54 a/b.]
2. See *The Practice of Lovingkindness (Metta),* trans. Ñanamoli, WHEEL No. 7.]
3. The tradition of "keeping the right side towards" respected persons and objects has a psychological basis. Also note in English right (for side) and right (good, correct).
4. See Nyanaponika, *The Four Sublime States,* WHEEL No. 6.
5. Jataka No. 33, see translation issued by the Pali Text Society.
6. See *The Mirror of the Dhamma,* WHEEL No. 54 a/b.
7. See *The Foundations of Mindfulness,* trans. Nyanasatta, WHEEL No. 19, p. 15; and Ledi Sayadaw, *A Manual of Insight,* WHEEL No. 31/32, pp. 25, 78.

Conclusion

Vipassana is not a rite or ritual based on blind faith. There is no visualization of any god, goddess or any other object, or verbalization of any mantra or *japa*. Neither is it an intellectual nor philosophical entertainment. The word *vipassana* is derived from "*passa*" (to look, to observe) and "*vi*" (in a special way). It means "observing oneself in a special way". It is a technique that purifies the mind, deconditioning the negativities of anger, hatred, greed, selfishness etc. by self-observation and introspection. It is insight meditation. It is looking at things *as they are* and not through coloured glasses. It is an effort to change the deep habit-pattern of the mind, which dwells in the continuous blind reactions of craving and aversion.

Modern life is moving at such a rapid pace that there is no time even to breathe. Our fiercely competitive world is like a rat-race where, in spite of all the technological and economic improvements and multifarious pleasures, people are still unhappy. Humankind has made tremendous progress in the fields of science, industry, and political systems, etc., resulting in materialistic development. Man is the promoter and consumer of these advancements, which aim at improving our standard of living and total well-being.

But does this really happen? Look at the so-called "developed countries" of the world, which try to ensure a high standard of living. Despite their advances in such fields as health, education and technology, they are experiencing an increased incidence of mental illness, delinquency, crime, drug addiction, alcoholism, and suicide, etc.

Every society is made up of individuals. The individual in a modern society is a victim of varying degrees of stresses and strains. His or her existence is full of constant conflict between the world within and the world outside. The materialistic world holds humans under a hypnotic spell. Engaged all the time in filling their stomachs by earning and spending money, people are slaves of their own cravings, euphemistically called ambition, aspiration, aims or ideals. These, alas, are seldom fulfilled, which causes deep distress, frustration and dissatisfaction, whether one belongs to the "Haves" or the "Havenots."

Suffering, then, is a common problem of humanity. It is a universal disease, not the bane of any one nation, or persons of any particular colour or creed. So the remedy must also be universal. *Vipassana* offers such a remedy.

The basis of any healthy, harmonious society is always the healthy, harmonious individual. Only if each individual has a pure, peaceful mind can we expect peace and harmony in the society. *Vipassana* is a unique technique for obtaining peace and harmony within an individual at the experiential level.

The great sage of India, Gautama the Buddha, discovered, or rather rediscovered this technique through his deep meditation. He attained enlightenment through this technique and was liberated from all the defilements of the mind. Then with great compassion and love, he distributed it to the suffering mankind. He did not establish any, "ism" or "cult." He taught *Vipassana*, a way to purify the mind of its negativities of craving and aversion.

Bibliography

A. Primary Sources:

1. *The Dîgha Nikâya,* Translated from the Pâli by Rhys Davids, *The Dialogues of the Buddha,* 3 vols, Delhi: Motilal Banarsidass, 2007 (reprints).
2. *The Majjhima Nikâya,* (Trans.) Bhikhu NâG◎amoli, Bhikhu Bodhi, *The Middle Length Discourses of the Buddha,* 3 vols, Boston: Wisdom Publications, 2009 (reprints).
3. *The SaC✢yutta-Nikâya,* (Trans.) Bhikkhu Bodhi, *The Connected Discourses of the Buddha,* 5 vols, Boston: Wisdom Publications, 2000; (Trans.) Rhys Davids & F.L. Woodward, *The Book of the Kindred Sayings,* 5 vols, Delhi: Motilal Banarsidass, 2005 (reprints).
4. *AE✢guttara-Nikâya,* (Trans.) F.L. Woodward & E.M. Hare, *The Book of the Gradual Sayings,* 5 vols, Delhi: Motilal Banarsidass, 2006 (reprints).
5. *The Dhammapada,* (Trans.) F. Max Muller, *A Collection of Verses,* Delhi: Motilal Banarsidass Publishers, 1992.
6. *The Udâna and Itivuttaka,* John D. Ireland, Srilanka: Buddhist Publication Society, 1997.
7. *The Visuddhimagga,* (Trans.) Bhikkhu Nanamoli, *The Path of Purification,* Colombo, Ceylon: Published by R. Semage, 1956.

B. Secondary Sources:

1. Bhikkhu ÑâG◎amoli (trans.), *Mindfulness of Breathing ✢ t"p✢✢"✢(Buddhist texts from the Pâli Canon and Extracts from the Pâli Commentaries),* Buddhist Publication Society, 2010.
2. D.K. Barua, *An Analytical Study of Four Nikâyas,* New Delhi: Munshiram Manoharlal, 2003.

3. Bhikkhu Bodhi (ed.), *In the Buddha t"p♈♈"♈words An Anthology of Discourses from the Pâli Canon,* Boston: Wisdom Publication, 2005.
4. Bhikkhu Bodhi, *A Comprehensive Manual of Abhidhamma: The Abhidhammattha Sangaha of Âcariya Anuruddha,* Seattle, WA: BPS Pariyatti Editions, 2000.
5. Bhikkhu ÑâG◉amoli (trans.), *Mindfulness of Breathing ♈ t"p♈♈"♈(Buddhist texts from the Pâli Canon and Extracts from the Pâli Commentaries),* Buddhist Publication Society, 2010.
6. Bhikkhu ÑâG◉amoli (trans.), *Visuddhamagga, The Path of Purification,* Buddhist Publication Society, Colombo, Srilanka.
7. Bhikkhu ÑâG◉amoli (trans.), *The Path of Discrimination (Patisambhidâmagga),* Oxford: The Pâli Text Society, 1991.
8. Harcharn Singh Sobti (ed.), *Vipassanâ the Buddhist way (The Based on Pâli Sources),* Delhi: Eastern Book Linkers, 2003.
9. U Ko Lay, *Manual of Vipassana meditation,* Dhamma Giri, Igatpuri, Maharashtra, 2010.
10. C.Alexander Simpkins & Annellen M. Simpkins, *Zen Meditation in Psychotherapy, Techniques for Clinical Practice,* Canada: John Wiley, 2012.
11. Mark Epstein, M.D., *Psychotherapy without the Self - A Buddhist Perspective,* London: Yale University Press New Haven, 2007.
12. K. Khao-suan-luang, *Reading the mind,* Buddha Dhamma education association Inc.
13. Soma Thera, *The way of Mindfulness the Satipatthana Sutta and Its Commentary,* 1998.
14. Nyanaponika, Thera, *The power of mindfulness,* San Francisco: Unity Press, 1972.
15. Bobrow, J., *Moment of truth—truths of moments,* In Safran, J. D. (ed.). *Psychoanalysis and Buddhism: An unfolding dialogue,* Boston: Wisdom Publications, 2003.
16. Oldenberg, H., *Buddha his life, His Doctrine, His Order,* Delhi: Motilal Banarsidass, 1997.

17. Rahula, W., *What the Buddha Taught,* London: Gordon Fraser, 1978.
18. A,C. Taylor (Ed) *Patisambhimagga* , Pali Text Society, Vol. 1905, Vol. II, 1907.
19. Ambassador Dato Dr.G.K.Ananda Kumaraser, Buddhist education and pedagogy Challenges and Opportunities Presented in UNDV Conference.
20. C.A.F.Rhys Davids (trs) *Buddhist Psychological Ethics* (Translations of Dhammasangani) Pali Text Society, 1974 (3rd Edition).
21. D.D. Kosambi (Ed) *Visuddhimagga,* Bhartya Bhavan, Bombay, 1940.
22. Edward Conze, *Buddhist Meditation,* Harper Torch Books, New York, 1956.
23. Erich Fromm, The Art of Loving, Harper Paper Planning classical publications,
24. F.L. Woodward (trs) *The Kindered Sayings* (Translation of Samyutta Nikaya) Pali Text Society, 1979.
25. Lancaster Pamphlets Series on "The Environmental and International Relations" ed. John.Volger & Mark Imber, Routledge, London: 1996.
26. *Report of Education Commission* (1964-66): Education and National Development, Ministry of Education, Govt. of India, 1966.
27. Schumacher, E. F., *Small is Beautiful: Economics as if People Mattered,* London: Hartley and Marks, 1999.
28. Venerable Nyanaponika Thera., *The Heart of Buddhist Meditation,* Rider, London 1962.
29. UNESCO Education Report, 2010.

Index